Indian Business in the Twent Century

T0371737

This book uses a combination of business history and political economy to chart the development of Indian business organisation from independence in 1947 through to the twenty-first century.

The Indian economy has undergone a dramatic transformation to become one of the leading global economies of the twenty-first century. After ending colonialisation and gaining independence in 1947, the economy moved from a reliance on the export of raw materials to an era of state-promoted development, followed by an era of liberalisation and integration in the world economy by the close of the twentieth century. This book looks at traditional industries, such as textiles, to industries of the second and third industrial revolution, ranging from chemicals and oils to telecommunications.

This book highlights how Indian businesses proved capable of importing both new managerial ideas and organisational developments while adapting them to the specific domestic context. The case studies underline the use of human resource management in the post-colonial 'indianisation' of foreign-owned multinationals and the rise of new business organisation and management training in the development of Indian multinational organisations such as Tata Sons.

The chapters in this book were originally published as a special issue of *Business History*.

Swapnesh K. Masrani is Assistant Professor at the Edinburgh Business School at Heriot Watt University, Edinburgh, UK. His research interest is in the area of Strategic Management and Management History, particularly the evolution of management practice in India during the twentieth century, history of management education, and family business. He is also interested in using capability approach, path dependency, and institutional theory.

Carlo J. Morelli is Senior Lecturer in Business and Economic History at the University of Dundee, UK. Carlo is interested in the generation of wealth in society and its re-distribution. His research examines industrial organisation and business/government relationships in the twentieth century. Current research in this area looks at our understanding of industrial decline, the jute and textile industries, and industrial transformation in Anglo-Indian economic relationships.

Amiya K. Bagchi is currently Emeritus Professor at the Institute of Development Studies, Kolkata, India, and Adjunct Professor at Monash University, Australia. He has taught and researched in the areas of economics and economic and social history since 1958. He has been awarded honorary doctorates by three universities in India and by Roskilde University, Denmark. His latest edited volumes are (jointly with Anthony D'Costa) *Transformation and Development: The Political Economy of Transition in India and China* (2012) and (jointly with Amita Chatterjee) *Marxism: With and Beyond Marx* (Routledge, 2014). He was the lead consultant for *Asia and the Pacific: A Story of Transformation and Resurgence, Economic and Social Survey of Asia and the Pacific 1947–2014* (United Nations, 2014).

Indian Business in the Twentieth Century

Development within an Era of Globalisation

Edited by
**Swapnesh K. Masrani, Carlo J. Morelli
and Amiya K. Bagchi**

Routledge
Taylor & Francis Group

LONDON AND NEW YORK

First published 2023
by Routledge
4 Park Square, Milton Park, Abingdon, Oxon, OX14 4RN

and by Routledge
605 Third Avenue, New York, NY 10158

Routledge is an imprint of the Taylor & Francis Group, an informa business

© 2023 Taylor & Francis

British Library Cataloguing-in-Publication Data
A catalogue record for this book is available from the British Library

ISBN13: 978-1-032-32937-6 (hbk)
ISBN13: 978-1-032-32938-3 (pbk)
ISBN13: 978-1-003-31742-5 (ebk)

DOI: 10.4324/9781003317425

Typeset in Myriad Pro
by codeMantra

Publisher's Note
The publisher accepts responsibility for any inconsistencies that may have arisen during the conversion of this book from journal articles to book chapters, namely the inclusion of journal terminology.

Disclaimer
Every effort has been made to contact copyright holders for their permission to reprint material in this book. The publishers would be grateful to hear from any copyright holder who is not here acknowledged and will undertake to rectify any errors or omissions in future editions of this book.

Contents

Citation Information

The chapters in this book were originally published in *Business History*, volume 63, issue 1 (2021). When citing this material, please use the original page numbering for each article, as follows:

Chapter 1
The rise of Indian business in the global context in the twentieth century: A review and introduction
Swapnesh K. Masrani, Carlo Joseph Morelli and Amiya Kumar Bagchi
Business History, volume 63, issue 1 (2021) pp. 1–17

Chapter 2
Reassessing FERA: Examining British firms' strategic responses to 'Indianisation'
Michael Aldous and Tirthankar Roy
Business History, volume 63, issue 1 (2021) pp. 18–37

Chapter 3
Regulating the post-independence textile trade: Anglo-Indian tariff negotiations from independence to the Multi-Fibre Arrangement
Carlo Morelli
Business History, volume 63, issue 1 (2021) pp. 38–51

Chapter 4
Internationalisation of the Indian telecommunication industry (1947–2004): A firm-level perspective
Ajit Nayak
Business History, volume 63, issue 1 (2021) pp. 52–71

Chapter 5
Internment as a business challenge: Political risk management and German multinationals in Colonial India (1914–1947)
Christina Lubinski, Valeria Giacomin and Klara Schnitzer
Business History, volume 63, issue 1 (2021) pp. 72–97

Chapter 6

Ambiguous decolonisation: a postcolonial reading of the IHRM strategy of the Burmah Oil Company
Neveen Abdelrehim, Aparajith Ramnath, Andrew Smith and Andrew Popp
Business History, volume 63, issue 1 (2021) pp. 98–126

Chapter 7

Getting together, living together, thinking together: Management development at Tata Sons 1940–1960
Swapnesh K. Masrani, Linda Perriton and Alan McKinlay
Business History, volume 63, issue 1 (2021) pp. 127–145

For any permission-related enquiries please visit:
http://www.tandfonline.com/page/help/permissions

Notes on Contributors

Neveen Abdelrehim is Senior Lecturer in Accounting and Finance at Newcastle University Business School, UK. Her research interests cover the role of accountability, disclosure and financial reporting, corporate social responsibility, risk, business history, and accounting history. Her research examines the performance of oil companies during nationalisation and independence.

Michael Aldous is Lecturer in Management at Queens University Belfast, UK. His work examines the long-run evolution of business ownership and organisation. His recent work has focused on the organisation of Anglo-Indian trade in the nineteenth and twentieth centuries.

Amiya K. Bagchi has taught and researched in the areas of economics and economic and social history since 1958. He has been awarded honorary doctorates by three universities in India and by Roskilde University, Denmark. He is currently Emeritus Professor at the Institute of Development Studies, Kolkata, India, and Adjunct Professor at Monash University, Australia.

Valeria Giacomin is Newcomen Fellow 2017/2018 at Harvard Business School, USA. She received her PhD from Copenhagen Business School, Denmark, in 2016 with a dissertation on the palm oil cluster in Malaysia and Indonesia in the twentieth century.

Christina Lubinski is Associate Professor at the Centre for Business History at Copenhagen Business School, Denmark, and Visiting Professor of Clinical Entrepreneurship (2018/19) at the Lloyd Greif Center for Entrepreneurial Studies at the University of Southern California, Los Angeles, USA.

Swapnesh K. Masrani is Assistant Professor at the Edinburgh Business School at Heriot Watt University, Edinburgh, UK. He is interested in cross-fertilisation of research between strategy and business history. Currently he is looking into the evolution of management practice in India during the twentieth century, globalisation of management education, and family business. He has also used capability approach, path dependency, and institutional theory.

Alan McKinlay is Professor of HRM at Newcastle University Business School, UK. He researches the long-run dynamics of employment relations and work organisation. He has also published extensively on Michel Foucault.

Carlo J. Morelli is Senior Lecturer in Business and Economic History at the University of Dundee, UK. Carlo is interested in the generation of wealth in society and its re-distribution. His research examines industrial organisation and business/government relationships in the twentieth century. Current research in this area looks at our understanding of industrial decline, the jute and textile industries, and industrial transformation in Anglo-Indian economic relationships.

Ajit Nayak is Senior Lecturer in Strategy at the University of Exeter Business School, UK. His research interests revolve around strategy process, practice, and decision-making in changing environments.

Linda Perriton is currently Senior Lecturer in HRM at the University of Stirling, UK. Her research interests are focused on the many ways in which managerial competence is developed, defended, and expressed. She has produced several historical studies of women's management of early philanthropic organisations, inter-war professional groups, the management of women only financial organisations, and institutions that allow women to independently manage their finances.

Andrew Popp is historian of business, focusing primarily on Britain in the nineteenth century. He has published two monographs, two edited volumes, and a number of book chapters and journal articles. He is Editor-in-Chief of *Enterprise and Society: The International Journal of Business History* and Secretary-Treasurer of the Business History Conference.

Aparajith Ramnath is Assistant Professor at Ahmedabad University, India. His teaching and research address topics in the history of science and technology as well as business history. Much of his work explores the history of industrial enterprises and the industrialisation process more generally. His monograph on the history of the engineering profession in pre-independence India was published in 2017.

Tirthankar Roy is Professor of Economic History at the London School of Economics and Political Science, UK. He is the author of *A Business History of India: Enterprise and the Emergence of Capitalism from 1700 (2018)*.

Klara Schnitzer holds a BA in Psychology at the University of Mannheim, Germany, and an MA in Organizational Innovation and Entrepreneurship at Copenhagen Business School (CBS), Denmark. After finishing her master's in 2017, she started working at Boston Consulting Group, USA.

Andrew Smith is Senior Lecturer in International Business at the University of Liverpool Management School, UK. He has published a monograph, three edited collections, and numerous papers in business-historical and other management journals. His work applies a diverse range of qualitative and mixed methodologies and has covered the evolution of business strategies in North America, Europe, and Asia. He also does research on social memory and how corporations use history to become more competitive.

The rise of Indian business in the global context in the twentieth century: A review and introduction

Swapnesh K. Masrani, Carlo J. Morelli and Amiya Kumar Bagchi

ABSTRACT
The focus of this special edition is on Indian business within its wider global context. Indian business was not immune to influences from the wider world. There is a considerable body of literature that establishes the history of the global interconnectedness of the Indian economy in the 18th and 19th centuries. This special edition of Business History seeks to build on this body of work to locate the development of Indian business in the wider world economy, the practices that have grown from this relationship of exchange and the transfer of knowledge, know-how and competences.

Introduction

The history of modern Indian business remains a largely unexplored area of research to a European and North American academic audience (Roy, 2017; Tripathi, 2007, 2014). However, it is an area of growing interest (MacKenzie, 2017) to which we hope to contribute in this special edition of *Business History*. Hitherto, Indian business has largely been addressed utilising a subaltern studies framework. First, domestically, in terms of a contextualisation of the importance of business state relationships in response to underdeveloped economic industrialisation (Bagchi, 1972; Harris, 1983, 1986; Kidron, 1965; Tomlinson, 2003; Tripathi, 2014) and second, internationally, in relation to Indian subordination, and exploitation, by western multinationals (Bagchi, 1982; Cain & Hopkins, 1993; Kumar & Desai, 1983; Sen, 2014). Subaltern studies itself maintains a central theme in the historiography of Indian labour history, and takes inspiration from Thompson's classic 1968 study *Making of the English Working Class*. While subaltern studies primary focus is upon the formation of class, gender and race, and the particular role of exploitation in a colonial context it is nevertheless extended into examining business organisation and development (Misra, 1999; Sen, 2008, 2014). While the institutional context in India was, as subaltern studies maintains, vastly different to that of any western economy recent contestation of this close linking of subaltern studies to Indian business history has also begun to emerge from a literature that insists that decisions and choices of Indian management instead require recognition in their own right (Austin et al., 2017; Roy, 2017).

A focus of this special edition is on Indian business within its wider global context. Indian business was not immune to influences from the wider world. There is a considerable body of literature that establishes the history of the global interconnectedness of the Indian economy in the 18th and 19th centuries (see for example, Aldous, 2015; Bagchi, 1999; Chapman, 1987; Jones, 2000; Riello & Roy, 2009). We seek to build on this body of work to locate the development of Indian business in the wider world economy, the practices that have grown from this relationship of exchange and the transfer of knowledge, know-how and competences.

Three broad periodisations are widely utilised in Indian business history. These are: the colonial era (1857 to 1947). Many of the fundamental elements of Indian business development were mature prior to 1947 and reflected the subordination of Indian business interests to those of British, European and the United States multinationals. The growth of Indian-owned businesses, associated with the agency form of organisation, operating within the primary goods sectors contrasted markedly with the dominance of foreign-owned multinationals operating within the industrial sectors of the second industrial revolution (Tomlinson, 2003).

The second period identified is that covering the traumatic events of independence and partition and the era of state-led development and import substitution (1947–1991). The post-independence era has been largely seen as a historiography of Indian contemporary business framed by the challenge of understanding the varying fortunes of large-scale business within a distinctive post-colonial institutional environment (Bagchi, 1972; Harris, 1983). The latter decades of the era, from the 1970s, is also discussed in a context of a recognition of lower economic growth relative to other newly industrialising economies, and relative economic decline in early established industries such as textiles (Bagchi, 1982; Harris, 1986; Wolf, 1982).

Finally, liberalisation and globalisation (1991 onwards) is identified as the third distinctive era. The 1980s onwards saw a growing weakening of the state-led model of development. Here the literature identifies liberalisation with economic success and rapid growth in newer industries in which higher levels of human capital were pre-requisites (Byres, 1997; Chenoy, 2015). The differing fortunes of the Indian economy across the two post-independence eras has unsurprisingly led to a focus on a wide range of factors and interpretations (Bagchi, 1999; Tripathi, 2004).

Additional sub-classifications have been made. For example, Roy (2011) divides the post-colonial period into Phase 1, covering 1950 to 1964 and ending with Jawaharlal Nehru's death, Phase II, covering 1965–1985 including famine and war with Pakistan, and Phase III covering the period from 1986 to the present.

Our interest, however, lies in the continuities and adaptiveness of Indian business across these periods and the three broad categories (pre-1947, 1947–1991 and 1991 onwards) provide a sufficiently broad analytical framework for this. Our primary approach is thematic rather than chronological but some chronological focus on the debates and scholarship found in the literature is necessary in order to put these themes into context.

Themes

The articles in this edition highlight the distinctive national elements of Indian development in each period, and emphasise the role of global influences and the continued

interconnectedness of Indian businesses to the global economy. In examining the interconnectedness during these periods, the papers in this edition will examine the following
themes: State and Industry Relationship, Multinationals, and Management Education and
Training.

Indian industrialisation and the legacy of colonialism

The dominance of European business houses over modern industry before the First World
War was supported and reinforced by a diverse set of administrative, political and financial
arrangements. This created a highly racially segmented business environment in which
European businessmen very consciously set themselves apart from 'native' businessmen.
They claimed a cultural and racial affinity with the British rulers of India that was denied to
Indians who might compete with them. Tomlinson (1979) highlights that these arrangements
were not unchanging and evolved to recognise the changing influences in Indian society
after the First World War. Sen (2008) shows that these were male environments in which
European women, if engaged in economic life at all, were relegated to roles in health and
social reform while Indian women faced extreme exploitation or, alternatively, exclusion in
industries such as cotton and jute textiles.

The late nineteenth and early twentieth centuries saw India's economic development
emerge in the areas of agricultural exports and textiles. Indian producers began to dominate
in these world markets, especially in the two classic cases of tea and manufactured jute
products (Goswami, 1985; Morris, 1979; Riello & Roy, 2009). From the post-First World War
era onwards, Indian producers were largely absent from the global markets that developed
in the industries of the second industrial revolution. In car manufacturing and transport
equipment, machine tool manufacturing, chemicals and oil, Indian development was either
absent or dependent upon the direct investment of European and US multinational organisations (Jones, 2000; Kidron, 1965). The first half of the twentieth century saw growth in
world trade that moved increasingly towards higher technology goods and away from agricultural and textile products. This led to developing economies such as India's falling behind
developed ones in terms of both output growth and their relative importance in world trade
(Maizels, 1963, pp. 178–179).

Between the two World Wars, the Indian state's industrial policy began to benefit domestic
producers due to the government policy of imposing import tariffs. However, these benefits
were also available to European businesses and as such can be said to be driven by the Indian
government's need to raise much needed revenue rather than by the promotion of industrialisation (Bagchi, 1972; Markovits, 1985). For Misra (1999), it was British business interests
that motivated the government while benefits to Indian-owned businesses were secondary.
Therefore, 'imperialism' was advocated more stridently by British businesses than by
government officials, and it was used to gain advantage over Indian enterprises (Misra, 1999,
p. 7). Gupta (2014), however, claims that differential access to social networks was the over-
riding influence. Whether driven by government or businesses, there is sufficient evidence
to suggest that some institutional barriers existed that limited the growth of Indian-
owned firms.

From the 1950s, once the social and political upheaval of independence and the Partition
had passed, debates over the continuing laggardness of Indian business in higher technology

industries began to be addressed more actively (Federation of Indian Chambers of Commerce, 1999). Harris (1986, pp. 18–29) provides a useful characterisation of the wider context of these debates. The role of the developmental state and the creation of conditions for the Rostovian 'Take-off' are central to understanding the framework of business-government relationships that emerged. Classical and Marxist approaches emphasise global market relationships and schools of thought that focus on 'underdevelopment and dependency'. As such, external international barriers to trade proved crucial (Bagchi, 1972; Majumdar, 2012, pp. 126–152).

Scholars including Kidron (1965) and Bagchi (1972) place an emphasis upon external barriers to development after independence. These focused on the continuing role of European and US imperial dominance as well as other advanced economies in restricting market entry through the creation of barriers to exporting. External control of the Indian economy was also evident through the continued ownership and control over industries reliant upon higher capital investment by imperial interests and the exclusion of indigenous managers in capital-intensive industries. For Bagchi (2007), with the exception of Western India where businessmen had a firm foothold in international trade and industry, Indian-owned businesses found themselves discriminated against by European-controlled banks in their access to much needed capital. This continued until the nationalisation of the Imperial Bank of India in 1956 (Bagchi, 2007; Ray et al., 2003) and was underpinned by the discriminatory attitude towards Indian-owned businesses that was prevalent in the state bureaucracy (Sinha, 1995).

A series of post-independence initiatives also sought to address the inadequacies of internal industrialisation. The 1948 Industrial Policy Statement extended state ownership into key sectors and introduced regulation into a wider set of industries. Financial support and preference for imports of raw material and capital goods for export orientated industries was also put into place in the first Five Year Plan from 1951–56. In this, Government sought to follow a macroeconomic policy with an orientation toward export-led growth. Internally, development policy focused on encouragement, and later enforcement, of indigenous ownership of domestic enterprises, first with the formation of the Industrial Finance Corporation of India in 1948, and still more aggressively with the system of industrial licensing from 1951 (Tripathi, 2004, pp. 282–325).

Developmental approaches linked to neoclassical economic ideas focus on weaknesses in the development of factors of production, market signals and the excessive concentration of resources in specific sectors for the restricting of more rapid internal development for modern industries (Gupta, 2005; Papendieck, 1978). In the neo-classical approach, entrepreneurial failure is a key component of the explanations provided for the limited success of industrialisation. Roy (2017) provides an overview of many of the elements of this entrepreneurial failure in a critical reflection of the 'transfer-cum-decline' thesis. The transfer of assets from British and other Western economies into Indian ownership is said to have witnessed an inevitable decline due to a lack of entrepreneurial know-how and capabilities, despite their promotion by government policy. The Foreign Exchange Regulation Act (FERA) 1973 was the culminating legislation in this process, ensuring that international organisations transferred ownership to Indian-based organisations, for Michael Aldous and Tirthankar Roy's in their contribution to this volume 'Reassessing FERA: Examining British firms' strategic responses to 'Indianisation'.

A further example of entrepreneurial failure is suggested by the contrasting performance of Calcutta (modern day Kolkata) and Bombay. The dominance of Marwari traders and bankers and their Calcutta-focused networks over Indian business is identified as indicative of an entrepreneurial failures in contrast to Bombay where British influence continued longer. The decline of the Calcutta region is thought to be caused by the narrow focus on speculation and trading rather than a lack of manufacturing knowledge (Federation of Indian Chambers of Commerce, 1999, p.159). Again, however, more recent scholarship has questioned the extent to which such supply-side explanations hold, and suggests that the dominance of existing social networks is a more plausible explanation for these economic outcomes than direct discrimination (Gupta, 2014).

Post 1947 state and industry relationship

The evolution of change in state-industry relationships and the development of legal frame-works for the development of business are understood to be at the heart of many of the more contemporary debates. International trading relations underwent liberalisation with the reduction in global tariff protection following the creation of the World Trade Organisation and increasing moves towards globalisation. However, liberalisation was not uniform. Significant barriers to international trade in manufactured goods remained and developed afresh as international trade was managed and regulated rather than 'free' (Hirst et al. 2009). As Carlo Morelli identifies in his paper 'Regulating the post-independence textile trade: Anglo-Indian tariff negotiations from Independence to the Multi-Fibre Arrangement', imperial prefer-ence gave way to voluntary export restraint in the 1960s and, in the case of the Multi-Fibre Arrangement, global quota limits on textile exports from developing economies were intro-duced. This management of trade nevertheless saw textile exports continue to play an important role in Indian exports, accounting for over 37 per cent of total export earnings in the 1970s (Vanathi & Swamynathan, 2016, p. 8).

The Indian economy increasingly integrated itself into global supply chains whereby new forms of development emerged, both in older manufactured goods sectors such as textiles, machinery and transport equipment, and in tertiary sectors of business services such as call centres and, in the case of Bangalore, software development. While the policy focus on comparative advantage increased the exposure of Indian firms to international competition, the state continued to play a major role in industrial development (Bagchi, 1999: Majumdar, 2012). In the organised sector of the economy, increases in public sector employment in the newer areas were rapid. In the area of Trade and Commerce, public sector employment rose from 37 percent to 64.7 percent while in manufacturing it rose from 10.9 percent to 24.9 per cent between 1961 and 1981 (Harris, 1983, table 7).

As Ajit Nayak demonstrates, co-operation as well as competition was a central require-ment for the investment necessary to establish new technologies. Nayak's paper 'Internationalization of the Indian Telecommunication Industry (1947–2004): A Firm-Level Perspective' demonstrates the importance of government in the contemporary development of mobile technology. Although a state monopoly, telecommunications did not become a strategic priority for the Indian government until the 1980s. Despite the government's ten-dencies towards favouring state monopolies public discourse on the status of telecommu-nications was shifting towards liberalization, leading to the development of strategic planning within the state sector. Nayak thus traces the evolution of the Indian telecommu-nication industry from a national monopoly to a liberalised sector. The entry of private sector competitors required the incumbent firm to develop strategic adaptability in order to survive in a newly liberalised market. Post-liberalisation, the dynamics within the industry changed dramatically for foreign firms whilst the nexus between business and government still proved to be important in terms of understanding the various changes in telecoms policy. Nayak's contribution demonstrates that Indian private sector companies were the main conduits for the activities of foreign firms. The main capabilities required by foreign firms were financial resources, technological expertise and, crucially, the political capabilities that enabled them to work with the Indian government. Once they gained entry and utilised joint ventures with Indian private companies to develop technical knowledge and capital investment, they also needed knowledge transfer capabilities.

Information technology is an important part of India's new economy and service sector. There remains scope for systematic analysis of implications on business practices of firms established during the early decades.[1] More broadly, research could also examine business practices in key service sectors such as tourism, hospitality, leisure, entertainment, and sports.

Our continued knowledge and nuanced understanding of state industry relationships will be further enriched as more case studies emerge. Firm and industry case studies will continue to raise new challenges to the economy-wide political economy approaches to Indian industrialisation that scholarship has predominantly focused upon.

Managing multinationals

Changing patterns of industrialisation also played an important role in understanding the evolution of foreign direct investment (FDI). The role of multinationals and FDI is crucial when analysing Indian business practices in the global context (Kumar, 2010). Analytically, this can be examined in the context of foreign firms operating in India (foreign multinationals), and in the later era of Indian firms operating overseas (Indian multinationals).

Indian inward FDI

Prior to independence, information on foreign firms operating in India can be ascertained by looking at inward foreign direct investments. During the early part of the 20th century, there very few restrictions in terms of investments, imports or exports from India (Bagchi, 1972). From 1914 to 1929, India rose from 8th to 3rd rank globally in terms of attracting inward FDI (Wilkins, 1994). At least three quarters of capital investment in India until independence was British owing to the government favouring the FDI of British firms (Bagchi, 1972; Kidron, 1965). Inward FDI was primarily concentrated in tea and jute (25%), trading (17%), finance and management (8%), utilities (6%) and transport (6%) (Kidron, 1965, p. 3). Thus, certain industries were almost wholly dominated by foreign capital. For example, in 1949–50, 85% of areas planted for tea was under foreign ownership, jute varied between 70% and 95%, wool 85% in 1945, and coal 65–75% (Kidron, 1965, p. 3). This shows that multinationals enjoyed a wide presence in the Indian industry up until the1940s.

The recruitment of Indian managers into these firms, 'Indianisation' is the subject of three of the papers in this volume.

Christina Lubinski, Valeria Giacomin & Klara Schnitzer's contribution to this volume, 'Internment as a business challenge: Political risk management and German multinationals in

Colonial India (1914–1947)', examines the changing patterns of racialized business relation-ships by examining the impact on German-owned multinational enterprises (MNE) of intern-ment during the two world wars. German MNEs, as with British, discriminated against local workers, were afraid of opportunistic behaviour, and wanted to keep a tight control on their offices. Lubinski et al. stress that the experience of MNEs' in India differed significantly depending on their country of origin, suggesting the category 'European business' requires a recognition of the variation in this framework of imperial advantage.

Neveen Abdelrehim, Aparajith Ramnath, Andrew Smith and Andrew Popp's contribution also examines the process of promoting local people to positions of real authority in their paper *'Ambiguous decolonisation: a postcolonial reading of the IHRM strategy of the Burmah Oil Company'*. They suggest it was a complicated process largely driven by pressure from local governments rather than something that was embarked on with willingness at a firm's headquarters. Moreover, the type of Indian even when selected for inclusion in the mana-gerial cadre reflected a strong desire to hire highly Anglicized Indians. The Burmah Oil Company (BOC) traditionally preferred candidates who somewhat fitted the model of a 'clubbable' young Englishman. The process of Indianisation at BOC was thus slow and halting. The company's move away from an ethnocentric IHRM strategy towards a polycentric one was extremely gradual, never entirely complete, and, apparently, grudging.

The era from independence to the 1980s is one in which industries in the manufacturing, chemicals and pharmaceutical sectors were the focus of attention for FDI while from the 1980s business services such as call centres, software and telecommunications played an important role in industrial development. After independence, the increasingly protectionist policies of governments led many MNEs to cease operations in India between the 1960s and 1980s (Nayak, 2018).

Aldous and Roy's contribution similarly considers the issue of the racialisation of British business in India after independence by examining moves to encourage the transfer of foreign-owned businesses into Indian ownership. Their article *'Reassessing FERA: Examining British firms' strategic responses to 'Indianization'* provides evidence based upon publications of the India Pakistan Burma Association to reassess how British businesses perceived the threats of Indianisation. Aldous and Roy show that British-owned firms used a diverse range of strategies, some drawing on their extensive experience, knowledge and networks built through long tenures in India. Although initial worries about 'Indianisation' were widely expressed, the balance of opportunity and risk remained somewhat favourable for British business. Their study reveals that strategic responses varied from outright divestment and sharing ownership, to expansion, investment, diversification, and making a case that the firms operated with sophisticated technologies even when no clear definition of the term existed. These studies demonstrate the continued importance and complexity of managing inward FDI in post-independent India. Collectively, they demonstrate the importance main-taining racial divisions played for MNE's in India both pre- and post-independence.

Indian outward FDI

One of the key changes of contemporary Indian business development is the shift from India as a recipient of FDI to a source. Evidence of Indian firms venturing overseas can be dated back to the early 1960s (Lall, 1983). Lall concludes that companies expanded overseas to mitigate the limitations imposed on domestic growth due to the Monopolistic and Restrictive Trade Practices (MRTP) Act of 1969 (Lall, 1983, p. 68). The restrictive regulatory environment was also responsible for the decision to set up production overseas instead of exporting from India (Lall,1983, p. 73). Between 1960s and 1980s, much of the outward investment went towards other similarly less developed nations in South East Asia, East Africa, West Africa and the Commonwealth of Independent States (CIS), which accounted for about 82% of the total investments (Pradhan & Sauvant, 2010, p. 5). However, Western governments' priorities rather than Indian also influenced these preferences towards outward FDI. As Morelli shows in *Regulating the post-independence textile trade: Anglo-Indian tariff negotiations from Independence to the Multi-Fibre Arrangement* the case of textile industry demonstrates that FDI provided a means of circumventing the increasing regulation of Indian exports into Western European and American markets under the Multi-Fibre Agreement.

The mode of entry chosen for outward FDI was predominantly joint ventures, which rose from 62% in the 1960s to 70% in the 1980s. According to Pradhan and Sauvant (2010, p. 10), in the 1990s with the relaxation of foreign exchange rules, the preference was clearly for wholly owned subsidiaries. Furthermore, between the 1960s and 1980s, the majority of outward investment was from the manufacturing sector, moving to service sector from the 1990s onwards (Pradhan, 2008, pp. 76–77).

The country went through a phase of state-led development from the 1950s, when the state set up public enterprises in steel, fertilisers, the exploration and distribution of oil, the making of heavy machinery for mines and minerals, electric turbines and telecom equipment. In 1969, it nationalized all major banks and subsidised agriculture with cheap fertilisers, electricity and cheap loans from public sector banks. Private sector industry was also sub-sidised with infrastructure built at public expense, and with cheap electricity and water (Bagchi, 1997, 1999; Byres, 1997; Rao, 1997). There was also some concentration among the largest Indian owned business organisations. Even before independence India had some large business groups, the biggest three being the Tata Group, the Birla Group and the Martin Burn Group. The first two were diversified across many industries with the encouragement of the government. Often in violation of government's own industrial policy resolution of 1956 (Chenoy, 2015, Chapter 6), the bigger business houses grew further (Hazari, 1966). The Birla Group under Aditya Vikram Birla was the first to go multinational. Its first venture outside India was a textile mill in Ethiopia in the 1950s. Further companies were floated in the 1960s and 1970s in Thailand, Malaysia, Indonesia and the Philippines. Companies were also floated in Kenya and Nigeria. Other important groups were the Lalbhais, Thapars, Shri Rams, Singhanias, Mafatlals, Walchands, Bombay Dyeing Group, Ruias and Kirloskars (Tripathi, 2004, pp. 286–296). In seeking to trace the patterns of development of outward FDI from India, Tumbe (2017, p. 651 and Figure 1) utilised migration records to highlight changing patterns of migration and the growth of internationalisation first towards Southeast Asia and Africa, and later towards the United States, Europe and West Asia.

This history of inward and outward FDI in the Indian economy demonstrates a more complex pattern than the accepted periodisation of Indian economic development suggests. Inward FDI was stifled by independence, and non-Indian firms, as shown above, took a range of approaches to demands for the Indianisation of senior managers. In contrast, outward FDI began during a period that pre-dates the liberalisation era, when the Indian state played its most direct role in the economy. During the state led development era Indian business developed and exercised a level of autonomy missing from much of the literature. In doing so they required a need to access knowledge, know-how and capabilities from outside of India.

However, in general we know very little about the challenges faced in terms of day-to-day management, either of foreign-owned multinationals operating in India or Indian multinationals operating abroad. It is not clear what internal governance systems were used to manage international ventures in terms of staff selection, training and knowledge sharing, or what impact, if any, the interaction with international markets had on domestic operations. Cross-cultural management, in particular the management of expatriates, is a topic with ample scope for future research. Harvey and Moeller (2009) framework for management of expatriates could be used to examine these issues in the Indian context.

Management education and training

As in the case with FDI patterns, management education and training is not easily understood within the periodisation of post-1947 state-led development and post-1970s liberalisation. Both pre- and post-1947, the global exchange continued. In the state-led intervention era, the government did not overlook the domestic need for managerial training. In fact, in a counter example to FDI, in the state-led development era, the Indian government actively encouraged the global exchange of managerial know-how and recognised the need for managerial expertise as a pre-condition to its growth planning.

Education and training in business and management in India during the 20th century was highly influenced by international exchange and this is addressed by two papers. The contribution of Swapnesh Masrani, Linda Perriton and Alan McKinlay 'Getting together, living together, thinking together: Management development at Tata Sons 1940–1960' examines the development and import, from Britain not America, of management training for in-house use.

Education in commerce related subjects can be traced back to the establishment of the Calcutta Presidency College in 1903, and later to 1913 at the Sydenham College, University of Bombay (Hill et al., 1973, p. 10). The University Education Commission, appointed by the Government in 1948 with the aim of facilitating post-war reconstruction and rapid industrialisation, found that the British modelled curriculum was better suited to those wishing to enter government civil service jobs or take up clerk positions than to those wishing to tackle the challenges of 'modern industrial management' (Hill et al., 1973, p. 10; Jain, 1968, p. 33; Myers, 1958, p. 110).

The period between 1947 and the 1960s was crucial for the development of management education and training (MET) in India. It was during this period that a systematic approach was introduced. Interestingly, as the Indian economy was entering a protectionist era, it was open to drawing on international expertise on MET. The University Education Commission recommended the establishment of a business and administration curriculum. Separately, the All India Council for Technical Education, a body established in 1945 on the recommendation of the Central Advisory Board of Education and the personal initiative of Ardeshir Dalal, director at Tata Industries, established the Industrial Administration Business and Management sub-committee under the chairmanship of Sir Jehangir Gandhy, also a director at Tata Industries. The subcommittee submitted its report in 1953 recommending the establishment of: a) an Administrative Staff College, b) a Board of Management Studies to formulate schemes at university level, and c) a National Institute of Management (Jain, 1968, pp. 33–34).

The Ford Foundation also played an important role in the 1950s by working with the government and other agencies to introduce American thinking to management programmes. Its association with India began in 1951 when Paul Hoffman, then President of the Foundation, in an interaction with the Indian ambassador to the US, offered his assistance to build the institutions of Western democracy in India. Hoffman had previously administered the Marshall Plan as head of the Economic Cooperation Administration in Europe and was concerned with the Communist takeover in China. He travelled to India and met Prime Minister Jawaharlal Nehru and prominent industrialists such as J.R.D Tata and G.D Birla. Since the Ford Foundation itself had limited resources, the discussions centred on contributing through 'demonstration and training projects', which would create multiplier effects. In 1952, Professor Paul Appleby visited India at the request of Nehru to survey the state of public administration and make recommendations for improving the functioning of the government (Staples, 1992, p. 44). During the 1950s, the Foundation sponsored visits by Indian industrialists and civil servants to business schools and management training centres in Europe and US. It also gave grants to the All India Management Association in collaboration with MIT Sloan School of Management. Its most significant contribution was assistance in the establishment of the Indian Institute of Management (Ahmedabad and Calcutta) (Staples, 1992, p. 45; Hill et al., 1973).

The 1950s also saw the introduction of various post-experience training activities. In 1950, the International Labour Organisation (ILO) invited several Asian countries to attend its courses in regional centres. At the request of the Indian government, the ILO conducted several training sessions in India between 1950 and 1953 under the Training Within Industry (TWI) schemes. A pilot scheme was held in Ahmedabad in association with the Ahmedabad Textile Research Association. Enthused by its success, the government requested a further roll-out of this scheme across India. Many large firms such as Tata, Burman-Shell and Lever Brothers introduced it to their supervisory staff (ILO, 1957).

The establishment of the Administrative Staff College of India (ASCI) in 1956 was an important milestone in providing post-experience managerial training. The college was modelled on the Administrative Staff College at Henley, England. In keeping with its emphasis on practice, ASCI's faculty comprised experienced executives from private and public sector organisations such as Tata, Hindustan Lever, Indian Railways and the civil service as well as defence personnel (Sinha, 2004, p. 144). The training was delivered using Henley's syndicate method. During the initial years, courses were designed mainly for senior executives in general management. But based on feedback from client organisations, additional courses were soon introduced such as a general management programme for young businessmen, functional courses such as human resources management, materials management, operations management, financial management and marketing management (Sinha, 1986).

The case of ASCI throws light on the role of Britain in the development of MET in India, showing that India did not rely on American ideas and was open to a variety of approaches (Maheshwari & Ganesh, 1974). However, it remains to be explored whether Britain's contribution to institution building was limited only to ASCI.

With the establishment of Institutes of Management (IIMs), the prominence of management related subjects and degrees began to grow during the 1960s. As a result, a wave of 'commerce colleges' began to introduce 'management' subjects leading to MBA degrees (Hill et al., 1973, p. 19). While the IIMs also ran executive education sessions, their focus was on 'education' or pre-experience degrees (Anubhai, 2011; Mohan, 2011).

Other parts of the economy also benefited from management education and training programmes. The Indian government placed heavy emphasis on the development of rural economy during the state-led intervention period. The Ford Foundation facilitated establishment of many programmes to introduce new techniques of farming to increase productivity (Stapes, 1992). On the 'management' side, the focus of programmes was mainly in small industries (p. 51). It resulted in establishment of institutions such as the Cottage Industries Emporium in 1952 and the National Institute of Design in 1961. In 1970s ASCI and IIM (Ahmedabad) initiated studies to look at issues and challenges of rural economies (Ramkrishnan, 1976). There remains scope for analysing wider implications of these programmes and trainings on rural and social entrepreneurship.

Not all imports of management techniques were channelled through institutions such as ASCI and IIMs. In some cases, the government directly sought assistance from international bodies. For example, in 1952, the United Nations Technical Assistance Administration was invited to help promote the concept of 'quality control' in Indian industries. As a result of this visit, dedicated units were established in Bombay in 1953 to provide assistance to local firms who wanted to gain more information or implement these systems. After a second visit from the UN team in 1962, additional units were established in Bangalore, Baroda, Bombay, Calcutta, Coimbatore, Delhi, Ernakulum, Madras and Trivandrum. However, industry showed very little interest in these programmes (Chatterjee, 1973). It was not until 1981 that Bharat Heavy Electricals (BHEL), a public sector enterprise, introduced the first quality circle in a systematic way (Srinivasan, 1991). However, there is very little information on the circumstances surrounding its introduction into BHEL. It is also not clear what type of, if any, quality control systems existed in Indian firms prior to 1980s. More broadly, the public sectors enterprises came to dominate the Indian economy during the state-led intervention period. Future research could look into their role as recipient and diffusor of such practices.

While institution building was taking place at the national level, it is interesting to explore how far individual firms took initiatives to develop their own training programmes. There is evidence of firms outside India developing in-house management training programmes (Friga et al., 2003; Russell, 2015). This also appears to be the case in India. Masrani et al's contribution (2018) shows that a managerial training programme was developed by Tata during 1950s. This was at a time when there were very few national institutions where training could be provided. Interestingly, Tata's in-house training was modelled on the Henley's Staff College as opposed to the American model. While there is evidence that other companies such as United Commercial Bank and Standard-Vacuum Oil Company started management training programmes during this period (Myers, 1958, p.113) there is a need to undertake further research on the variety of in-house training programmes during this early period, and on their impact on practice.

The global inter-connected nature of management education also contributed to the 'modernisation' of many family owned businesses. Throughout the three periods covered in this issue, a large section of the Indian economy continued to be under the control of family owned firms (Roy, 2018). Children of the many business families pursued education in Western countries. There are many anecdotal stories on how, upon return, they introduced new practices inspired by their Western education. A case in point is that of Rajiv Bajaj, of Bajaj Auto, who established new manufacturing unit 1990s inspired by knowledge gained from his education overseas (Aiyar, 2005). However, there is scope for a systematic analysis of this phenomenon within and between periods, looking into the range of business practices where contribution from management education were made and its implications through a fine-grained analysis.

Concerning family businesses more broadly, future research could study the implications of the changing government policies on the flow of global exchanges on their wider business practices and response to it.

Governance structures

While the subject of the managing agency is not directly addressed in this issue, its dominance as a major form of governance in Indian industry for much of the 19th and 20th centuries merits some discussion. Managing agencies were distinctly Anglo-Indian in origin. According to one estimate, by 1915 the agency houses controlled more than 70% of industrial capital in India (Misra, 1999). Up until the 1950s, industries such as jute, iron & steel, cotton, tea plantations, coal and railways were dominated by large agency houses, thus concentrating power into just a handful of firms (Sarkar, 2010; Nomura, 2014). The agency system was used by the British merchant houses as far back as the 1790s for investments in indigo plantations in India (Chapman, 1992). The first evidence of a local managing agent in India can be traced back to the establishment of Carr, Tagore and Company in 1834 (Kling, 1966, p. 38).

While managing agencies were both British- and Indian-owned, there were two important differences in how they operated. First, the British-owned agencies normally appointed external members to their boards of directors, especially for their technical and managerial expertise. Indian agencies, on the other hand, were a family affair and rarely appointed outsiders to the board. Therefore, while the Indian agencies were able to provide financial support to the companies they managed, they were often found to be lacking in technical and managerial expertise. Second, the majority of Indian agencies oversaw one or two firms in the same sector, whereas the British agencies were typically highly diversified and managed many companies (Loknathan, 1935, pp. 314–317).

A major advantage of the agency system was that it could provide centralised and coordinated control, especially where a large number of companies were managed and operated across different sectors (Loknathan, 1935, p. 348). In reality, the agency houses tightly controlled the companies they managed. The control was exercised in two ways: by actively protecting their shareholding and by having favourable agency contracts in the managed firm in their favour (Nomura, 2014). Through centralised control, the agency system is claimed to have also stifled the growth of the professional managerial class' in India (Patel, 1965). The agents were more interested in ensuring their steady commission than in making long-term investment decisions for the companies they managed (Lokanathan, 1935; Patel, 1965).

The agency system, it is argued, had a negative impact on industrial development in India. The system came under close scrutiny through the Companies Act of 1956 and was formally abolished on 3rd April 1970. However, some have questioned this negative perception, finding that managing agents were flexible in their practices, sometimes charging a commission based on profit rather than on sales in the interests of the company (Oonk, 2001).

One of the key functions they performed was to oversee the day-to-day running of the companies they managed. With the exception of Wearmouth (2014), there is very little detailed case studies of the managerial expertise they provided to the managed companies. Large agency houses typically managed many firms in diversified sectors. These firms were often located in different parts of India. It is not clear what system of control was employed to manage them. There is potential for future research to document and analyse managerial practices of large and small agencies, difference among Indian owned and difference between Indian and foreign owned agencies.

While the agency structure pre-dates the period of interest in this set of papers, it nevertheless demonstrates a pre-history of the Indian global interconnectedness that we focus upon. The replacement of the agency structure is a major area for future research in Indian business. Of particular interest would be the source of inspiration, Indian or Western, for the structure that replaced it, and the impact on the day-to-day governance of companies. According to Goswami (2016), there was very little change in the way companies operated after they moved away from the agency structure in the 1970s. The kernel of the agency form remains very much intact in modern Indian business groups. However, this hypotheses need to be supported by systematic fine-grained empirical analysis.

Concluding remarks

The articles in this edition have shown that the development of Indian business continued to be highly dependent upon global relationships of exchange, and transfer of knowledge, know-how and competences within the world economy throughout the twentieth century. While interconnectedness provided a means to frame the on-going relationship between Indian business and the global economy, it was the ability to embed this knowledge and know-how into Indian business that was a precondition to the success of these transfers. Over time, it is evident that many Indian businesses proved to be highly adaptive and responsive to the changing institutional environment within the economy.

With a thematic rather than a chronological approach, it is evident that many of the changes identified with later periods can be found to have their origins and establishment in the early post-independence era (Bagchi, 1999). In particular, the state-led import substitution and licensing policies proved to be far more open to international integration than might traditionally be assumed.

This arose from both political and economic changes, from the shift away from lower technologies of the first industrial revolution to the higher levels of value in the industries of the second, third and even fourth industrial revolutions including software, call-centres and services.

Finally, another common feature of the articles in this special issue is the cross-disciplinary approach to investigating these issues, drawing from international business, management and political economy. The contributions incorporate suggestions for greater methodological consistency in the analysis of Indian business (Jones & Zeitlin, 2008). This thematic analysis contributes a theoretically grounded approach to research on Indian business history that has, until recently, been overly dominated by biographies of prominent individuals and company histories.

Note

1.   For example, International such as IBM and International Computers and Tabulators; Domestic such as Electronics Corporation of India Limited, Hindustan Computers Limited, DCM Data Products, and Operations Research Group.

Disclosure statement

No potential conflict of interest was reported by the author(s).

References

Abdelrehim, N., Ramnath, A., Smith, A., & Popp, A. (2018). Ambiguous decolonisation: A postcolonial reading of the IHRM strategy of the Burmah Oil Company. *Business History*, 1–29. https://doi.org/10.1080/00076791.2018.1448384

Aiyar, A. S. (2005). Swaminomics: Rahul vs. Rajiv, The Bajaj Saga. *Times of India*, http://swaminomics.org/rahul-vs-rajiv-the-bajaj-saga/

Aldous, M. (2015). Avoiding Negligence and Profusion: The failure of the Joint-Stock form in the Anglo-Indian Tea Trade, 1840–1870. *Enterprise & Society*, *16*(3), 648–668. https://doi.org/10.1353/ens.2015.0005

Aldous, M., & Roy, T. (2018). Reassessing FERA: Examining British firms' strategic responses to 'Indianisation. *Business History*, 1–20. https://doi.org/10.1080/00076791.2018.1475473

Anubhai, P. (2011). *The IIMA story: The DNA of an institution*. Random Business.

Austin, G., Dávila, C., & Jones, G. (2017). The alternative business history: Business in emerging markets. *Business History Review*, *91*(3), 537–569. https://doi.org/10.1017/S0007680517001052

Bagchi, A. K. (1972). *Private investment in India 1900–1939*. Cambridge University Press.

Bagchi, A. K. (1982). *The political economy of underdevelopment*. Cambridge University Press.

Bagchi, A. K. (1997). Public sector industry and the political economy of Indian development. In T. J. Byres (Ed.), *The state, development planning and liberalisation in India* (pp. 298–339). Oxford University Press.

Bagchi, A. K. (1999, November 6). Globalisation, liberalisation and vulnerability: India and the third world. *Economic and Political Weekly*, *34*(45), 3219–3230.

Bagchi, A. K. (2007). State Bank of India. In K. Basu (Ed.), *The Oxford book of the Indian Economy* (pp. 495–498). Oxford University Press.

Byres, T. J. (Ed.). (1997). *The state, development planning and liberalisation in India*. Oxford University Press.

Cain, P. J., & Hopkins, A. G. (1993). *British imperialism: Innovation and expansion, 1688–1914*. NY: Longman. https://doi.org/10.1086/ahr/99.5.1685

Chapman, S. D. (1987). Investment groups in India and South Africa. *The Economic History Review*, *40*(2), 275–280. https://doi.org/10.2307/2596694

Chapman, S. (1992). *Merchant Enterprise in Britain: from the Industrial Revolution to World War I*. Cambridge: Cambridge University Press.

Chatterjee, A. K. (1973). Quality control. *ASCI Journal of Management*, *3*(1), 42–50.

Chenoy, K. M. (2015). *The Rise of Big Business in India*. Aakar Books.

Federation of Indian Chambers of Commerce. (1999). *Footprints of enterprise, Indian Business Through the Ages*. Oxford University Press.

Friga, P., Bettis, R., & Sullivan, R. (2003). Changes in graduate management education and new business school strategies for the 21st century. *Academy of Management Learning & Education*, *2*(3), 233–249. https://doi.org/10.5465/amle.2003.10932123

Goswami, O. (1985, September). Then came the Marwaris: Some aspects of the changes in the pattern of industrial control in Eastern India. *The Indian Economic & Social History Review*, *22*(3), 225–249. https://doi.org/10.1177/001946468502200302

Goswami, O. (2016). *Goras and Desis: Managing Agencies and the Making of Corporate India*. Penguin Books, India.

Gupta, B. (2005). Why did collusion fail? Archival evidence from the Indian Jute Industry. *Business History*, *47*(4), 532–552. https://doi.org/10.1080/00076790500132985

Gupta, B. (2014). Discrimination or social networks? Industrial investment in colonial India. *The Journal of Economic History*, *74*(1), 141–168. https://doi.org/10.1017/S0022050714000059

Harris, N. (1983). *Of bread and guns: The world economy in crisis*. Penguin.

Harris, N. (1986). *The end of the third world: Newly industrialising countries and the decline of an ideology*. Penguin.

Harvey, M., & Moeller, M. (2009). Expatriate managers: A historical review. *International Journal of Management Reviews*, *11*(3), 275–296. https://doi.org/10.1111/j.1468-2370.2009.00261.x

Hazari, R. K. (1966). *The structure of the corporate private sector: A study of concentration, ownership and control*. Asia Publishing House.

Hill, T., Haynes, W., & Baumgartel, H. (1973). *Institution building in India: A study of international collaboration in management education*. Harvard University Press.

Hirst, P., Thompson, G., & Bromley, S. (2009). *Globalization in question* (3rd ed.). Cambridge, UK/Malden, MA, USA: Polity Press.

International Labour Office. (1957). *Expanded programme of technical assistance: Report to The Government of the Republic of India on Training Within Industry for Supervisors*. International Labour Office.

Jain, S. (1968). New breed of managers. In S. B. Prasad & A. R. Negandhi (Eds.), *Managerialism for economic development* (pp. 20–44). Martinus Nijhoff.

Jones, G. (2000). *Merchants to multinationals: British trading companies in the nineteenth and twentieth centuries*. Oxford University Press.

Jones, G., & Zeitlin, J. (2008). *Oxford handbook of business history*. Oxford University Press.

Kidron, M. (1965). *Foreign investments in India*. Oxford University Press.

Kling, B. B. (1966). The origin of the managing agency system in India. *The Journal of Asian Studies*, *26*(1), 37–47.

Kumar, D., & Desai, M. (Eds.). (1983). *The Cambridge Economic History of India. Vol. 2, C.1757–C.1970*. Cambridge University Press.

Kumar, R. (2010). *The strategic implications of Indo-U.S. private-sector ties*. Center for a New American Security.

Lall, S. (1983). *The new multinationals*. Wiley.

Lokanathan, P. S. (1935). *Industrial organisation in India*. London: George Allen and Unwin, London.

Lubinski, C., Giacomin, V., & Schnitzer, K. (2018). Internment as a business challenge: Political risk management and German multinationals in Colonial India (1914–1947). *Business History*, 1–26. https://doi.org/10.1080/00076791.2018.1448383

MacKenzie, N. G. (2017, December). Entrepreneurs and Indian Transnational Business. *The NEP-HIS Blog*. Retrieved July 20, 2018. https://nephist.wordpress.com/2018/01/30/entrepreneurs-and-indian-transnational-business/

Maheshwari, B. L., & Ganesh, S. R. (1974). Management by objectives: The Indian experience. *ASCI Journal of Management, 4*(1), 1–13.

Maizels, A. (1963). *Industrial growth and world trade: World trends in production, consumption and trade in manufactures*. Cambridge University Press.

Majumdar, S. (2012). *India's late, late industrial revolution: Democratizing entrepreneurship*. Cambridge University Press.

Masrani, S. K., Perriton, L., & McKinlay, A. (2018). Getting together, living together, thinking together: Management development at Tata Sons 1940–1960. *Business History*, 1–19. https://doi.org/10.1080/00076791.2018.1458840

Markovits, C. (1985). *Indian Business and Nationalist Politics 1931–39: The Indigenous Capitalist Class and the Rise of the Congress Party* (Cambridge South Asian Studies). Cambridge: Cambridge University Press.

Misra, M. (1999). *Business, race, and politics in British India, c.1850–1960*. OUP Catalogue, Oxford University Press. https://doi.org/10.1086/ahr/105.4.1281-a

Mohan, R. (2011). *Brick by red brick: Ravi Matthai and the Making of IIM*. Rupa & Co.

Morelli, C. J. (2018). Regulating the post-independence textile trade: Anglo-Indian tariff negotiations from Independence to the multi-fibre arrangement. *Business History*, 1–14. https://doi.org/10.1080/00076791.2018.1517751

Morris, M. D. (1979). South Asian entrepreneurship and the Rashomon Effect, 1800–1947. *Explorations in Economic History, 16*(3), 341–361. https://doi.org/10.1016/0014-4983(79)90024-X

Myers, C. A. (1958). *Labor problems in the industrialization of India*. Harvard University Press.

Nayak, A. (2018). Internationalisation of the Indian telecommunication industry (1947–2004). *Business History*, 1–20. https://doi.org/10.1080/00076791.2018.1492553

Nomura, C. (2014). The origin of the controlling power of managing agents over modern business enterprises in colonial India. *The Indian Economic & Social History Review, 51*(1), 95–132.

Oonk, Gijsbert (2001). "Motor or millstone? The managing agency system in Bombay and Ahmedabad, 1850-1930." *Indian Economic Social History Review, 38*: 419.

Papendieck, H. (1978). British managing agencies in the Indian coalfield. In D. Rothermund & D. C. Wadhwa (Eds.), *Zamindars, mines and peasants* (pp. 165–224). Manohar Publications.

Patel, I. G. (1965). *Report of the managing agency system in India*. New Delhi: Government of India, Ministry of Law, Department of Company Affairs.

Pradhan, J. P. (2008). The evolution of Indian outward foreign direct investment: Changing trends and patterns. *International Journal of Technology and Globalisation, 4*(1), 70–86.

Pradhan, J. P. & Sauvant, K. (2010). Introduction: The Rise of Indian Multinational Enterprises. Revisiting Key Issues, In Karl P. Sauvant & Jaya Prakash Pradhan, with Ayesha Chatterjee & Brian Harley (Eds)., *The Rise of Indian Multinationals: Perspectives on Indian Outward Foreign Direct Investment* (pp. 1–23). New York: Palgrave Macmillan.

Ramkrishnan, V. (1976). Rural development: Human resource utilisation approach. *ASCI Journal of Management, 6*(1), 42–58.

Rao, J. M. (1997). Agricultural development under state planning. In T. J. Byres (Ed.), *The state, development planning and liberalisation in India* (pp. 127–171). Oxford University Press.

Ray, A., Mathai, J., Roy, S., & Sarkar, U. (2003). *The evolution of the State Bank of India, Vol 3, The era of the Imperial Bank of India 1921–1955*. Sage.

Riello, G., & Roy, T. (Eds.). (2009). *How India clothed the world: The world of South Asian Textiles, 1500–1850. Global economic history series*. Brill.

Roy, T. (2011). *The economic history of India 1857–1947* (2nd ed.). Oxford University Press.

Roy, T. (2017). Transfer of economic power in Corporate Calcutta, 1950–1970. *Business History Review, 91*(1), 3–29. https://doi.org/10.1017/S0007680517000393

Roy, T. (2018). *A business history of India: Enterprise and the emergence of capitalism from 1700*. Cambridge University Press.

Russell, J. (2015). Organization men and women: Making managers at Bell Canada from the 1940s to the 1960s. *Management & Organizational History*, *10*(3–4), 213–229. https://doi.org/10.1080/17449 359.2015.1098546

Sarkar, J. (2010). Business groups in India. In A. M. Colpan, T. Hikino, & J. R. Lincoln (Eds.), *The Oxford handbook of business groups* (pp. 294–321). Oxford University Press.

Sen, S. (2008). Gender and Class: Women in Indian Industry, 1890-1990. *Modern Asian Studies*, *42*(1), 75–116. https://doi.org/10.1017/S0026749X07002818

Sen, S. (2014). Gender and the jute industry: The Calcutta chapter. *International Journal of Management Concepts and Philosophy*, *8*(2/3), 126–144. https://doi.org/10.1504/IJMCP.2014. 063849

Sinha, D. (1986). Collaboration and innovation: Strategy for growth of management development programmes at ASCI. *ASCI Journal of Management*, *16*(1), 1–24.

Sinha, D. (2004). *Management education in India: Perspectives and challenges*. The ICFAI University Press.

Sinha, M. (1995). *Colonial masculinity: The 'Manly Englishman' and the 'Effeminate Bengali' in the Late Nineteenth Century*. Manchester University Press.

Srinivasan, A. V. (1991). Quality circle movement in India: A status report. *ASCI Journal of Management*, *21*(1), 56–75.

Stapes, E. S. (1992). *Forty years, a learning curve: The Ford Foundation programs in India, 1952-1992*. Ford Foundation.

Thompson, E. P. (1968). *The making of the English working class*. Penguin.

Tomlinson, B. R. (1979). *The political economy of the Raj, 1914–1947: The economics of decolonization in India*. Macmillan Press.

Tomlinson, B. R. (2003). British business in India 1860–1970. In R. P. T. Davenport-Hines & G. Jones (Eds.), *British business in Asia since 1860* (pp. 92–116). Cambridge University Press.

Tripathi, D. (2004). *The Oxford history of Indian business: Business enterprise in free India*. Oxford University Press.

Tripathi, D. (2007). *Oxford handbook of business history in India*. Oxford University Press.

Tripathi, D. (2014). Introduction. *Business History Review*, *88*(1), 3–8. https://doi.org/10.1017/S00076 80513001396

Tumbe, C. (2017). Transnational Indian business in the twentieth century. *Business History Review*, *91*(4), 651–679. https://doi.org/10.1017/S0007680517001350

Wearmouth. (2014). *Thomas Duff & Co and the Jute Industry in Calcutta, 1870–1921; Managing Agents and Firm Strategy* [Unpublished PhD thesis]. Economic Studies, University of Dundee.

Wilkins, M. (1994). Comparative hosts. *Business History*, *36*(1), 18–50. https://doi.org/10.1080/00076799400000002

Wolf, M. (1982). *Indian exports*. Oxford University Press.

Reassessing FERA: Examining British firms' strategic responses to 'Indianisation'

Michael Aldous and Tirthankar Roy

ABSTRACT
The Foreign Exchange Regulation Act, introduced in India in 1973, was the culmination of efforts to 'Socialise' economic policies and 'Indianise' corporate ownership. It resulted in a flight of foreign capital as Multinational Enterprises exited India to avoid these risks, finally driving out long-established British commercial interests. This article uses new sources to reassess how British businesses perceived the threats of Indianisation and analyses how they strategically responded to them. It shows that British-owned firms used a diverse range of strategies, some drawing on their extensive experience, knowledge and networks, built through long tenures in India, to adapt successfully.

Introduction

British commercial interests in India have a long and storied history. The arrival of the East India Company (EIC), and its dramatic expansion in the eighteenth century, saw British mercantile and political interests well established throughout India. The passing of the EIC's monopoly in 1813 did little to halt the growth of British business, with entrepreneurs pouring into India throughout the nineteenth century to pursue opportunities in emerging industries including tea and jute, to provide services such as banking, insurance and shipping, and to undertake the building and management of railways, ports and telegraphs (Chapman, 2004: Chapter 4).

Favoured by the colonial British government, British and European mercantile firms came to dominate many industrial and service sectors. This process was supported by the evolution of a model of business ownership and organisation known as the managing agency system. This allowed partnership firms, often former British trading firms, to manage and control a portfolio of joint-stock firms in diverse industries (Jones, 2000: Chapters 2 & 3; Jones & Wale, 1998). Through this system, the managing agent firms came to control around 75 per cent of industrial capital in India by the early twentieth century (Misra, 1999, p. 4).

The managing agent system was not solely the preserve of British interests, and control of industry in areas such as Mumbai and Ahmedabad was dominated by Indian owners (Lokanathan, 1935). However, in Bengal and Eastern India, where the largest concentration of economic power resided, corporate control was entrenched in the hands of British partners of managing agent firms and the directors of Multinational Enterprises (MNEs).

The story of what happened to the British commercial interests in India over the twentieth century is less well known and researched. Indian Business and Economic History has tended to focus on rather reductionist arguments about the relatively pro or anti-business nature of the post-independence Nehru government (Chaudhury, 1984; Chenoy, 1985; Mukherjee, 2002). It is, though, broadly accepted that from a position of dominance, British control over the Indian economy was weakened through the 1930s, and fundamentally reversed by Indian independence in 1947. Indianisation' policies introduced regulation that mandated the transfer of ownership and managerial control in foreign-owned firms (Tomlinson, 1981).

The role and response of British firms to these developments have been understood as one of passive decline, with little effort made to adapt to the post-independence environment (Tripathi & Jumani, 2012). Lingering outposts of British commerce were finally polished off by the Foreign Exchange Regulation Act (FERA) in 1973. This replaced an earlier Act passed in 1947, and ostensibly set out to regulate foreign currency flows, restricting firms' capacity for investment and the repatriation of revenues. Faced with these restrictive policies, many British firms, and a number of high-profile multinationals such as Coca-Cola and IBM, quit the Indian market (Encarnation, 1989). The outcome of the act has generally been negatively perceived, both for British firms forced to exit or significantly reduce their position in the Indian market and for the Indian economy, which saw capital flight and a loss of managerial and technological expertise hinder growth and the modernisation of certain industries (Desai, 1993; Panagariya, 2008, pp. 60–62).

There is, however, a growing interest in reassessing the trajectory of British commerce in India across the twentieth century, challenging the narrative of British decline. This has come from a number of directions. One strand has sought to demonstrate the role and importance of Indian entrepreneurship (Goswami, 1989, p. 302). A better understanding of Indian business interests in the early twentieth century, particularly considering how they acted in partnership with British business, may reveal different long-run trajectories for the ownership and management of business in India.

Another strand has focused on analysing the evolution of British firms, both MNEs and the managing agencies, to understand how they responded to these political shocks. A more complicated narrative of adaption, and transference of economic power has emerged (Jones, 2000). This narrative emphasises the particular circumstances of the firms, suggesting that a range of options was open to them, and paints a more diverse and differentiated pattern of response to political risk. In this article, we advance this project with new sources.

In their analysis of the response of British and American MNEs to the FERA act, Choudhury and Khanna (2014) showed that British firms were far less likely to exit India than their US counterparts, using a range of strategies to adapt to the evolving political situation. They asked whether this was, 'endogenous to other firm/managerial-level variables or whether there is a deeper causal story related to the home country of the MNE and/or historical ties between the home country and host country' (Choudhury & Khanna, 2014, p. 162).

They approach this question through International Business theory centred on the analysis of the response of MNEs to Country and Political Risks, such as arbitrary government intervention in the economy or discrimination against foreign firms (Choudhury & Khanna, 2014, pp. 145–148). Theory posits that these responses are driven by firms' capabilities and experience in managing in risky markets or the personal perceptions and understanding of individual managers to market risk (Buckley, Chen, Clegg, & Voss, 2016; Delios & Henisz, 2013). Alternatively, MNEs emanating from home markets with weak institutional constraints will be more likely to accept high political risks and may seek host markets with these characteristics, believing they have an advantage vis-à-vis firms from more institutionally developed markets (Holburn & Zelner, 2010).

The extensive experience of British firms in India, providing them with knowledge and connections to host country political actors, is identified as a factor allowing them to effectively negotiate and mitigate the effects of the FERA regulations. British firms had, therefore, greater capabilities and appetite to address political risks. The authors do, however, note that the research should be extended, 'to "unpack" the antecedents of what drives different MNEs to follow these different dynamic trajectories' (Choudhury & Khanna, 2014, pp. 162–163).

This article specifically aims to 'unpack' these antecedents by re-examining the response of a range of British firms to the political economy of post-independence India. It asks how the institutional environment evolved in India in the period between independence and FERA. What strategies did British businesses pursue in response to these changes? How were these strategies shaped by their experiences and operations in India? To answer these questions, the strategic responses of British firms to the institutional changes in India in the years around independence and the period leading to the 1973 FERA act are analysed. This includes examination of how British entrepreneurs understood the opportunities and risks they saw emerging in the post-independence period. Extending the periodisation allows analysis of temporal effects, such as path dependence, on the strategic choices, and examination of whether the endogenous firm level and historical variables, alluded to by Choudhury and Khanna, varied responses to the FERA act.

The article extends Choudhury and Khanna's (2014, pp. 143–145) analysis, which focused on a sample of British MNEs with operations in India, selected from the FTSE 50. While this sample provides a comparable set of firms it does not capture the range of British commercial interests in India. Smaller firms that were more limited in their range of activities and markets, but with longstanding operations in India are ignored. It also does not capture the response of an important segment of British business in post-independence India, the managing agencies or Indo-British firms.

This analysis seeks to advance Indian business history towards a more nuanced understanding of the impact of economic policy on foreign capital in the twentieth century. It also seeks to deepen understanding of the history of British business in India, more fully assessing the post-independence period, recognising that this was not simply a story of decline and failure, and that a range of responses to Indianisation emerged, some of which were successful.

The rest of the article has six sections. The next section develops a typology of British firms in India and describes the role of the IPB and the value of these sources. The subsequent sections develop the discourse of British firms on regulation to 1947, the regulatory environment after 1947, the response of British business to this environment, the turning point of the FERA, and the response of British firms to FERA. The conclusion reflects on the broad patterns of adaptation to regulation of foreign capital.

Typology of British firms in India

It is useful to start with a typology of British firms in India in 1947. When British colonial rule ended in South Asia, there were two types of British companies working in India. The first type can be called Indo-British companies, that is, British-owned companies that operated in India alone. Some of them were registered in London, and known as sterling companies, and others were registered in India. The managing agents, usually partnership firms, which managed these companies headed highly diversified conglomerates, with the managed companies having interests in manufacturing, services, plantations and commerce. These interests included tea, jute, paper, mining, engineering, inland transport, international ship- ping, financial services, real estate, agriculture and trade. The prominent examples of man- aging agencies were Bird (mainly jute and coal), Andrew Yule (jute, tea, engineering), McLeod (jute and tea) and Duncan Brothers (tea). The second type consisted of subsidiaries of British MNEs. The subsidiaries were all registered in India, but the majority shareholder was a British firm. Prominent examples include Imperial Chemical Industries, Guest Keen and Williams (GKW), Mather and Platt, British American Tobacco, the Anglo-Dutch conglomerate Unilever, Dunlop Rubber and Metal Box (Various sources taken from Graces guides, http://www.grac-esguide.co.uk/Main_Page).

Almost without exception, the Indo-British companies had either originated in nineteenth century commodity trade in the Indian Ocean rim (tea, textiles, opium and indigo), or depended on exports for their main market (jute, tea). Therefore, the India-based companies necessarily formed agency relationships with London firms. Managerial personnel, know- how and capital circulated between the two principal nodes of their business, London and Kolkata. In the case of the jute industry of Kolkata, a third node was Dundee. This circulation of 'factors' was indeed one of the major sources of their adaptive capacity. Post-independence Indian regulation struck precisely at this capacity by making circulation of people and money more difficult than before. The British MNEs in India typically started as a trading arm of a British engineering or chemical company, which moved into manufacturing in the interwar period when government protection was available. The MNEs, like the Indo-British firms, relied on links between London and Kolkata, but in this case the link mattered because of the transfer of specialist technology. The government of India took technology seriously, especially in fields such as chemicals, metallurgy and machinery, where MNEs were encouraged.

In business history scholarship on India, the segregation of British and Indian capital has been seen in two ways. One view is that the British firms monopolised privileges and access to resources thanks to support from the British Empire. In this view, a 'crisis of the British Empire' late in the interwar period allowed Indians to make some gains (Gupta, 2016, pp. 82–83). A second view is that British and Indian businesses specialised in different fields according to their comparative advantage (Morris, 1983). Indians, such as the cotton mill owners of Mumbai, made use of their knowledge of cotton trade, indigenous banking and markets in India and China; the Europeans made use of their access to the British money market, world shipping and networks of managerial personnel across continents. Some would say that the two fields were more interdependent than these two alternatives suggest. Struck by the Great Depression, Kolkata's British firms relied increasingly on Marwari bankers for financial accommodation, for example (Goswami, 1985). Still, British corporate enterprise in India did rely on distinct resources and strategies from Indians, for example, a successful combination of deep knowledge of Indian production conditions and international markets. This inherited knowledge capital would have made many of them reluctant to leave India when the government changed in 1947.

The article uses new sources from a trade body, the India Pakistan Burma Association (IPB), to examine the perceptions and responses of British firms to Indian Independence and the FERA acts. Established in 1942, the association was an interest group that sought to promote British industrial and commercial interests involved in these markets. In 1971, it was amalgamated into the Confederation of British Industry. The association represented the interests of British business across the spectrum of firm types.

One of the association's main functions was to collate and distribute market information to its members. To do this, it produced a bimonthly bulletin and commissioned reports that provided news on political, social and economic developments, considering how the changes affected the markets and their potential impact on their member firms. These bulletins and reports are used to identify what the association's members perceived as important issues, allowing analysis of the attitudes and perceptions of British business owners to the challenges of independence, and the policies of Indianisation, and their responses in terms of ownership and management structures.[1]

The article proceeds with a section analysing the IPBs bulletins in the years prior to and post-independence. This reveals that many British business owners remained guardedly optimistic of their position and the opportunities in India, in part, owing to an ongoing change in business ownership through growing involvement of Indian owners, both as shareholders and through direct participation in joint-ventures.

Discourse on regulation of foreign capital to 1947

Founded in 1942, the IPB had two dominant concerns in its early years. The first was the outcome of the Second World War, and India's position in any subsequent settlement. The second was to understand the direction of political and economic policy in India in the post-war period. Initially, the association sought to ensure that British business interests were recognised for their wartime contributions, and well positioned to take advantage of the post-war settlement. However, as the movement for Independence gathered pace, the major concern rested on the nature of the political settlement determining India's status and the position of British political and economic interests.

The political system had already undergone several significant shifts in the early part of the twentieth century. The Government of India Acts in 1919 and 1935 had granted significant autonomy and decision-making powers to Indian administrators, but India remained a British dominion. However, Gandhi and elements of the Congress Party called for full Indian sovereignty; an outcome an increasing number of Indians desired, as witnessed by the growth in self-rule and the Quit India movements. The nature of some of these movements was explicitly anti-British in sentiment. The obvious concern was that a post-war settlement would lead to a fully sovereign India in which British business was driven out and assets expropriated (Matthews, 1943).[2]

These threats were embodied in a series of clauses inserted in the Government of India Acts (1919 and 1935) which prohibited discrimination against British firms or individuals. In 1945, elements of the Indian government called for these clauses to be removed and replaced instead by a compact of mutual goodwill (British Library (BL ST856), IPB Bulletin Vol. 3, 11

October 1945, 'Trade with India'). The IPB's response was to demand that the clauses were retained, not because they provided an advantage to British firms, but rather because their removal was indicative that discrimination would occur in the future.

Yet, the needs of the Indian economy were such that links to Britain remained an imperative element of economic development. Sir Ardeshir Dalal, a key contributor to the post-war economic plan, noted that,

> In the immediate post-war years India has to look to the United Kingdom to a large extent for the supply of capital goods and the expert advice and assistance in the development of its industries which India so sorely needs. Co-operation should be welcome if it does not involve control or domination. (BL IPB Vol. 3, 29 March 1945, 'Future of British trade in India')

More generally, the Reconstruction Committee set up by the government of India indicated that the economy would be organised along broadly capitalist lines, 'Where industries are left in private hands, government control should interfere as little as possible with the actual management, so as to provide free scope to efficiency' (BL IPB Vol. 3, 1 February 1945, 'Planning for Indian industry'). However, there was to be far greater control over the direction and nature of future foreign investment. Assistance was particularly sought to develop high-tech industries, through the provision of machinery and expertise.

Where capital investment was required,

> care should be taken to see that the capital is issued in India, that the majority of the capital, as well as the directorate is in India and final control over policy rests in Indian hands. In cases where it is necessary to entrust the management of such industries to outside firms, provision should be made for the training of Indians in all technical processes and the ultimate transfer of control to Indian management' (BL IPB Vol. 3, 1 February 1945, 'Planning for Indian industry')

This approach was manifested in the range of policies, broadly termed 'Indianisation', through which the control and management of industry and commerce were to be increasingly vested in Indian hands.

Regulatory environment after 1947

The interplay between the threat of discrimination and the risk of expropriation, and the need for British assistance in industrial reconstruction, remained the key focus of the IPB's bulletins. In the years after Independence, the balance between risk and opportunity shifted in response to various political developments.

Independence required significant changes to the political infrastructure of India. A new Constitution was gradually drafted and negotiated, coming into effect in 1950. Similarly, a new Companies Act was enacted in 1956, with other bills such as the Industries Control Bill and Labour Relations Bill strongly impacting on commerce and industry. This created a volatile environment in which competing interests sought to influence the legislation. The IPB noted pressures against their interests coming from left-wing political actors, who disliked free trade and the movement of capital, and local industrialists, seeking to reduce the impact of more productive and competitive foreign firms dominating Indian markets. There were calls for the confiscation of foreign capital and assets and the protection of infant industries (BL (8229 aa 44), IPB Pamphlet 1953, 'A note on foreign investment in India').

Yet, the tenor of industrial and commercial policy remained guardedly friendly towards foreign investment in general, and British business more specifically (BL IPB Vol. 9, 9 February 1950, 'India and Pakistan today, Impressions of a Business Man'). In contrasting the situation in India with similar emerging markets such as Argentina and Egypt, the IPB was generally favourable towards the Indian government. It was recognised, and accepted, that investment would need to be focused, no longer being allowed in older and simpler manufacturing industries, or in purely trading concerns, which were to be given over to Indian business. There was also greater regulation of service industries, and targeted efforts by the government to increase Indian ownership in the key areas of banking, insurance and shipping, often by forcing foreign firms to use Indian services (BL IPB Pamphlet 1953, 'A note on foreign investment in India').

By 1953, the IPB had identified five main criteria for sanctioning foreign investment: that it went to a genuine programme of manufacture, in a field where indigenous investment is inadequate or technical know-how lacking, to increase productivity, and improve the balance of trade, and that provision is made for the training of Indian personnel to senior technical and administrative posts (BL IPB Pamphlet 1953, 'A note on foreign investment in India'). These, and the wider policies on Indianisation, were, though, viewed as moderately elastic and open to interpretation and lobbying.

However, from the mid-1950s, there was a shift towards an overarching social and political agenda described as 'Socialisation'. These policies sought to address the massive levels of poverty in India, by increasing levels of employment, improving labour conditions and wages, and investing in social services. The extent to which the government would involve itself in the economy to achieve these aims became a source of great debate that was still raging in the 1960s (BL IPB Vol. 23, 31 January 1964, 'A turning point for India'). Policies from price controls, the unionisation of labour, to nationalisation of certain industries and sectors, were all proposed in support of these aims. The Indian government was still, however, 'particularly anxious to reassure British visitors that in spite of the "socialisation" programme there is still a large and worthwhile field for British enterprise' (BL (T 50231 (a), IPB, Pamphlet 1955, 'A report on Indian conditions').

The 1960s saw efforts to balance the aims of socialisation with the desire to attract foreign investment. The IPB lobbied for improved conditions for investment, carefully analysing budgets to see where they might provide relief and benefits, in particular through changes to taxation (BL IPB Vol. 25, 28 February 1965, 'A balanced budget'). This period also saw growing external pressure, particularly from the USA, to open the economy up. It was notable, though, that the IPB rather than back the demands for greater market freedom actually emphasised the importance of the role of the state in growing the economy, while emphasising the need for fewer controls and more efficient government operations (BL IPB Vol. 25, May 1966, 'The unplanned economy').

Response of British business to the environment

How, then, did British business interests respond to the rapidly evolving political and economic landscape in India? The bulletins provide some insight into changes in the ownership and organisation of British business in India and the rationale that drove them. The policies of Indianisation, which gathered pace in the years around Independence, were an obvious threat to British control and management, requiring owners to dilute their ownership and allow Indians into management positions. The perception of further political risk, in the form of discrimination and the expropriation of assets, was also high in the immediate period around Independence. One obvious response would be rapid divestment of holdings in India.

In 1948, the total market value of foreign investments in India was Rs. 5,960 million, of which Rs. 5,190 million, or 87 per cent, was long-term business investment. Direct investments totalled Rs. 4,310 million, of which direct British investments were Rs. 3,220 million, followed by the US with Rs. 300 million (BL IPB Vol. 9, 5 October 1950, 'India's Foreign Investments – Reserve Bank report'). Between 1947 and 1953, it was calculated that the total foreign capital withdrawn from India was Rs. 580 million. The total British divestment was Rs. 420 million, of which Rs. 410 million was made up of the sales of shares and securities, and the liquidation or sale of business interests. A conservative estimate was that around 12 per cent of British-owned business in India was divested. This was, however, offset by Rs. 82 million of new foreign investment in this period, of which Rs. 68 million came from British sources (BL IPB Pamphlet 1953, 'A note on foreign investment in India').

There was clearly a degree of capital flight, but it was not a rout. The divestments were targeted in 'older forms of trade and long-established staple industries', such as jute and cotton, and import/export style trading ventures, industries most likely to be targeted by Indianisation policies (BL IPB Pamphlet 1953, 'A note on foreign investment in India'). It was also suggested that the majority of firms that divested ownership to Indian interests were comparatively small. Many of the larger firms rejected attractive offers to sell-out, believing India continued to offer good prospects (BL IPB Vol. 4, July 10 1947, 'Business transfers Big British firms unaffected'). The new investments were indicative that British business still saw opportunities in India, particularly in high-technology sectors where the Government welcomed new investment. The IPB surmised that the data 'does not support the frequently heard allegation that British enterprise has deserted the field in favour of its American and Continental competitors' (BL IPB Pamphlet 1953, 'A note on foreign investment in India').

If British business did not leave India, how did it react to the risks of Indianisation and Socialisation? The managing agent system, particularly in Bengal and Eastern India, was dominated by British owners and managers. Through this mechanism, British ownership and control of large swathes of industrial capital were entrenched, and thus faced significant threats from Indianisation. Indeed, post-independence, there were periodic investigations and proposed legislative changes aimed at dismantling the system (BL IPB, Pamphlet 1955, 'A report on Indian conditions').

In the face of these threats the IPB bulletins sought to justify and lobby for the importance of the managing agent system, both in the role it played in providing capital and expertise that supported Indian industrialisation, and in the benefits it provided to British exporters and manufacturers (BL IPB Vol. 4, December 19 1946, 'Managing Agencies'). This points to a degree of intransigence in the British response to the threats, clinging to the old-established models, yet the bulletins reveal quite a range of responses, both before and after Independence.

Writing in 1947, the position of the IPB was that,

'The British business which remains in India after August 15 will not be the British business of the past. Outwardly there may be little change, but under the surface will be found a complete reorientation of policy. This change will not cause any upheaval for the simple reason it has been going on for some considerable time' (BL IPB Vol. 4, 24 July 1947, 'Future for British Business in India, services in the new regime')

The bulletins identify a series of fundamental changes in the ownership and organisation of British-owned firms that had occurred well before 1947.

Ownership of joint-stock firms, particularly in established low-technology industries such as jute and tea, had been steadily transferred, handing control to Indian shareholders as early as the late nineteenth century (BL IPB Vol. 2, 25 May 1943, 'Britain's economic stake in India'). This process had seen many London listed sterling companies converted to rupee companies in Kolkata and Mumbai. In the years after Independence, some of this transfer occurred owing to pressure from the Indian government in certain sectors, and there were also elements of stock market manipulation (BL IPB Vol. 9, 24 February 1955, 'Indian interest in British firms'). There was, though, a significant transfer of ownership and control as Indian shareholders took controlling stakes that gave them seats on the board of directors of many corporations (BL IPB Vol. 2, 25 May 1943, 'Britain's economic stake in India').

Various factors encouraged these patterns of ownership transfer. There was recognition that integration of upstream raw material suppliers, often Indian-owned, with downstream production and marketing ventures, predominantly British-owned, could offer cost and supply advantages. While partition disrupted the supply of raw materials from the newly created East Pakistan, and independence led to growing labour disputes in West Bengal, significantly reducing the profitability in these industries, encouraging British owners to exit.

The managing agents also evolved, rather than waiting for government intervention to force the issue. Prior to 1947, many of the British-dominated agents opened up and added Indian partners (BL IPB Vol. 3, 2 August 1945, 'A trade link with Great Britain, Working of the managing agency system'). Some that were private limited companies incorporated, with Indian shareholders acquiring control through seats on the board. Well before official policy mandated Indianisation, British businesses had sought to diversify ownership (BL IPB Vol. 4, 24 July 1947, 'Future for British Business in India, services in the new regime'). It was estimated that by 1948, 85 per cent of equity in British-owned managing agencies now resided in Indian hands (Choudhury & Khanna, 2014, p. 136). Since the managing agency contract secured control by the firm over the companies managed, the company shares were allowed to be widely held.

The result of these processes was that capital and management became increasingly diverse (BL IPB Pamphlet 1953, 'A note on foreign investment in India'). Partnerships and joint ventures became a widespread approach to business ownership. Writing in 1953, it was expected that,

> the joint venture, which brings together in a common objective both Indian and foreign capital resources, would seem to come nearest to meeting the requirements of the situation, for it carries the assurances which both sides – as well as government itself – wish to secure. (BL IPB Pamphlet 1953, 'A note on foreign investment in India')

In the face of the political risks that emerged around independence, the dominant response of British business owners was one of adaption, seeking to find solutions that would allow them to remain in the market. Although Independence was a shock that forced out some unable to adapt, 'For the many more who are adaptable to changing circumstances – and adaptability has always been a British quality – the future holds definite prospects for a new Indo-British business even stronger than ever' (BL IPB Vol. 4, 24 July 1947, 'Future for British Business in India, services in the new regime').

In part, the rationale for adaption seems to have been driven by the generally positive attitude towards British business that emerged in the years after Independence. Mr Elkin,

President of the Indian Associated Chamber of Commerce, noted the 'surprising measure of good will towards us there, a reaction which many perhaps who left India in the difficult days … may find hard to believe' (BL IPB Vol. 9, 1 June 1950, 'Economic Prospects of India'). The historical links and scale of British commercial interests made collaboration and partnership a preferable solution to expulsion, for both British and Indian businesses. British business maintained close relationships with both the government and Indian commercial interests post-independence (BL IPB, Pamphlet 1955, 'A report on Indian conditions').

A further significant factor was the nature of British business investments in India. It was noted that, 'the great bulk of British investment in India was built up over the last seventy or eighty years from the re-investment of profits earned in the country' (BL IPB Vol. 9, 15 June 1950, 'Indo-British trade outlook'). The IPB's chairman, Sir Percival Griffiths, noted that although large well-established ventures were having success in issuing equities, new share issues were problematic for smaller and less well-known firms, so raising new capital proved difficult (BL IPB, Pamphlet 1955, 'A report on Indian conditions'). Many British owners had, therefore, significant capital tied up in firms through initial investments and reinvested profits. A prevailing attitude was that,

> 'Owners of capital are usually tenacious of their saving … foreign enterprise, will always do its best to adjust itself to each fresh turn of the screw (short of actual expropriation) in the hope that that the original investment, or at least some of it, may be preserved' (BL IPB Vol. 9, 24 March 1955, 'Ends and means').

Various managerial challenges were created by the policies of Indianisation. Increasing the proportion of Indian management, and demanding that new investments be accompanied by technical expertise, caused a change in the British commercial community (BL IPB, Pamphlet 1955, 'A report on Indian conditions'). A growing number of technicians and engineers were increasingly employed on short-term contracts, which resulted in a decline in the number of managers who had extensive knowledge and experience of India. This was exacerbated by changes to tax policies and rising prices, which reduced the standard of living for expatriate managers, making careers in India less attractive for both young Europeans and more established managers (BL IPB Vol. 9, 9 February 1950, 'India and Pakistan today, Impressions of a Business Man'; BL IPB Vol. 9, 24 March 1955, 'Ends and means'). The 'screw' was, however, relentlessly tightening, and the late-1960s became a decisive turning point. FERA was a culmination of this tendency.

Late 1960s turning point and the FERA

There was a demonstrable negative change in attitude and policy from the Indian government, with a corresponding deterioration of British attitudes, from the late 1960s. The challenge to adapt was becoming harder, and pessimism about Indian politics was gathering force among British MNEs. A confidential and unpublished survey of large British firms' attitudes towards India conducted by a faculty member of the University of Glasgow is revealing (British Library (Mss .Eur D982), 'Papers compiled by John R Castree … concerning the attitudes of British Companies with investments in India, their opinions on Indian economic and industrial policy, and an analysis of aid/trade relationships,' 1967–68).[3] The tone of the responses was one of uncertainty, with concern growing over the potential use of tax, foreign exchange and work permit rules as regulatory instruments to deter foreign firms. The response from Dunlop noted, 'Although Government's policy, as repeatedly stated, is to encourage foreign investment, in practice numerous conditions and controls become major irritants to the would-be investor' (BL Mss. Eur D982, 'Papers compiled by John R Castree'). The comments of J. and P. Coats note irritants such as indirect restraints placed on the business through income taxation, remittance of dividends and employment of foreign nationals through the restriction of visas.

The point of emphasis was increasingly 'distrust' of the Indian government, as highlighted in the comments from English Card Clothing: 'Indian government's distrust of the foreigner breeds a mutual distrust of the Indian government by the foreigner' (BL Mss. Eur D982, 'Papers compiled by John R Castree'). The response also mentioned that the prospect of 'communism on Burmese and Ceylonese models' was a deterrent to further investment in India. The responses clearly stressed 'the aversion of the Indian Government to foreign investors holding a majority interest in any undertaking' (BL Mss. Eur D982, 'Papers compiled by John R Castree').

The political economy of the early 1970s drove the Indian legislature towards tighter regulation of foreign capital, and the complete Indianisation of these companies. The first oil shock and persistent foreign-exchange shortages placed the balance of payments in serious crisis. Protectionist industrialisation, with an accent on chemicals, metals and machinery at the expense of traditional manufactures such as textiles and tea, had reduced the export capability of the country while increasing the import intensity of production. Politically, communism had grown in strength and influence in the 1960s, especially after a major food crisis in 1967. In the 1970s, Maoist intellectual critiques of Indian policy identified imperialism and industrialisation as the causes of underdevelopment, and foreign capital as the agent of imperialism (Chandra, 1973; Frank, 1966). The country was dependent on foreign aid, and foreign capital represented a degree of dependence on foreign know-how and money that was never totally acceptable to Indian politicians. The general stance of the Indian Parliament towards foreign investment became increasingly hostile, and hardened further in the 1970s.

FERA was approved by the Parliament in 1973 and in force from 1 January 1974. It replaced the Act of the same name passed in 1947. The new Act shared with the latter two general aims, to regulate the entry and operation of foreign firms, to regulate the employment of 'nationals of foreign states' in India (Section 30 of the Act), and to monitor and reduce outward remittance of foreign exchange. Unlike the more benign 1947 predecessor, the 1973 FERA made it mandatory on all firms to register in India. But it became famous for another provision that represented an extreme version of Indianisation. The provision was that companies incorporated abroad but operating in India, or predominantly foreign-owned Indian companies, were required to reduce the proportion of shares held by non-Indians to no more than 40 per cent, ensuring control of the firms remained in Indian hands.

Although conservation of exchange was an obvious rationale behind the law, other motivations got mixed up with it. The rhetoric of exploitation by foreign capital had a political impact. Contemporary reports suggest that lobbying by a section of Indian business was a further factor. Soon after Indian independence, Marwari traders, bankers and stockbrokers took control of several British companies in Kolkata. Subsequently, there were credible allegations of asset stripping, and induced bankruptcy (Roy, 2017). The adverse publicity that this episode created had the effect of slowing down the takeover spree. FERA came as an opportunity for a second round of takeovers. In 1973, 'Indian houses based in Kolkata' were again 'imagining themselves as the natural choice' as successors in an episode of forced divestment by foreign companies (Anonymous, 'FERA disappointment', 1977a). There were reports of 'hectic behind the scenes activity' to induce foreign firms to induct Indians as majority shareholders. Whether or not these groups also lobbied for FERA before it came into being, we cannot say, but FERA was compatible with their interests.

Of the 881 companies that reported themselves as potentially subject to the Act, about 50 were large industrial concerns with shareholding of foreign owners well above the mandated 40 per cent. Some of the largest British firms were Hindustan Lever (subsidiary of Unilever), ITC (British American Tobacco), Godfrey Philips (Philip Morris), Cadbury, Indian Duplicators (Gestetner), Britannia Biscuits (subsidiary of Associated Biscuit Manufacturers), Metal Box (Metal Box Co.), Lipton Tea, Gramophone Co. (EMI), and Remington Rand. US firms such as Pond's (Cheesborough Manufacturing) and Colgate-Palmolive dominated sectors such as pharmaceuticals and cosmetics. Other significant European firms included the Swedish engineering firm Asea, and Swedish-controlled Western India Match Co (WIMCO).

In its role of monitoring remittances, the Reserve Bank of India became the gatekeeper for the implementation of FERA. On the act's passage, foreign companies were required to immediately seek permission from the Bank to continue in business. Companies that needed to divest shares to achieve the 40 per cent foreign-owned shareholding limit were given some time to divest. The time, it turned out, was somewhat negotiable.

Companies could escape the provision altogether if they could make a case that they (a) operated in 'core' areas (such as utilities, essential chemicals and industries deemed to be of national importance), (b) operated in mainly exportable products or (c) worked with 'sophisticated technology.' It was difficult, almost impossible, for companies to claim that they fulfilled the first condition. Many tea companies could make a credible claim that they fulfilled the second condition. Several firms, possibly the majority, submitted applications stating that they employed sophisticated technology. The application of the FERA provisions to these firms became caught up in an unsophisticated discussion about technology, irrespective of the product line. Ultimately, such arguments only bought the firms' further time to avoid divestment and, in the case of large conglomerates like Hindustan Lever, some authority to influence the negotiation process.

The room to negotiate decreased in 1977, as compliance with FERA was ensured by more 'rigorous enforcement' than in the first four years of its existence. A new government came to power in 1977.[4] Arguing that 'the Congress government had in the last few years ... progressively relaxed ... restrictions on foreign companies,' the ruling Janata Party raised the heat on foreign firms (Anonymous, 'Expansion through FERA', 1977b). The Law Minister in the new government declared that 'big foreign companies' could not be 'allowed to exploit the country' any longer (Chaudhuri, 1979). In the first few months of the new government, there was reportedly a disagreement between a pro-business and an anti-business view within the party. Eventually the latter won, and George Fernandes, a trade unionist with a reputation for bullying capitalists, was appointed the Minster of Industries. The Janata Party remained in power for about two years. During this period, Coca-Cola and IBM left India rather than having to conform to FERA. It was said that Fernandes personally ordered them to leave. Fernandes also called up Hindustan Lever and WIMCO and ordered them to stop producing soaps and matches, deemed to be low priority, within three years, but he was to be out of the job in two. There were several other less publicised cases of discriminatory treatment at the behest of politicians. The General Secretary of the Janata Party and socialist activist Madhu Limaye was said to have personally intervened to deny Indian Explosives' bid to set up a naphtha cracking unit on the ground that government companies were already making the product.

Response of British firms to FERA

There were two patterns of response to FERA. Firms selling in the Indian market expanded shareholding, diluted foreign shareholding and used the proceeds to make new investment commitments. These new commitments forced them to move somewhat further away from their core areas of operation. Export-oriented firms, such as tea companies, restructured ownership without a plan to expand shareholding.

Companies registered in London owned 40 per cent of the tea plantation area and controlled 44 per cent of the production in the late 1970s. These companies were asked to comply with the provisions of FERA by incorporating in India, but the foreign owners were allowed to retain 76 per cent holding. Between 1973 and 1977, a few large companies did register in India. Macneill Magor merged with Williamson to form Williamson Magor, a B.M. Khaitan company, Kannan-Devan Hill Plantations, a James Finlay company, sold its stake to Tata and Harrisons, and Crosfield estates were sold to the R.P. Goenka group of Kolkata.

In 1977, pressure built up on the Reserve Bank of India to force the remaining companies to Indianise. The Bank issued a stern warning and threatened stoppage of all repatriation at the very least, and criminal prosecution at worst. Tea producers usually sold tea in collaboration with a London agent, often an affiliated firm. The Reserve Bank of India required that such arrangements be subject to license (B.M., 1982). The Bank oversaw valuing the estates in the case of a sale. Several British owners were said to be interested in a sale of the estates to Indians; the fear was that the Bank would undervalue the shares under political pressure (Anonymous, 'Tea', 1977c).

At least two large transfers were initiated by FERA, but these were completed in an unplanned manner over several years. In 1976, Jokai (Assam) Tea Co. Ltd, a wholly owned subsidiary of Jokai Tea Holdings, Ltd UK, sold its stake to a UK company called Frendial. A few years later, Frendial sold the shares to Sethia. At the time of the sale, there was a rumour that Frendial was acting on behalf of Indians interested in the firm, but this was not proven. The company, later renamed Rossell India, was owned by an Indian group (B.M. 1979). The other case was Warren Tea Holdings, a company that owned James Warren, which managed and owned some of the best tea companies in Assam and Dooars. FERA induced Warren Tea to Indianise, and the two companies merged into one. After a brief takeover by a tea group, Guthrie, Warren Tea was bought by an Indian resident in the UK, A.K. Ruia. In the 2000s, a battle for control broke out between Ruia and an offshoot of the Goenka family over control of these companies, and as a compromise, the company split into two, named Warren Tea and James Warren (Mukherji, 2012).

Foreign interest continued in tea, one major example being Goodricke, which reformed itself as an Indian company with foreign control. Goodricke originated in two mid-nineteenth-century Kolkata firms, Duncan Brothers and C.A. Goodricke. Duncan Brothers' London agent was the firm Walter Duncan. C.A. Goodricke was a London tea merchant who had spent a part of his youth in Assam and held the agency of several Eastern Assam tea estates. In 1949, Walter Duncan merged with C.A. Goodricke to form Walter Duncan and Goodricke Ltd (WDG). This company sold its estates in Assam to the Goenka group in Kolkata within a few years after independence, while expanding in tea in East Africa. In the 1960s,

British-owned Camellia Investments acquired a significant stake in WDG (Camellia PLC. History http://www.camellia.plc.uk/history (accessed 27 March 2017)).

As mentioned before, in several cases, firms desiring to stay on in India made an investment plan, raised fresh equity and, by a variety of means, tried to ensure that the equity went to trusted hands. Private placement with retired employees, existing employees and financial institutions was the common methods adopted. The companies were generally well managed, so that the divestment raised a great deal of interest. Several of these sales were hugely oversubscribed. The fact that some of them were gradually Indianising their shareholding from some time past (such as Hindustan Lever) ensured that they could take this step without running into takeover threats. Careful planning and help from public-sector financial institutions eased the process. Between 1973 and 1977, intense negotiations took place as companies sought permission, formally or informally, to set their own schedule for Indianisation or even to avoid it altogether.

One of the most cited cases was Hindustan Lever. Lever Brothers (India) was established in 1933 to produce soaps and detergents, and Hindustan Vanaspati Manufacturing Company some years earlier in the production of hydrogenated vegetable oil, both being subsidiaries of Unilever. A separate trading company marketed toilet preparations. In 1956, these companies were merged to form Hindustan Lever Limited (HLL). Between 1956 and 1973, HLL expanded in dairy products and animal feed, and continued to produce Vanaspati, but its core businesses remained soaps and detergents. HLL owned three top brands in these fields, namely, Lifebuoy soap, Surf detergent and Dalda Vanaspati.

In the wake of the FERA, HLL chose not to dilute its stake to 40 per cent and Indianise, but to remain a 51 per cent owned subsidiary of Unilever. HLL negotiated with the government that they would subsequently export 10 per cent of their production and diversify in high-technology fields. Between 1973 and 1982, the share of soaps and detergents – the two core businesses – in HLL sales fell from 70 to 63 per cent. The export obligations were met by trading unrelated goods such as shoes, clothing and seafood, and the promise to diversify into high-technology fields was met by vertical integration into sodium tripolyphosphate and linear alkyl benzenes, components of detergents. HLL remained a potential target of punitive action because its core products were consumer goods, and it was not obvious that the successes of its main brands owed to innovation. In 1982, HLL divested from its food products, transferring these to Lipton, a subsidiary company that, owing to the level of foreign ownership being under 40 per cent, was not affected by FERA.

Analysts of HLL saw its strategy as 'direct contravention of FERA with the government turning a blind eye to its activities', which allowed the firm to carry out 'foreign exchange drain' year after year (Rath, 1982). The company, however, had to pay a price for losing sight of its core business, soaps and detergents. Its pricing and branding strategies suffered. In the 1980s, a small firm called Nirma emerged as a significant threat in its main market, prompting HLL to change its marketing and advertising system. Later accounts of restructuring in HLL suggest that investments had slowed during the 1980s, to pick up pace after the economic liberalisation in the 1990s (Pandey, 1985).

The business strategy of Imperial Chemical Industries (ICI) after FERA displayed a similar pattern to HLL. One of the four constituent companies of the speciality chemicals manufacturer ICI, Brunner Mond, opened a trading office in India in 1911 and converted into a manufacturing firm in the 1950s, with its main plant located near Kolkata. Unlike HLL, there never was a question that ICI's expertise was both 'sophisticated' and of great value to the industrial strategy pursued in India. The company expanded steadily in the 1950s and the 1960s, in new fields such as explosives, and diluted its shareholding to conform to the 1956 Indian Companies Act. After FERA, it expanded Indian shareholding (in 1978 and 1979) and used the proceeds to make new investments. All along, ICI UK provided the Indian subsidiary technical support. The company still ran into labour and production difficulties because of labour disputes and strikes in Kolkata, where one of its main plants was based. In the early 2000s, there was a conscious attempt to strengthen links between the parent company and the subsidiary. In 2011, with ICI UK changing ownership, the Indian subsidiary became a subsidiary of Akzo Nobel (Akzo Nobel N.V. https://www.akzonobel.com/in/news/pressre-leases/2010/worlds_largest_paint_company_akzonobel_concludes_ici_india_transition.aspx (accessed 27 March 2017)).

If HLL and ICI were shaken by and eventually survived FERA, in two other cases, we see decline and bankruptcy, as the British owners of the Indian subsidiary simply gave up on India.

In the 1920s, a series of amalgamations of British tinplate manufacturers and traders, box-making firms and printers led to the emergence of the Metal Box Company, registered in that name in 1930. The Indian subsidiary of Metal Box was started in 1933 in the company's traditional business, containers of various types, and was based in Kolkata. The company was profitable through the 1950s and the 1960s. Following the reinforcement of FERA in 1979, the two large foreign shareholders – Metal Box Overseas, and Continental Can Co. Inc – divested from the Indian firm. Metal Box Overseas continued to remain a large shareholder, but the company was effectively an Indian company, now named Metal Box India Ltd. No major Indian business group seemed to be seriously interested in the company, whereas direction from London ceased to be of much importance. The company appeared to lack vision as well as direction thereafter. From 1980 onward, an almost unending sequence of financial crisis and labour disputes led to the eventual closure of the company (Gupta, 1991; Mathai, 1988). In 1989, the company was referred to the Board of Industrial Finance and Reconstruction, the government body in charge of rehabilitating bankrupt companies. Conflicting views of the prospects of the company were voiced. Metal Box Plc, still a signifi-cant shareholder, came onto the scene expressing hopes of a recovery but was apparently unwilling to stake any fresh equity. After 2000, few media reports appeared on Metal Box, except for occasional news about attempts to sell real estate. Its manufacturing units were closed.

The Indian branch of the Midlands metallurgy firm Guest Keen Nettlefolds (GKN) was known as GKW after one Henry William partnered with GKN to start GKW in Kolkata in the 1920s. The Kolkata firm produced nuts, bolts, fasteners and railway material. The relationship between GKN and GKW was always arm's length, though they did work in similar lines of manufacturing. After FERA, GKW was allowed to carry on with the existing foreign holding of 59 per cent, on condition that the firm diversified into 'sophisticated technological fields'. Between 1973 and 1978, GKW expanded its share capital, the majority being held by resident Indians. But the promise to diversify did not materialise. In fact, there was growing divergence in the lines of business between the two companies, and FERA may have hastened that process. As GKN moved towards higher-technology automotive engineering, military vehi-cles, aerospace and industrial services, GKW remained committed to fasteners, nuts and bolts, in which lines it faced tough competition from small firms. In the 1980s, GKW succumbed to labour disputes and heavy debt burden, and in 1994, GKN divested its 47 per cent stake to a trading company.

Notwithstanding these two examples of decline, in the 1980s, FERA pressures eased off. A robust inward flow of foreign remittance from labour migration to the Persian Gulf had made the foreign-exchange management less of a worry for the government of India and the Reserve Bank. In the late 1980s, Reserve Bank's data on company accounts revealed that FERA had failed to change levels and percentages of remittance in the previous decade, while import-intensity of investment had increased after the spate of expansions and diversification. 'The overall BOP [Balance of Payments] effect is negative,' and therefore, 'FERA had failed' (Anonymous, 'Foreign Companies', 1988).[5] Despite such stark results, FERA continued to be applied with less and less force. Licensing requirements in import and investment were relaxed, and there was more openness to foreign investment. Actual inflow of foreign investment did not respond to these changes dramatically, but in several cases of new entry, the concerned Ministry relaxed the FERA norms.

Goodyear was one such example. Its expansion plan in industrial rubber in 1980–1981 ran into two obstacles, the now government-owned company Andrew Yule had also planned a similar enterprise, and Goodyear stake would increase to 60 per cent after the expansion. Andrew Yule did not have the marketing experiences of Goodyear. The Ministry negotiated a deal – 'said to be the first arrangement of this kind' – where the public-sector firm and Goodyear would jointly produce, and the former would market. Goodyear was allowed to raise its stake (B.M., 1982).

Conclusion

This article investigates the response of British firms to regulatory policy of post-independence India, especially the response to 'Indianisation' and its major instrument, FERA. The first part shows that the political situation in the years post-independence presented various risks for British firms. The proposed policies of Indianisation, both of the ownership and management of firms, and the decision to block access to certain industries, potentially threatened existing assets and limited opportunities for future investment. British firms responded through a series of adaptions, divesting holdings and assets from certain industries and investing in more technologically advanced sectors, while using long-established relationships to build joint ventures with Indian owners. They also exploited relationships with the government to lobby for the benefits of foreign capital investment and knowledge transfer in technologically advanced industries.

Although initial worries about Indianisation were widely expressed, the balance of opportunity and risk remained somewhat favourable for British business. For many firms, it was also the case that their Indian operations formed such a significant portion of their business that exiting represented a major threat to ongoing operations and loss of capital. The second part of the article deals with the FERA, analysing the rationale for its passage and effects on foreign businesses. The study reveals that strategic responses varied from outright divestment, sharing ownership, to expansion, investment, diversification and making a case that the firms operated with sophisticated technologies, even when no clear definition of the term existed.

The limitations of the case-study methodology used in this article make the identification of systematic patterns of strategic responses to FERA difficult. Broadly, however, explaining the diverse responses ranging from to exit or stay and adapt requires a deeper understanding of the managing agency and wider typology of forms of ownership employed by British owners. The extent to which the policies to Indianise capital, labour and corporate ownership could be manage varied both between and among the different forms. Indo-British firms had extensive experience of shared ownership and management, having adapted to significant political economy changes throughout the 19th and 20th centuries. Indianisation pushed through FERA, ostensibly, was no more a challenge than those they had faced previously.

Although the antecedents influenced the firms' responses, the decisions in the 1970s to remain or exit were driven by the future prospects of the industry and the firms' relative exposure to the Indian market. The tea companies, where prospects remained reasonable, and exposure was often high, saw continued adaption. While Metal Box and GKN were forced to divest away from their core industries, and with British and foreign investors less exposed to the Indian market exited, large MNEs such as HLL saw opportunities and had the capacity to innovate and negotiate, allowing them to diversify and remain in the market. Again, longstanding experience and continued proximity to the government were assets that enabled adaption. Further research encompassing more cases should help to clarify the relative importance of the key factors identified in this article: experience and proximity to the Indian government and investors, alongside industry structure and the firms' capacity for innovation and deployment of advanced technologies, in shaping the exit/adapt strategies followed by the British firms. If firms' responses to Indianisation were mixed, so were the macro-implications of forced Indianisation and not entirely negative. The rather simplistic pro and anti-business readings of FERA, and its negative effects on foreign capital can be reassessed. From the few cases (Hindustan Lever, Cadbury, McLeod Russell, Britannia Biscuits) where large-scale divestment did occur, the episode stimulated the share market and public shareholding. The link between issuing fresh equity and diversification into fields that the firms could project either as high-technology or as export-oriented strategies induced investment and innovative marketing. The Indian economy had run into an industrial stagnation from the mid-1960s. The investment boom led by the government sector was proving unsustainable (Nayyar, 1994). Growth, however, was depressed during 1965 and 1975, and then mysteriously recovered. The recovery has not yet been satisfactorily explained. The consequences of FERA in stimulating diversification and issue of fresh equity may have contributed to the recovery (Vikraman, 2017).

This article, more generally, seeks to encourage efforts in Indian Business History to reassess and move towards a more nuanced understanding of foreign capital, particularly manifested in British business, and its intersection with both Indian political and commercial interests in the twentieth century. It also offers some interesting opportunities to further explore ideas in International Business theory related to MNE strategy in managing country risk. Indo-British firms challenge the concept of having a clearly delineated home market, in effect being multinational in ownership and management, with attendant capabilities and knowledge. The extent to which such firms perceive and respond to country risk may vary from more traditional MNEs. This opens interesting opportunities to reassess the trajectories of Indian MNEs later in the twentieth century, considering their antecedents, particularly the development of capabilities and knowledge of global markets built through joint ownership and management with British business.

Notes

1. We should note the potential biases of these sources in explaining the perception of British Business interests in India. The membership had clear vested interests in preserving their position and assets, possibly leading to overly positive descriptions of the market, and downplaying threats to maintain confidence. At the same time, there is an incentive for the compilers to provide as good an understanding of the market as possible, to support their members decision-making. On balance, these sources represent a good insight into the understanding of British business owners towards the Indian market.
2. Sequestration of British assets was feared by European respondents and demanded by Indian respondents to the interviews conducted in 1942 by the *New York Times* journalist Herbert Matthews in India, 'India Challenges.' More broadly, the expropriation and nationalisation of oil resources that occurred in Mexico in 1938, and Iran in 1951, were tangible warnings of the threats facing foreign capital in periods of political uncertainty.
3. The firms in the survey were Tube Investments, Associated Electrical Industries Ltd, Imperial Chemical Industries, The Metal Box Company Overseas Ltd, Reckitt and Coleman Overseas, British India Steam Navigation, The English Card Clothing Co. Ltd, Glaxo International Ltd, The Dunlop Company Ltd, Chloride Overseas Ltd Leyland Motors Ltd, and Turner and Newall Ltd.
4. The Janata Party was formed of a coalition between socialists, farming lobbies, and pro-business groups, united in their opposition to the Congress led by Indira Gandhi. As a political party, it did not project a single ideology, but being a coalition, individual leaders wielded considerable power in policy-making.
5. According to World Bank data, net inward foreign direct investment as a percentage of GDP was negative in India during the peak years of the FERA, 1975–1977. Thereafter, net inflow turned positive, but it was less than one-tenth of the world average until the 1991–1992 reforms, after which it rose sharply. These trends suggest that the FERA and its aftermath may have had an effect on the direction of the net flow, but made little difference to the scale of foreign investment either way (http://data.worldbank.org/indicator/BX.KLT.DINV.CD.WD?locations=IN (accessed 8 August 2017).

Disclosure statement

No potential conflict of interest was reported by the authors.

Archival Sources

British Library (BL) (ST856), IPB Bulletins Vol. 1 - 25
BL (T 50231 (a)), IPB, Pamphlet 1955, "A report on Indian conditions."
BL (8229 aa 44), IPB Pamphlet 1953, "A note on foreign investment in India."
BL (Mss Eur D982), "Papers compiled by John R Castree … concerning the attitudes of British Companies with investments in India, their opinions on Indian economic and industrial policy, and an analysis of aid/trade relationships," 1967-68.

Bibliography

Akzo Nobel N.V. 2010. World's largest paint company AkzoNobel concludes ICI India transition. May 5. Retrieved March 27, 2017, from www.akzonobel.com/in/news/pressreleases/2010/worlds_largest_paint_company_akzonobel_concludes_ici_india_transition.aspx

Anon. (1977a). FERA: Disappointment for Indian big business. *Economic and Political Weekly, 12*(30), 1160–1161.

Anon. (1977b). Expansion through FERA. *Economic and Political Weekly, 12*(49), 1992–1993.

Anon. (1988). Foreign companies: Aftermath of FERA. *Economic and Political Weekly, 23*(42), 2138–2139.

Anon. (1977c). Tea: The pruning process. *India Today*.

B.M. (1982). FERA in reverse. *Economic and Political Weekly, 17*(37), 1484–1485.

B.M. (1979). Not-So-Strange case for Jokai India. *Economic and Political Weekly*, 1788–1789.

Buckley, P., Chen, L., Clegg, J., & Voss, H. (2016). Experience and FDI risk-taking: A microfoundational reconceptualization. *Journal of International Management, 22*, 131–146.

Camellia PLC. History. Retrieved March 27, 2017, from www.camellia.plc.uk/history

Chandra, N. (1973). Western imperialism and India Today, I and II. *Economic and Political Weekly, 8*(7), 221–244, 403-8.

Chapman, S. (2004). *Merchant enterprise in Britain: From the industrial revolution to World War I.* Cambridge: Cambridge University Press.

Chaudhuri, S. (1979). FERA: Appearance and reality. *Economic and Political Weekly, 14*(16), 734–743.

Chaudhury, S. (1984). Indian Bourgeoisie and foreign capital, 1931-1961. *Social Scientist, 12*(5), 3–22.

Chenoy, K. M. (1985). Industrial policy and multinationals in India. *Social Scientist, 13*(3), 15–31.

Choudhury, P., & Khanna, T. (2014). Charting dynamic trajectories: Multinational enterprises in India. *Business History Review, 88*(1), 133–169.

Gupta, D. (2016). *State and capital in post-colonial India: From licence Raj to open economy.* New Delhi: Cambridge University Press.

Delios, A., & Henisz, W. (2013). Political hazards, experience, and sequential entry strategies: The international expansion of Japanese firms, 1980–1998. *Strategic Management Journal, 24*, 1153–1164.

Desai, A. (1993). *My economic affairs.* New Delhi: Wiley Eastern.

Encarnation, D., & Mutlinationals, D. (1989). *India's strategy in comparative perspective.* Ithaca: Cornell University Press.

Frank, A. (1966). The underdevelopment of development. *Monthly Review, 18*(4), 17–31.

Goswami, O. (1985). Then came the Marwaris: Some aspects of the changes in the pattern of industrial growth in Eastern India. *Indian Economic and Social History Review, 22*(3), 225–249.

Goswami, O. (1989). Sahibs, Babus, and Banias: Changes in industrial control in Eastern India, 1918-50. *Journal of Asian Studies, 48*(2), 289–309.

Grace's Guide to British Industrial History. Retrieved January 16, 2016, from http://www.gracesguide.co.uk/Main_Page

Gupta, S. (1991, February 13-28). Metal box: Saving grace. *Business World,* 80–81.

Holburn, G., & Zelner, B. (2010). Political capabilities, policy risk, and international investment strategy: Evidence from the global electric power generation industry. *Journal Strategic Management, 31*, 1290–1315.

Jones, G. (2000). *Merchants to multinationals: British trading companies in the 19th and 20th centuries.* New York, NY: Oxford University Press.

Jones, G., & Wale, J. (1998). Merchants as business groups: British trading companies in Asia before 1945. *Business History Review, 72*(3), 367–408.

Lokanathan, P. (1935). *Industrial organization in India.* London: George Allen and Unwin.

Mathai, P. (1988, May 15). Cutting links. *India Today*.

Matthews, H. (1943). India challenges British finance. *Current History (pre-1986), 3,* 496–498.

Misra, M. (1999). *Business, race, and politics in British India, c. 1850–1960.* New York: Oxford University Press.

Morris, M. D. (1983). The growth of large-scale industry to 1947. In D. Kumar (Ed.), *Cambridge economic history of India, vol. 2: 1757-1970* (pp. 551–676). Cambridge: The University Press.

Mukherjee, A. (2002). *Imperialism, nationalism and the making of the Indian capitalist class, 1920–1947*. New Delhi, Thousand Oaks and London: Sage Publications.

Mukherji, U. P. (2012, August 15). Warren tea to be split into two companies. *Times of India*.

Nayyar, D. (Ed.). (1994). *Industrial growth and stagnation: The debate in India*. Bombay: Oxford University Press.

Panagariya, A. (2008). *India: The emerging giant*. New York and Oxford: Oxford University Press.

Pandey, I. M. (1985). Hindustan lever limited. IIM Ahmedabad Case Studies No IIMA/F&A0405.

Rath, A. K. (1982). Local and global operations of multinational corporations: Unilever in India. *Social Scientist, 10*(10), 30–43.

Roy, T. (2017). Transfer of economic power in Corporate Calcutta 1950-1970. *Business History Review, 91*(1), 3–19.

Tomlinson, T. (1981). Colonial firms and the decline of colonialism in Eastern India 1914–1947. *Modern Asian Studies,* 455–486.

Tripathi, D., & Jumani, J. (2012). *Oxford history of contemporary Indian business*. New Delhi: Oxford University Press.

Vikraman, S. (2017, August 8). How 'Draconian' FERA clause triggered flush of retail investors. Retrieved from   http://indianexpress.com/article/explained/express-economic-history-series-3-how-draconian-fera-clause-triggered-flush-of-retail-investors/

Regulating the post-independence textile trade: Anglo-Indian tariff negotiations from independence to the Multi-Fibre Arrangement

Carlo J. Morelli

ABSTRACT

Based upon UK and Indian government archives the article innovatively informs our understanding of business/state relationships in the areas of the regulation of post-colonial international trade. The abandonment of Imperial Preference for tariff protection in Britain proved problematic in the case of the Indian textile industry, whose entry into the British market, tariff free under Imperial Preference, was being replaced first by quota regulations and then by duties from the early 1970s. This article examines the negotiations between British and Indian textile interests in the period before the Multi-Fibre Arrangement as an environment where conflicting interests were negotiated.

Introduction

The introduction of the Multi-Fibre Agreement (MFA) in 1974 was the culmination of international negotiations which sought to protect declining domestic industries of the advanced western economies of Europe and North America from import competition from newly industrialising developing economies. Textiles as an example of an industry of the first industrial revolution that was particularly vulnerable to international competition from emergent economies acts as a key example of this process. The Anglo-Indian negotiations and the MFA provide a case study for our understanding of the relationship between governments' management of economic transitions within their own economies and their management of international trade between economies in response to their domestic concerns.

This case, however, also suggests that the regulation of the textile trade between Britain and India, while an important example of this form of regulation, cannot be understood in the traditional simplistic contextualisation of competition between the developed and developing economies. Indian producers and the Indian state were not simply powerless recipients of decisions made by dominant western powers. Instead, Indian producers rapidly moved into higher technology production and internationalised production of low-cost textiles in order to circumvent barriers to trade imposed by the MFA. At the same time the Indian state actively encouraged production in higher-value, export-orientated artificial fibres. In doing so the article questions the entrepreneurial failure identified in the historiography of the

Indian textile industry and the failure of the Indian state in developing strategies to maintain employment in the sector.

The growth of textile industries has historically been associated with the development of the first industrial revolution in modern economies (Goodman & Honeyman, 1988). Textiles not only provided a means for industrial revolutions to develop internally within economies but also provided a mechanism for the growth of internationalisation of economies through the trade of raw materials, semi-finished products, and finished consumer goods (Deane, 1979). Thus, the domestic development of indigenous textile industries and the subsequent domestic management of the transition from textiles into more complex manufacturing processes, combined with management of the international textile trade, have consistently been the focus of government industrial and commercial policy in industrialising economies.

In the case of Britain and India the political context within which the management of these trade relationships occurred from the end of the Second World War to the introduction of the MFA in 1974 was one in which the end of the British Empire and Indian independence, in 1947, ensured that Indian economic interests could no longer be subordinated as easily to those of British industrial interests, as had been the case under empire. As a result, the attempts of the British government to dictate terms of trade to the Indian government by limiting imports of low-value goods were met with the economic reality that saw Indian producers responding proactively by organising production into higher value-adding sectors of the trade. In doing so the Indian producers were replicating changing patterns of production which British producers had followed in the decades earlier when the first international competition emerged from Indian textile producers.

The article demonstrates that in both Britain and India government trade policies, aimed at protecting domestic employment while promoting industrialisation, had very different impacts; while both economies grappled with a similar problem: that of managing an economic transition from low-value textile production into higher-value internationally competitive textile production and simultaneously dealing with the emergence of competition from newer, lower-cost centres of production. In this respect the questions faced by the Indian government and the Indian textile industries were in many respects similar to that of the British industries.

The following sections of the article show how India's industrialisation before independence came to be understood as highly racialised, with the promotion of indigenous ownership becoming one of the key themes dominating political thinking before and after 1947. The article then examines the role played by the Indian government's industrial policy in protecting domestic employment and demand along with promoting export-led growth. The article then turns to the problem the British government faced in managing Indian imports into the British market. Using original archival sources from the Indian and British governments' archives the article demonstrates how the regulation of Anglo-Indian international trade in textiles was used to manage industrial development in both economies. The article concludes that while international regulation restricted Indian exports of low-value textiles into British markets rather than protecting British producers, it promoted trade diversion, with Indian manufacturers of low-cost production moving to countries exempt from British import restrictions, and simultaneously encouraged the development to higher value-adding production of textile exports among the Indian producers.

Independence and the industrialisation of the Indian economy

Indian development during the colonial period before independence in 1947 was characterised by an economy with world-leading sectors yet set within a wider economy with limited indigenous development of modern industries. Already by the mid-twentieth century India had become the world's largest tea producer and the centre for global production of other commodities, including jute, cardamom, and ginger. In a yet wider area of agricultural exports India also held a dominant world position, including coffee, rubber, cashews, and pepper (Agarwala, 2002, p. 535). Beyond agricultural exports and the textile-based industries of the first industrial revolution, Indian industrialisation until 1947 was, however, much more limited (Bagchi, 1982). In so far as industries of the second and third industrial revolutions were concerned, Indian business was highly dependent upon the foreign direct investment (FDI) of British, European, and American multinationals. It was not until the interwar period before 1940 that investment by Indian firms in capital-intensive processing industries began to emerge. Originating from the reinvestment of profits made by the managing agencies during the First World War, firms such as the Tata Iron and Steel Company developed prior to 1940 (Ramnath, 2012, pp. 62–66). Nevertheless, in more technically advanced sectors such as chemicals and dyestuffs, while its history could be dated back to the 1880s, the industry remained dominated by the European multinational companies of Bayer, BASG, and Hoechst, the British company ICI, and the US firms Du Pont, Monsanto, and Carbide until the 1970s. The same role for FDI can also be seen in the oil and car industries (Agarwala, 2002, pp. 531–551). Thus, colonial rule was understood to be restricting indigenous development to primarily agricultural goods production for export, with the Indian domestic economy restricted to becoming a market for advanced manufacturing of European multinationals rather than a centre of global production in its own right.

Once independence was won the state took a much greater interventionist and developmental approach to industrialisation. State monopolies in key industrial sectors, including iron and steel, the manufacture of telephone and telegraph networks, and mineral oils, were formed along with regulation and control over 18 further private industries following the 1948 Industrial Policy Statement. The Industrial Policy Statement was then reinforced with three further measures, industrial licensing from 1951, government protection for infant industries, and finally import substitution in what Tripathi (2007, pp. 282–325) has described as the 'four pillars' of post-independence industrial policy.

In so far as indigenous industrial enterprises had developed in areas of textile production including cotton and jute the large firms that had emerged were dominated by diversified firms in which a management structure encouraged the separation of ownership and control. The managing agency structure ensured private finance from individual shareholders was centralised in a managing agency while third-party firms were contracted to own and manage production units and so a divorce of ownership from control was an essential element of these large organisations. Agency organisations derived a fee from the principal investors for their operation of the agency relationship. As Wearmouth (2014) describes, the 'managing agent was a firm delegated by another firm's principals [shareholders] with responsibility for the day-to-day operational management in return for a fee, often a commission on the managed firm's sales or profits (p. 42). In doing so the agency's management held significant sway in both the creation and distribution of profits and returns to the principal investors.

But as a consequence the managing agency firm did not then have access to capital markets independently of the principal investors.

One consequence of this structure was, Misra (1999, pp. 210–214) maintains, that while indigenous Indian capital rapidly flowed into managing agencies in sectors where export markets had emerged, especially in cotton, jute, tea, and other agricultural goods, this led to a highly racially segregated form of industrial capitalism in India itself and limited diversification opportunities into more technically advanced and capital-intensive sectors. Marcovits (1985) shows the interconnectedness of the managing agencies through a system of interlocking directorships, and while Chandavarkar (1985) challenges the normative assumption of a defined path of industrialisation, it is difficult to resist Misra's conclusion that the managing agency structure, although highly effective at developing specific export-focused sectors, simultaneously hinders wider Indian industrialisation.

As Indian independence arrived, indigenous Indian business was identified as 'behave[ing] more like speculators and traders than industrialists' (Federation of Indian Chambers of Commerce, 1999, p. 159), requiring an interventionist and developmental state to foster domestic industrialisation. This was compounded by the economic dislocation of the catastrophic events involving the partition between India and Pakistan (Khan, 2007). Partition had a disproportionate impact on the agency firms operating in the textile sectors of cotton and jute, separating the areas of raw material production from the areas of manufacturing across the newly formed states' boundaries. In cotton, of 394 cotton mills only 14 were in Pakistan after 1947, but almost all the raw cotton originated in Sind and west Punjab provinces of Pakistan (Federation of Indian Chambers of Commerce, 1999, p. 154). The significance of this impact can be understood from the fact that, in the case of cotton, domestic demand in 1947 after partition was twice that of domestic production (Singh, 1999, p. 139). Similarly, for jute, 81% of raw jute production took place in East Pakistan (subsequently Bangladesh) yet 100% of jute processing mills were in the newly formed state of India.

Regulating the domestic textiles industry: 1947 to the textile plan

The textile industry has remained throughout the twentieth century of crucial importance to the Indian economy. Fifty years after independence it still accounted for one-fifth of total industrial output of the economy, yet only contributing some 4% to gross domestic product and only 2.3% of world trade in textiles (Nageswara Rao, 1999, p. 117). The textile industry was deemed to be one of the 18 industries identified in the 1948 Industrial Policy Statement to be important for the national interest and in 1951 also came under the Industries (Development and Regulation) Act for allocating import and raw material licences. Controls introduced over the industry during the Second World War were retained in the Cotton Textiles (Control) Order in 1948 and remained in operation for the next four decades. Misra (1993, p. 24) suggests that the Indian textile industry was probably one of the most tightly regulated industries in the world. He charts the post-independence evolution of India's domestic textile policy through the development of five related policy goals: the regulation of intersectoral competition; the provision of cheap cloth; the fibre policy; modernisation; and the rehabilitation of 'sick mills'.

Economic dislocation after 1947 and the low levels of industrial development saw government undertake a systematic attempt to direct investment into industrial production. In the case of cotton the areas under cultivation increased 55% from 58.8 to 90.06 lakh hectares[1] with a corresponding increase in output of 422% from 1951 to 1997 (Singh, 1999, p. 140). By the 1990s India was the third largest producer of raw cotton behind China and the United States (Karunakaran Pillai, 1999, p. 160).

The low value adding of the manufacturing elements within the sector acted as an impediment to the industry's potential to act as a key sector in the development of higher technology industries such that little development took place associated with related and supporting industries. Profits from the sector were instead used to diversify into other extractive and agricultural industries, such as coal and tea production, by the managing agents dominating the larger firms and thus provided evidence for the criticism of weak Indian entrepreneurship both pre- and post-independence. Raw material costs thus continued to constitute the overwhelmingly largest component of total costs in these low capital-intensive production technologies. Across all textile sectors from cotton to silk, jute to woollen products, raw material expenditure constitutes a minimum of 50% of total sales and in some areas such as textile processing as much as 80% (Nageswara Rao, 1999, table 10).

The diversity of production technologies included modern mill production encompassing 'composite' mills engaged in both weaving and spinning sitting alongside traditional handloom production at home or in small-scale factory settings, powerloom production in specialised weaving factories, and fine hosiery production in knitting factory production settings. Domestic industrial policy therefore identified two specific areas for intervention, employment and productivity enhancing investment (Kumar Sinha and Sasikumar 1999).

Protection of the continued employment of handloom weaving and its evolutionary transition from handloom to powerloom weaving was one of the government's policy goals, with limitations placed on the growth of the higher productivity industrial production methods embodied in composite mill operations. Thus, while composite mill expansion was blocked, powerloom take-up was such that from 1951 to 1964 a sixfold increase took place according to official estimates (Misra, 1993, pp. 24–45). As a result, while the larger composite mills were responsible for the production of 80% of cloth in the 1950s, this had fallen to just 20% by 1989 (Misra, 1993, p. 120). However, production from the composite mills was still of major importance to the industry's export development as almost all exports derived from just 10–12 of the private composite mills (Karunakaran Pillai, 1999, p. 161).

Price controls operated in the industry to ensure cheap cloth was available within the domestic market. Limiting prices first through voluntary means and then through statutory measures after 1964 affected the profitability of mills, leading to the creation of loss-making 'sick' mills. The impact of a lack of rationalisation and capital investment in new large-scale productive technologies led to an environment whereby relatively low-cost entry could take place. Over-supply of output and falling prices in periods of growth led to mill closures and mothballing of plant in what were described as 'sick mills'.

Protection of agricultural employment also affected innovation within the industry. Not only did the composite mills not invest in new technology, but the fibre policy preventing the use of non-cotton fibres had the additional impact of limiting the development of a domestic market for the synthetic fibre industry in the 1960s within the composite mills sector.

Growing industry concerns over profitability by the 1970s saw greater government regulation of the industry with the development of the Cotton Corporation of India in 1970 as a state trading body aimed at seeking to boost marketing and sales in order to alleviate the sick mill phenomenon. The creation of the National Textile Corporation also saw direct government ownership emerge in the sector with the taking over of 103 sick mills by 1973.

Further intervention followed in 1985 with the introduction of the textile policy. This development sought to address failings in the private sector through investment and modernisation (NAI 1973a, 1973b). The textile policy provided further financial support for rationalisation and modernisation conditional upon enforcement of managerial and labour changes to alter work practices (Bagchi & Das, 2014; Misra, 1993, p. 130).

Overall, Indian government policy towards the textile industry, while aiming to encourage production of raw materials and also that of modern small-scale production technologies as a means to manage employment levels, also deterred development of large-scale integrated technologies. The industry was one in which state control and latterly ownership under the National Textile Corporation played an increasingly dominant role in the industry from the 1950s onwards. Attempts at industry-level co-ordination were facilitated by government but increasingly failed to resolve the problems of the industry and more direct intervention incrementally emerged as a policy response in different economies (Bagchi & Das, 2014; Ditt & Pollard, 1992; Tomlinson, Morelli, & Wright, 2011).

The experience of the domestic Indian textile industry from the 1950s through to the 1990s was in many ways similar to that of many other established textile industries in the developed world. Singleton's (1990, 1991) work on the Lancashire cotton industry identifies similar problems of adjustment, while Tomlinson, Morelli, and Wright (2011) chart the management of this decline in the case of the Scottish jute industry. Problems of maintaining employment while promoting modernisation and rationalisation were difficult to solve within diverse and highly fragmented sectors. What is identified as entrepreneurial failure in the Indian experience can be readily identified as operating in other mature textile industries, such as in the UK and Europe more widely, and may reflect more accurately the industry entrepreneur's recognition of the lack of opportunity for profit in the industry. Where new opportunities emerged, particularly in the development of artificial fibres, investment was not slow in emerging. Indian producers were gaining government licences for the production of polypropylene, rayon, polyester, and other synthetic yarns and fibres from the early 1970s onwards (Indian Government Department of Commerce and Industry, Industrial Policy and Promotion 276, 1973–1975). Thus, if there was an entrepreneurial failure in textiles manufacturing it must be identified as an international phenomenon (Morelli, 2014).

Not all agree with this analysis. Wolf (1982, p. 50), for instance, concludes that exports of textile manufacturers in general and cotton goods in particular were a lost opportunity for the Indian economy before the 1970s. This is predicated on the view that Indian modernisation and industrialisation in its production technologies would not have had an impact on domestic employment levels due to their sole focus upon export markets and, in addition, that increased export potential would have found access to the growing markets of the developed economies, particularly those of Britain, western Europe, and the United States. Yet a central part of the explanation of the limited success of the Indian government's domestic policy towards the textile industry lies with the fact that the domestic Indian textile industry was itself linked to and an integrated part of a wider global trade in raw material production, unfinished cloth, and finished garments (Vanathi and Swamynathan, 2014). As such international regulation of the trade played a large part in determining the ability of firms (and the Indian government) to influence the development of the domestic industry.

Within the international regulatory environment Indian interests were also much less powerful than those of first world governments and firms. While new international production centres, such as Hong Kong in the 1950s, Bangladesh in the 1970s, and still more recently

China, could emerge it was at the expense of existing centres of production that these developments took place due to the fact that international regulation limited potential growth opportunities of existing centres. As a result, increasing output of low-cost raw materials, yarns, and unfinished cloth acted to encourage the development of producers in newly industrialising economies rather than within India itself. It is to the regulation of the international trade and in particular linkages between the British and Indian industries that we therefore now turn.

Market regulation after 1945: negotiating Anglo-Indian textile trade

The post-Second World War settlement in Europe was ideologically predicated on the development of deeper trading relationships between the conflicting powers under the premise that trading nations were less likely to resolve conflict militarily. Thus, Milward identifies the development of the Marshall Aid programme, the European Iron and Steel Agreement, and the European Payments Union in 1950 leading to the Treaty of Rome in 1957 as central to our understanding of the European rescue of the nation state (Aldcroft, 1993; Milward, 1992). This regulatory framework extended into a wider range of other industries, including agriculture with the Common Agricultural Policy and also that of the textile industries with common tariffs on imports of raw materials and finished goods (Aldcroft, 1993, p. 150). In the British case, despite its refusal to participate in the developing Common Market, similar regulatory frameworks emerged. Again the emphasis of regulation on the British textile industry can be broadly understood in terms of promoting domestic investment leading to rationalisation and the boosting of productivity, the encouragement of export capabilities, and consequentially the maintenance and management of full employment (Cairncross and Watts, 1989; Grove, 1962; Singleton, 1991).

In the case of the British textile industries Rose (1997) and Dupree (1992) show, particularly for the cotton industry, that the development of any new regulatory framework after 1945 was impeded by the continuation of pre-existing colonial economic relationships and in particular Imperial Preference. Imperial Preference ensured a free trade area existed within the British Empire, and later the Commonwealth countries, but in the post-war era acted to impede the development of trade relationships outside the Commonwealth economies for both British and Indian firms. In the context of textiles this relationship meant that the British government acted to seek protection for domestic producers who inevitably faced a cost disadvantage relative to Indian imports.

The British government's Board of Trade (BoT) and Foreign and Commonwealth Office (FCO) together played a major role in the Anglo-Indian textile trade negotiations. Immediately after British government controls were relaxed in 1954 the cotton industry began to demand further protection from the threat of rising Indian imports of 'grey cotton'. Unbleached or dyed and unprinted cloth imports, referred to as 'grey cotton' imports, were encouraged by those parts of the textile trade linked to processing rather than the manufacture of grey cloth, whereas those parts of the trade producing cloth from raw cotton or cotton yarn were facing cost disadvantages in this environment. In the case of both the British cotton and jute industries the dominant voice of these trades originated from those firms who were spinners and weavers of raw materials, with firms whose only role was garment production from finished cloth having less of an influence. With Indian imports accounting for half of all UK imports of grey cotton cloth any change in import regulations, duty, or quota restrictions would inevitably place a heavy strain on the development of Anglo-Indian trading relation-ships (Board of Trade 1954-55, PRO BT 11/5606, 1 March 1955).

Immediately on the withdrawal of wartime restrictions on the economy in 1954 concerns over the impact of low-cost textile imports became a focus for government thinking. Potential retaliation involving 'the whole shooting match' could develop from the Indian Congress if the British government raised restrictions warned Jha, the Indian joint secretary for com-merce and industries, in discussions with BoT officials in 1954 (Board of Trade 1954-55, PRO BT 11/5606, 13 October 1954). While initially resistant to renewed intervention within three years the BoT had accepted that avoiding action was no longer a viable strategy. As Board officials recognised '… after years of skilful fencing, [we] have reached a point where we have to decide whether or not the Lancashire cotton industry is to be protected' (Board of Trade PRO BT205/234, 24 June 1957). Initial attempts to develop industry-level co-ordination referred to as the 'Crossley Plan' faced difficulty from the fact that Crown Immunity would be required for a new collusive agreement following the passing of the 1956 Restrictive Trade Practices Act (Board of Trade PRO BT 258/742, 3 June 1958).

The textile industry posed a significant dilemma for the British government's approach to industrial policy in the late 1950s. While government was moving towards increasing competition policy and the abandonment of industry-level collusive agreements as a means to force private industry to act more competitively, it was increasingly identifying the need to sanction the development of more restrictive collusive agreements in order to address the lack of competitiveness within the differing sectors of the textile industry. In the case of the British jute sector of the industry, while the introduction of competition policy in 1956 was the catalyst for internal transformation such transitions were complex and took place over extensive time periods. Direct government import controls had been regulated through the continuation of wartime body Jute Control, beginning in 1941 and not ending until 1969 (Morelli, 2014). In the case of the alteration of international relationships such transitions took place over a much longer timeframe. In cotton, wartime controls introduced in 1941 with the formation of the Cotton Board evolved into the 1962 quota agreements, which evolved into duty tariffs in 1972, and ultimately the MFA after 1974 (Morelli, 2013; Rose, 1997; Singleton, 1991). As Beckerman (1972, p. 148) argues, this approach was, however, dictated by domestic rather than international concerns.

The BoT's attitude to the differing textile sectors was not, however, uniform. Recognising the political importance of the wider and larger Lancashire cotton industry ensured cotton had greater political weight than was the case in other sectors. As BoT officials recognised, political campaigning by the Labour Party in Lancashire meant government had to behave more sym-pathetically. In addition, their less sympathetic approach to the decline of jute production, concentrated just in the Scottish city of Dundee, might then also be used as a bargaining chip with Indian officials. As the president of the Board of Trade recognised 'We are about to help India over jute and it might be that the Indian Government, whom we are bound to consult, would agree to a reasonable cotton quota' (Board of Trade PRO BT205/234, 25 June 1957).

As described above in the Indian textile industry, British industry also saw similar attempts at controlling imports. However, while the British government could unilaterally impose tariff protection on textile imports from non-Commonwealth countries, it had to seek agreement on bilateral voluntary quota restrictions on finished imports from Commonwealth economies.

Quota controls were agreed by 1962 limiting Indian imports of cotton cloth and continued until 1972 when regulation moved to financial duties on imports rather than quantity-based controls from Commonwealth countries. As the British textile industry became more integrated and larger firms dominated both production of untreated grey cloth and that of finished garments, this shift was a reflection of the changing requirements of protectionist policies. Tariff protection now took the form of restricting finished products rather than raw materials, with tariff ramping identifying the extent of processing by the exporting economy for the level of duty. Anthony Crosland MP, as president of the Board of Trade, had signalled the move away from quotas to tariffs in a speech to the House of Commons in July 1969. From 1972 a tariff was to be imposed on imported cotton, which was to fall heavily on Indian producers, amounting to a 7.5% tariff on cotton yarn, 15% on cloth, and 17% on most garments (Foreign and Commonwealth Office PRO FCO67/537, 1972).

The British government's move towards application and entry into the European Common Market also provided a further rationale for the shift in tariff policy. Common Market entry required a common external duty-based tariff barrier by all member states. As a result, the need to 'modify' and abandon the quota agreements became a policy goal particularly of the British government but also accepted by other Commonwealth economies by the late 1960s (Cairncross and Watts, 1989, pp. 96–97).

As with the original introduction of quantitative restrictions the dominant position of the British government in the negotiations ensured Indian economic interests were secondary. The FCO calculated that by 1970 India imports totalled £106m, of which £8m were imports of tea duty free, £12m of cotton goods that were regulated via bilateral quotas, £26m of other goods incurring tariff duties for the protection of British manufacturers, and £30m of other goods with no tariff protection. Indian imports accounted for 53% of total cotton imports under the Commonwealth quota arrangements (Foreign and Commonwealth Office PRO FCO67/537, 1971). Again, as with the debates in the 1950s, government concerns over insufficient investment, low productivity growth, and continuing high unemployment in the domestic cotton textile area of Lancashire provided the rationale for further government intervention. The publication of the Textile Council's *Report on Cotton and Allied Textiles* in 1969 acted to provide government with the validation required to move away from quota restrictions on cotton imports to duty protection as it sought a means both to address the sector's concerns and to prepare for future entry into the Common Market (Foreign and Commonwealth Office PRO FCO67/718, 1972).

Board of Trade and FCO officials nevertheless recognised that the move to greater restrictions on textile imports would have a significant impact on Indian cotton producers. Crosland himself recognised the problem and stated that the 'Government will … when the time comes to determine the level of aid to India after 1972, take into account, against the background of India's general aid requirements at that time, any adverse effects on her exports arising from the tariff' (Hansard, 1969, p. 1509).

However, Crosland's stated intention of providing aid in compensation for the dislocation of trade proved more controversial within government itself. Opposition from within the FCO and the Department for Overseas Development Aid (ODA) developed on the issue of compensation to Indian producers for the loss of markets. The FCO were concerned that any payments might set a precedent for other economies in their negotiations with the British government, while the ODA sought to avoid explicitly linking aid to compensation for changes in trade relations and trade negotiations. Thus, in a letter from officials at the ODA to the FCO setting out the principles for negotiations, FCO officials included the handwritten instruction that 'None of the above should of course be passed to the Indians' (Foreign and Commonwealth Office PRO FCO67/373, 1970).

A further element in the negotiations between the British and Indian governments lay in the potential diversion of production from tariff to non-tariff produced goods. The FCO were keen to ensure that 'We should not say anything which they [the Indian government – author's addition] could interpret as encouragement to invest in man-made fibre capacity ... in the belief that they would find a ready market in the UK' (Foreign and Commonwealth Office PRO FCO 67/141, 1969). This was especially the case as the FCO were further concerned that the offer of £10m additional aid for the changes might provide producers with the investment required for such diversification (Foreign and Commonwealth Office PRO FCO67/718, 1972, p. 4). Yet despite British government concerns Indian producers were already making these decisions independently and grasping the new opportunities in artificial fibres. Garwara Nylons Ltd of Bombay gained government licences for the production of polyester in December 1973, Rajasthan State Industries Mineral Development Corporation Ltd of Jaipur and Sri Sakthi Textiles Ltd in Pollachi were similarly was licensed to produce synthetic yarns and fabrics, respectively, in 1975, while the manufacture of polypropylene was being pursued from 1973 (NAI 1973a., Department of Commerce and Industry, Industrial Policy and Promotion 276, 1973–1975).

Anglo-Indian negotiations over the regulation of bilateral trade was mirrored by and eventually superseded by multilateral regulation. The 1974 MFA can be understood as a culmination of these processes towards multilateral regulation of trading arrangements. The MFA itself was a multilateral arrangement to limit imports from the developing economies into the developed economies of the United States, Britain and the European Union. The MFA was also the outcome of a process preceded by the Short Term Arrangement in 1961 and the Long Term Arrangements in 1962, both of which were organised with the United States (Bagchi, 2004, p. 25). The MFA subsequently then went through a series of changes with new arrangements being negotiated every three years (Majmudar, 1989). These changes were generally to tighten the voluntary export restrictions placed on exporting countries and to extend the restrictions across an increasingly specific and targeted range of textile products. The British government's response to these agreements, while in general favourable, was that they failed to offer sufficient protection for its textile industries, particularly that of cotton. However, Prime Minister Jim Callaghan accepted the view that the renewal of the MFA arrangement and the additional continuation of Common Market restrictions on imports provided the greatest protectionism available (Cabinet Office PRO PREM 16 1470, 1977). The alternative was further isolation of the UK's interests in the Common Market and fears of a rapid increase of imports without restriction if no agreement was reached. As David Owen, foreign secretary, wrote to Prime Minister Jim Callaghan in December 1977, 'There would be bitterness if another blow were struck at the community's credibility. The United Kingdom would ... be entirely isolated and should not expect autonomous measures to look after the United Kingdom's interests' (Cabinet Office PRO PREM 16 1470, David Owen MP to Prime Minister Jim Callaghan, 16 December 1977).

Majmudar's (1989) study of Indian textile exports following the introduction of the MFA suggests that the impact of tightening quota restrictions and rising duty tariffs failed to limit imports. Indeed, evidence suggests Indian imports increased and the Indian textile industry responded by increasing value-added production into garment production and away from raw material and unfinished cloth production (Karunakaran Pillai, 1999, p. 167). Between 1976 and 1985 the number of firms exporting grew from 3929 to 8260 (Majmudar, 1989, table 4). In each of the three periods the MFA was renegotiated from 1976 to 1987 the value of exports also grew more rapidly than the volume of exports (Majmudar, 1989, p. 5), while the concentration of Indian exports into restrained countries grew from 68.9% by value to 80.5% from 1985 to 1987 (Majmudar, 1989, table 5).

Similarly, in the area of artificial fibres Indian capabilities increased during this era. As with British producers, Indian firms with weaving and textile knowledge readily diversified into artificial fibres once the market for these products emerged and the technological impediments to mass production were resolved. This again provided existing textile producers with opportunities to avoid areas of production where low value adding and low-cost competition was developing. This process of diversification into higher capital intensity production methods also developed with the move away from the agency structure of ownership and management. Large Indian firms began to develop more recognisable financial and managerial structures, while often retaining a high degree of family control (Roy, 2017; Tomlinson, 2003).

Conclusions

This article suggests that the post-independence Indian textile industry's evolution was a function of a number of domestic governmental political influences. Government action to protect domestic employment while promoting the development of more efficient production technologies was linked to the desire to encourage larger firms to focus upon export markets with more capital-intensive technological production technologies. However, the potential for larger Indian firms to gain access to international markets, primarily those in the United Kingdom, the United States, and Europe, was itself highly constrained by the rapid re-emergence of the regulation of trade at the bilateral and latterly multilateral levels. Quotas and duties were means by which the importing governments in the developed economies provided protection for their own indigenous, but declining, textile industries. As such this regulation acted as a means to slow and manage the decline of traditional textile industries in advanced economies in response to the cost advantages available to newly industrialising economies. Yet at the same time this limited the degree to which Indian producers could find profitable outlets for increased investment in larger mills.

This highly constrained environment for established textile industries, such as those in India, led to the emergence of new centres of production facilitated by accessing the expansion of supply of low-cost raw materials. These new centres initially also had the advantage of unconstrained access to developed markets outside the quota agreements until they too were brought into the agreements framework via the MFA. Once new low-cost producers emerged the established Indian producers themselves moved towards higher value-added garment manufacture and away from lower-value unfinished cloth production. This was combined with the process of diversification into artificial textiles as larger firms took advantage of new opportunities combining their existing production capabilities with innovation in yarn production. Export-led diversification was supported and promoted as part of the Indian government's trade and commercial policies while protection of small-scale domestic producers of traditional textiles continued. This developmental path of the Indian textile industry had previously been followed by textile industries in developed economies once low-cost producers, India being a key example, emerged at the end of the nineteenth century. Thus, the Indian textile industry's development echoed many of the features of the textile industries' developments in advanced economies. However, viewing the demise of low value-added textiles as economic failure within the domestic setting misses the wider global framework within which the industry was developing: low value adding was giving way to higher value adding, domestic-focused production was giving way to internationally-focused production technologies. Governments themselves in the developing world, as had been the case in the developed world, increasingly actively undertook the management of these transitions in order to maintain employment and promote technological development.

Acknowledgment

I am grateful to Swapnesh Masrani for his editorial role in overseeing the publication of this paper.

Note

1.   A lakh in the Indian numbering system refers to 100,000.

Disclosure statement

No potential conflict of interest was reported by the author.

Primary Sources

Board of Trade BT 11/5606. (1957 June 25). Economic Policy Committee, Note by the President of the Board of Trade: Imports of cotton textiles from India, Pakistan and Hong Kong, National Register of Archives (NRA hereafter), PRO BT205/234.
Board of Trade (1954–55), Imports of Indian Grey Cloth: Review of Possible methods of control, NRA PRO BT 11/5606.
Board of Trade. (1958 June 3). Correspondence to Ryder, Board of Trade, NRA PRO BT 258/742.
Foreign and Commonwealth Office. (1969 March), Trade Talks with India, Cotton Textiles, New Delhi, NRA PRO FCO 67/141.
Foreign and Commonwealth Office. (1970 December). Letter from HEJ Hale at Overseas Development Aid to PJE Male at the Foreign and Commonwealth Office Commodities Dept, NRA PRO FCO67/373, (New Delhi); December 1970.
Foreign and Commonwealth Office. (1971). Trade effects of tariffs: Quotas on imports of textiles from India to UK 1971 NRA PRO FCO67/537.
Cabinet Office. (1977). The problem of the British footwear and textiles industries, NRA PRO PREM 16 1470.
Hansard, (1969 July 22), Cotton and Textiles (Report), House of Commons debate, (787) published online retrieved 3rd June 2017, pp. 1507-16, http://hansard.millbanksystems.com/commons/1969/jul/22/cotton-and-allied-textiles-report,.
Department of Commerce and Industry, Industrial Policy and Promotion, National Archive of India (hereafter NAI), (1973-76), 276.
NAI. (1973a). 36, LI:23/73/DU, 82/74/DU, 24/73/DU, 28/73/DU, 27/73/DU, 26/73/DU and 25/73/DU, Letters of intents for the manufacture of Polypropylene Box Strapping dated 27/11/1973.
NAI, (1973b). 39, C:IL:25/73/DU, M/s. Garwara Nylons Ltd, Bombay – Industrial License for the manufacture of Polyester Filament yarns dated 10/12/1973.

NAI (1974). 1010, C:IL614/74/DU, M/s Rajasthan State Industries Mineral Development Corporation Ltd., Jaipur – Industrial licence for the manufactures of Cotton/Synthetic yarn, 1974.

NAI (1975). 1447: IL:396/75/DU, Sri Sakthi Textiles Ltd, Pollachi – Industrial Licence for the manufacture of Cotton and Synthetic Fabrics dated 18/08/1975.

Secondary References

Agarwala, P. N. (2002). *A comprehensive History of Business in India*. New Delhi: Tata McGraw Hill.

Aldcroft, D. H. (1993). *The European Economy 1914–1990*. 3rd edition. London: Routledge.

Bagchi A. K. (1982). *The Political Economy of Underdevelopment*. Cambridge: Cambridge University Press.

Bagchi, A. K., and Das, P. (2014). Indian Jute Manufactures: Adaptation and survival in a 'sunset industry'. *International Journal of Management Concepts and Philosophy*, 8(2–3), 181–195.

Bagchi, J. (2004). *Indian Textile Industry: Liberalisation and World Market*. New Delhi: Samskriti Press.

Beckerman, W. (1972). *The Labour Government's Economic Record 1964–70*. Essex: Gerald Duckworth.

Cairncorss, A., and Watts, N. (1989). *The Economic Section 1939–61: A study in economic advising*. London: Routledge.

Chandavarkar, R. (1985). "Industrialization in India before 1947: Conventional approaches and alternative perspectives", *Modern Asian Studies*, 19(3), 623–668.

Deane, P. (1979). *The First Industrial Revolution*. Cambridge: Cambridge University Press.

Ditt, K., and Pollard, S. (1992). *Von Der Heimarbeit in die Fabrik: Industrialisierung and arbeiterschaft in Leinen und baumwollregionen Westeruopas während des 18 und 19 Jahrhundrets*. Paderborn, Germany: Ferdinand Schöning Press.

Dupree, M. (1992). The Cotton Industry: a Middle Way Between Nationalisation and Self- Government?. In H. Mercer, N. Rollings and J. Tomlinson (Eds). *Labour Government and Private Industry, the Experience of 1945–51*. (pp. 137–162). Edinburgh: Edinburgh University Press.

Federation of Indian Chambers of Commerce (1999). *Footprints of Enterprise, Indian Business Through the Ages*. Delhi: Oxford University Press.

Goodman, J., and Honeyman, K. (1988). *Gainful Pursuits: The making of industrial Europe 1600–1914*. London: Edward Arnold.

Grove, J. W. (1962). *Government and Industry in Britain*. London: Longmans.

Karunakaran Pillai, G. (1999). Restructuriung the Textile Industry to Reach a Level of Global Competitiveness. In A. Kumar Sinha and S.K. Sasikumar, (Eds). *Restructuring of the Textile Sector in India*. (pp. 157–168). New Delhi: Indian Economic Association.

Khan, Y. (2007). *The Great Partition: The making of India and Pakistan*. New Haven, USA: Yale University Press.

Kumar Sinha, A., and Sasikumar, S. K. (Eds.). (1999). *Restructuring of the Textile Sector in India*. New Delhi: Indian Economic Association.

Majmudar, M. (1989). The Economic Consequences of Voluntary Export Restraints on Indian Garment Exports to the USA and EEC Countries 1980–87, *Economics and Management Working Papers, No.15*. Glasgow: Paisley College.

Marcovits, C. (1985). *Indian Business and Nationalist Politics 1931–39: The indigenous capitalist calls and the Congress Party*. Cambridge: Cambridge University Press.

Milward, A. S. (1992). *The European Rescue of the Nation State*. London: Routledge.

Misra, M. (1999). *Business, Race, and Politics in British India, c.1850–1960*. Oxford; Oxford University Press, pp. 210–214.

Misra, S. (1993). *India's Textile Sector: A policy analysis*. New Delhi: Sage Publications.

Morelli C. J. (2013). Jute, Firm's Survival, and British Industrial Policy: Government Action under Globalization, in M. Umemura and R. Fujioka (Eds). *Comparative Responses to Globalization* (pp. 141–158). London: Palgrave Macmillan.

Morelli, C. J. (2014). The Dutch Disease: The role of industrial policy for industrial transformation – the case of the jute industry. *International Journal of Management Concepts and Philosophy*, 8(2–3), 156–167.

Nageswara Rao, K. (1999). Problems of the Textile Industry: A review, in A. Kumar Sinha and S.K. Sasikumar, (Eds.) *Restructuring of the Textile Sector in India* 117–120. New Delhi: Indian Economic Association.

Ramnath, A. (2012). *Engineers in India: Industrialisation, Indianisation and the State, 1900–47.* Unpublished PhD, Imperial College London, London.

Rose, M. (1997)."The politics of protection: an institutional approach to government industry relations in the British and United States cotton industries, 1945–73" *Business History, 3*(4), 128–150.

Roy, T. (2017). Transfer of Economic Power in Corporate Calcutta, 1950–1970, *Business History Review 91*, 3–29, published online: 02 May 2017, doi.org/10.1017/S0007680517000393

Singh, B. N. (1999). Indian cotton in the Global Market: Problems and Prospects; in A. Kumar Sinha, and S.K. Sasikumar. (Eds). *Restructuring of the Textile Sector in India* (pp. 139–143), New Delhi: Indian Economic Association.

Singleton, J. (1991). *Lancashire on the Scrapheap: Cotton Industry, 1945–70, Pasold Studies in Textile History.* Oxford: Oxford University Press.

Singleton, J. (1990). Showing the White Flag: The Lancashire Cotton Industry, 1945–65. *Business History 32*(4), 129–149.

Tomlinson B. R. (2003). British Business in India 1860–1970. In R. P. T. Davenport-Hines and G., Jones. (Eds.). *British Business in Asia since 1860.* Cambridge: Camridge University Press, pp. 92–116.

Tomlinson, J., Morelli, C.J., and Wright V. (2011). *The Decline of Jute: Managing industrial change.* London: Pickering and Chatto.

Tripathi, D. (2007). *Oxford Handbook of Business History in India.* Oxford: Oxford University Press.

Vanathi R., and Swamynathan R., (2014). Competitive Advantage Through Supply Chain Collaboration: An empirical study of the Indian textile industry. *Fibres and Textiles in Eastern Europe, 22*(4), 106, pp. 8–13.

Wearmouth, (2014). Thomas Duff & Co and the Jute Industry in Calcutta, 1870–1921; Managing Agents and Firm Strategy, Unpublished thesis, Economic Studies, University of Dundee, Dundee.

Wolf, M. (1982). *Indian Exports.* v Oxford: Oxford University Press.

Internationalisation of the Indian telecommunication industry (1947–2004): A firm-level perspective

Ajit Nayak

ABSTRACT
While the importance of the telecom revolution in India has been recognised, little attention has been paid to the diverse international influences at the firm level. This article addresses this gap by developing a firm-level framework, drawing on the resource-based view, institution-based view and the knowledge-based view of the firm, and by drawing on data related to the various foreign firms' entry strategies during the pre-liberalisation period (1980–1991) and the liberalisation period (1991–). The article demonstrates that the two periods required foreign firms to have different capabilities to enter the Indian telecom industry. The article also sheds light on the international knowledge-transfer process in the Indian telecommunications industry with a specific focus on the differences between different foreign-country firms.

Introduction

The Indian telecommunications revolution has been a significant success story of India's liberalisation in the 1990s and its rise as one of the fastest-growing economies in the world (Panagariya, 2008). Telephone density, or teledensity, the number of telephones per 100 people, provides an aggregate measure of the state of telecommunications in a country. The increase in teledensity in India demonstrates India's telecom revolution. Teledensity in 1980–81 was 0.3 and increased marginally to 0.7 in 1990–1991. In comparison, the following decade saw a marked improvement. Teledensity increased to 1.3 in 1995 and, with the entry of private mobile telecom companies in the latter half of 1990s, was 4.3 in 2000–2001. The following decade saw a remarkable rise to 52.74 in 2010 (Panagariya, 2008, p. 372). By mid-2017, the teledensity was 93.98 (TRAI, 2017).[1] Bearing in mind India's large population (over a billion people) and vast geography (over 3 million square kilometres) spread across urban and rural areas, a national teledensity of 93.98 demonstrates the extent to which India is now connected through telecom.[2]

In explaining the transformational story of Indian telecom, much scholarly attention has focused on the role of the state, its economic policies and the deregulation of the telecom sector (Jain, 2006; McDowell, 1997; Mody, 1995; Petrazzini, 1996; Sridhar, 2011). While this has undoubtedly played a major role, an important part of the story is the contribution of other actors. In particular, we know little about the role of foreign companies in the transformation. Given the broader changes in India's economic liberalisation (Corbridge & Harriss, 2013; Panagariya, 2008), the role of foreign companies is distinctively different in the time period before liberalisation and after. Post-independence and pre-liberalisation (1947–1991), for the most part India relied upon foreign technology to develop its telecom infrastructure. This changed in the liberalisation period (1991–), starting a multitude of foreign-firm influences on the industry.

The central thrust of this article is to adopt a firm-level perspective on the Indian telecom story. By firm-level, I mean that the focus is on the firm as a bundle of resources and capabilities. Furthermore, I draw on the capabilities literature that highlights the strategic needs of firms in forming alliances and entering new markets. I also draw on the literature on political capabilities of firms to influence the institutional and regulatory environment. By adopting a firm-level perspective, I demonstrate that the Indian telecom story is a story of international technology and knowledge transfer, international joint ventures, financial capabilities and political capabilities of firms. Pre-liberalisation, the relationships between the Indian government and other international governments and institutions played an important role in transferring telecom technology. In this context, the foreign firms relied on their respective governments to lobby and negotiate access to the Indian telecom industry. This changed post-liberalisation. It is the Indian private companies in joint ventures with foreign companies that delivered the infrastructure and connectivity across the vast country. Indian telecommunication changed from being based on outdated and inefficient technology with long waiting lists for telephones pre-1985 to state-of-the-art technology and one of the lowest prices for consumers by 2010. Foreign firms, with their Indian partners, played an important part in enabling this transformation by providing access to technology, capital and business practices.

Unlike Japan's or China's telecom transformations, both of which were driven by limited foreign participation, India's route to a modern telecom industry is the result of global participation. In Japan, the government played an important role in nurturing Nippon Telegraph and Telephone Company (NTT). Started in 1952, NTT benefitted from the Japanese government's drive towards technological self-sufficiency. By initially importing foreign technology and expertise, and investing in national R&D, Japan steadily moved towards creating its own telecom infrastructure (Anchordoguy, 2001). Similarly, in China, the government focused on developing competition between Chinese state-owned enterprises and breaking up the monopoly of China Telecom (Liu & Jayakar, 2012; Loo, 2004). In contrast, India's telecom industry witnessed global participation during its deregulation.

The 1990s saw the deregulation of the Indian telecommunication sector, which opened the industry to several Indian and foreign private sector companies. There have been several studies into telecom deregulation in India. For example, two key institutional actors, T.H. Chowdary, who drafted the National Telecom Policy 1994 (NTP-94) and was CEO of one of the privatised telecom companies, and M.B. Athreya, who headed an influential committee that reported on restricting the telecom industry, have written several articles on the shift in telecom policy (Athreya, 1996; Chowdary, 1998a, 1998b, 2004). McDowell's (1997) book provides a detailed analysis of the liberalisation period. His account of the changes in government policies in telecom, and in particular the public narratives surrounding telecom deregulation provide a comprehensive chronology of the events. Panagariya (2008) provides a comprehensive account of India's liberalisation, including the telecom sector. Several studies have also focused on the telecom policies in 1994 and 1999, which aimed to establish the regulatory framework for businesses and the incumbent state monopoly (Dokeniya, 1999; Dossani, 2002; Mukherji, 2009; Singh, 2000).

I draw on these studies that focus on the political and institutional arrangements. However, my focus in this article is on the foreign firms entering India, rather than on the challenges of economic reforms. Whereas previous studies have examined the reasons for the nature and pace of telecom liberalisation, they have not focused on the perspective of foreign firms looking to enter a deregulated market. Three important exceptions are Subramanian (2010), Desai (2006) and Levi (2007). Subramanian's book on the history of Indian Telephone Industries (ITI) provided useful data on the pre-liberalisation period. While the focus of the book is on the challenges facing ITI, the public sector monopoly for manufacturing telecom equipment, it provided insights into the role of foreign companies in transferring technology. Desai's book provides a comprehensive account of the different Indian and foreign firms operating in India. And Levi's book provides interesting insights into entry strategies of Swisscom, Alcatel, Avaya and First Pacific. Her study demonstrates the need for greater focus on individual firms. These books have provided useful data for charting the trajectories of foreign firms in India. I draw on two other sources to identify foreign firm involvement. The legal battle between the government and various companies over the issue of mobile licences in 1992, and the subsequent court case judgements, provided information of joint-venture partnerships between Indian firms and foreign firms. I also drew on accounts in the Indian newspaper, *The Times of India*, about the entry of foreign firms and their partnerships. The article has also benefitted from personal conversations with key actors in the industry during the liberalisation of the industry.[3]

Theoretical background

The firm-level perspective developed in this article draws on the resource-based view (RBV), institution-based view (IBV) and knowledge-based view (KBV) in strategy and international business. By bringing these literatures together, I develop a firm-level framework to analyse the evolution of the Indian telecommunications industry and to identify the key capabilities that led to foreign firm success. I begin by outlining the theoretical background of these literatures and position its potential contribution relative to the telecom industry research.

As a discipline, strategy focuses on the question of why some firms outperform others. The central premise of RBV is that firms differ in their resources and capabilities, and these differences are difficult to imitate, copy or replicate for other firms. This explains why some firms have a competitive advantage and achieve superior performance. In other words, valuable, rare, inimitable and organised heterogeneity in resources and capabilities is the cornerstone of RBV (Barney, 1996; Peteraf, 1993; Wernerfelt, 1984). An organisational capability is defined as a firm's capacity to perform an activity reliably over time (Amit & Schoemaker, 1993; Collis, 1994; Dosi, Nelson, & Winter, 2000; Ethiraj, Kale, Krishnan, & Singh, 2005). The label, organisational capabilities, can span a wide range of activities that a firm can perform, such as marketing capabilities, operational capabilities, R&D capabilities and so on. For the purposes of this article, the focus is on financial, technological and joint venture capabilities. By financial capabilities, I mean the capacity of a firm to raise capital to fund the telecom installation and expansion. By technological capabilities, I mean the capacity to deliver telecommunication services, which includes telecom equipment manufacture, network infrastructure and client management. And by joint-venture capabilities, I mean the capacity to find and partner with other firms. This includes the capability to work with partners on market entry, establishing terms for technology transfer and financing, and, once operational, developing a cooperative relationship to establish the business (Barkema, Shenkar, Vermeulen, & Bell, 1997; Gulati, Wohlgezogen, & Zhelyazkov, 2012; Ireland, Hitt, & Vaidyanath, 2002; Schreiner, Kale, & Corsten, 2009).

In recent years, several strategy and international business scholars have focused on the institutional conditions informing strategy (Ahuja & Yayavaram, 2011; Meyer, Estrin, Bhaumik, & Peng, 2009; Peng, Sun, Pinkham, & Chen, 2009). Under the umbrella of IBV, scholars have theoretically argued and empirically demonstrated that 'institutions directly determine what arrows a firm has in its quiver as it struggles to formulate and implement strategy, and to create competitive advantage' (Silverman & Ingram, 2000, p. 20). This has led to identifying a different category of organisation capabilities, one that focuses on a firm's ability to influence government policies that can lead to competitive advantage. Sometimes labelled non-market strategies, this capability underpins a firm's capacity to engage with rule-makers (Doh, Lawton, & Rajwani, 2012; Hillman & Hitt, 1999; Oliver & Holzinger, 2008; Peng, 2003). This includes the capacity to influence the formal rules, but more importantly, it also includes the capacity to understand and play by the 'informal rules of the game' (Baron & Diermeier, 2007; Bonardi, Holburn, & Bergh, 2006; Frynas, Mellahi, & Pigman, 2006; Henisz & Delios, 2004; Henisz & Zelner, 2005; Holburn & Bergh, 2008; North, 1990).

A final capability that informs my firm-level perspective is the capacity of firms to transfer technology and know-how to other firms. While there is an overlap with the literature on technological capabilities, the inter-organisational knowledge transfer capability is distinct and is based on KBV of the firm that posits that knowledge is the key productive resource that differentiates firms (Grant, 1996; Grant & Baden-Fuller, 1995; Spender, 1996). Based on KBV, the literature on inter-organisational knowledge transfer recognises the importance of three key success factors: (1) the nature of knowledge being transferred; (2) the capacities of donor and recipient firms to teach and learn, respectively; and (3) the inter-organisational dynamics. Technology transfer involves tacit and explicit knowledge that a donor firm has. It is not just a case of selling or licensing the technology (explicit knowledge), but the significance of practices and processes that accompany it (tacit knowledge). While some of the practices and processes can be codified and made explicit in training manuals and standard operating processes, a donor firm needs to have the capability to transfer the knowledge by providing training and embedding the technology in a host firm. Equally important is the recipient firm's capacity and willingness to learn the new technology. The recipient firm must see the new technology as significant and be motivated to develop its internal technological capabilities. Here, the inter-organisational dynamics plays an important part in establishing trust and communication between donor and recipient firms. Past experiences and culture matter in establishing successful technology transfer capabilities (Dhanaraj, Lyles, Steensma, & Tihanyi, 2004; Dyer & Singh, 1998; Eisenhardt & Schoonhoven, 1996; Lane & Lubatkin, 1998; Lucas, 2010; Mowery, Oxley, & Silverman, 1996).

These five capabilities – financial, technological, joint venture, political and inter-organisational knowledge transfer – form the basis of a firm-level framework and play an important role in explaining the success of telecom firms in India. Figure 1 illustrates how these capabilities combine to explain the relationship between donor firms, recipient firms and the

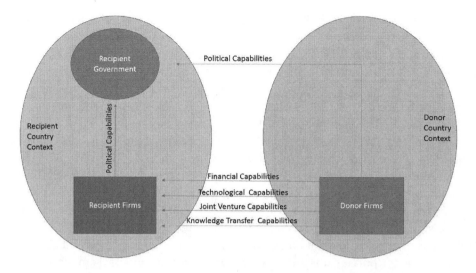

Figure 1. Theoretical framework: A firm-level perspective on internationalisation.

government. On the left-hand side, the broad oval-shape indicates the institutional context in the recipient country within which all actors operate. The recipient government represented by the small oval shape (which is the Indian government in the context of this article) sets the institutional environment and the policy for telecom firms. The rectangular box represents the firms operating with the country. For this article, these are the Indian telecom companies. The arrow between the recipient firms and the government indicates the political capabilities of firms to shape and influence government policies. The right-hand side of Figure 1 represents the donor firms and their institutional context. The arrows flowing from the donor firms depict the key capabilities needed for success, which is the focus of this article.

Empirical background

The telecommunications industry has played an important role in globalisation in the 1980s and 1990s. Foreign direct investment by telecom companies in the 1990s contributed significantly to global corporate activities. For example, the US and European telecom companies invested in 60 countries between 1986 and 1991 (Serrano, Bane, & Tunstall, 1991; Thomsen, 1997). In explaining the changes in telecommunications, the dominant focus has been on broad macro-issues such as deregulation, globalisation and privatisation of national monopolies. However, a few studies have pointed to the importance of firm-level actions and strategy. Sarkar, Cavusgil, and Aulakh (1999) identify key strategic drivers at the firm level. They argue that deregulation of the home markets and the loss of monopoly status prompted firms to explore foreign markets that were also deregulating. This enabled firms to transfer their existing technology and know-how to new markets. To benefit from first-mover advantage, firms attempted to establish presence in international markets. A large multinational telecom company also benefitted strategically by having economies of scale and influence in terms of global technology standards and developing new technology. Sarkar et al. also highlight that this internationalisation of telecom firms features several joint ventures. As firms addressed the multiple challenges of gaining market entry, investing in new technology and developing costly infrastructure and operations in different countries, they formed various alliances (Jamison, 1998). Clifton, Comín, and Díaz-Fuentes (2011) build on Sarkar et al.'s firm-level focus to demonstrate that firms from Europe that faced the same regulatory changes followed different internationalisation strategies. This highlights that although deregulation and liberalisation were important, European firms responded differently to these changes. Moreover, they argue that 'significant investment abroad was undertaken both by firms that had experienced substantial inward liberalisation pressures, as well as those who were based in countries where liberalisation lagged behind'. A more recent study by Nevalainen (2017) also demonstrates the role of key strategic actors within the Finnish Post and Telecommunications Department (PTL), the Finnish national carrier. Facing deregulation across Europe, the firm entered 'the nearby areas of the Baltic Countries and north-west Russia in the early 1990s, and only a little later to more distant markets like Hungary and Turkey, in which a small but relatively skilled operator could seize the opportunity' (Nevalainen, 2017, p. 375). Focusing on the Indian market, Nayak and Maclean (2013) also point to firm-level activities. Although they focus on the entrepreneurial field and the role of key actors, they demonstrate the significance of firms such as Bharti Airtel in changing the telecommunications industry in India.

Whereas previous firm-level studies have focused on reasons for companies internationalising from their home countries, the focus of this article is on the differences at the firm level between various foreign companies. Unlike previous studies that have highlighted firm-level differences in their timing and scope of international activity, the focus here is on one international market – India. The changing nature of the Indian telecom industry provides interesting insights into how different foreign firms approached their entry into the industry.

I divide the article chronologically: (1) pre-liberalisation (1947–1991); and (2) liberalisation (1991–2005). Within each time period, I focus on three main issues – the government policy related to telecom, which sets the backdrop for the different actors, Indian companies involved and their responses, and foreign firms involved and their engagement. I use the theoretical framework (Figure 1) to analyse firms and demonstrate the significance of the five capabilities. In the final section, I discuss the variation in the way different foreign companies engaged with the Indian context and the implications of knowledge transfer, country entry and country exit.

Pre-liberalisation (1947–1991)

India became independent from British rule in 1947. In 1948, the Indian government published its first Industrial Policy Resolution (IRP) in which it divided industry into four main categories – Sole Ownership of the Central Government, Reserved for the Public Sector, Regulated by States, Private sector. These represented the order of importance of the different sectors in terms of government/private ownership. The first category included key security and defence industries such as atomic energy, railways and military equipment. The telecommunications industry was listed in the second category, where the government excluded all private-sector involvement. Along with coal, iron and steel, aircraft manufacturing, shipbuilding and minerals, participation in telecommunications was the sole reserve of the public sector. The telecommunications company at the time of independence, Indian

Radio and Cable Communications Limited, was nationalised to create the Department of Post and Telegraphy (P&T). This period saw the founding of ITI in 1948 in Bangalore (now Bengaluru), creating a national monopoly in manufacturing telecom equipment. At its inception, ITI, the telecom equipment manufacturer, had some foreign company involvement. The British Automatic Telephone and Electric Company (ATE) held a minority stake in ITI from its inception until 1977 (Subramanian, 2010, p. 45).

Recognising the lack of technical know-how to build a telecommunications network, the P&T sent a technical officer to Europe to identify technology partners (*Minutes of the Nineteenth Estimates Committee,* 1957; Subramanian, 2010, p. 70). The officer received four offers, but the names and nationality of two of these companies remain unknown. The government considered two offers – one from a Swiss company (name unknown) and the other from ATE. The government also received an offer from International Telephone and Telegraphy (ITT). The decision to award the contract was based on (1) technological capabilities and (2) price. On both issues, ATE was seen as a better choice, providing favourable terms for the technology licensing and the cheapest bid. The existence of British telecom technology prior to independence also worked in ATE's favour. Prior to independence, ATE had worked with the Indian government to install India's first automatic exchange in 1914. The chief engineer at ATE, Mr A.F. Bennett, had developed the capabilities to negotiate and implement the Strowger technology in the UK, Canada, Poland and Lithuania. Drawing on the old British Empire network, ATE also expanded to South Africa and India (Emerson, 1989). ATE and the Indian government agreed a 15-year collaboration to transfer the Strowger technology to India. In line with international knowledge transfer theory, ATE sent its staff to design, install and train personnel at ITI. Twenty-three employees of ATE were deputed to ITI, occupying key posts such as works manager, chief inspector, personnel and recruitment, and training. ATE developed 'methodical procedures to regulate all aspects of the factory's activities. The transfer of know-how was thus confined not solely to technical expertise, but also extended to practical expertise pertaining to the overall organisation of work' (Subramanian, 2010, p. 73).

In 1964, the P&T engaged in another foreign technology transfer, this time for the production of crossbar switches, with Bell Telephone Manufacturing Company (BTM), which was part of ITT. Although Ericsson and Nippon EC bid for the technology tender, the P&T chose BTM because of its low bid and two main capabilities. First, BTM's parent company agreed to provide loans and bought an equity stake in ITI to enable ITI to purchase machinery and finance factory expansion. This cash injection was an important consideration for selecting BTM. Second, BTM was perceived (wrongly, as it turned out) to have the technological capabilities. The committee that recommended BTM stated that BTM had 'vast experience in the manufacture of varied types of telecommunication equipment' (COPU 1975–76, 1975, p. 6; cited in Subramanian, 2010, p. 89).[4]

In principle, the technology transfer model with BTM was the same as with ATE. BTM was expected to provide the know-how and practical expertise. However, the realities turned out to be very different; the 'crossbar agreement … represented a textbook case of all that went wrong in the diffusion of know-how from a developed to a developing country' (Subramanian, 2010, p. 86). BTM faced challenges in coordinating its own operations in Europe and with its parent company. The technology was ill-suited to the Indian conditions, and required adaptation. Managerial practices also suffered because the Belgian managers were not fluent in English (Subramanian, 2009, p. 207). In other words, BTM struggled to meet its obligation of providing the crossbar technology, illustrating poor knowledge transfer capabilities.

India's reliance on foreign company technology continued in the 1980s. As ITI moved from the crossbar switching technology to electronic switching system (ESS), the foreign technology provider changed. The main foreign company active in the telecom sector in this period was the French government-owned CIT-Alcatel, which provided the technology and the capital to enable India to upgrade its telecom infrastructure. The mode of technology transfer was the same wherein the foreign company would provide the technical know-how and training. Although CIT-Alcatel had not participated in the initial tender process, the contract was awarded to them after discussions at the highest level between the two countries. India also agreed to buy fighter jets and enriched uranium from France at the same time (Ramesh, 1982). Technologically, as with the BTM crossbar technology, arguably India did not buy the best ESS technology available at that time. The Ericsson AXE switch was more popular in developing countries in the 1980s (Bhushan, 1987; Mani, 1989). However, it is the political capabilities of CIT-Alcatel and the Indo-French relationship that proved to be the key capability ('French pressure pays off,' 1982). In contrast to the previous two technology transfer deals (with ATE and BTM), the political capability worked indirectly, mediated by the French government.

Although a state monopoly, telecommunications did not become a strategic priority for the Indian government until the 1980s. Despite the tendencies of state monopolies to resist change, public discourse on the state of telecommunications was shifting towards liberalisation. As Das (2002, p. 208; also cited in Panagariya, 2008, pp. 371–371) noted:

> The telephones that existed were not dependable – it was rare to get a number on the first attempt. The employees of the telephone department were arrogant and corrupt. If the lines were down, it could take months to fix unless one bribed the linesman. When an MP complained in Parliament of these breakdowns, C.M. Stephens, Mrs. Gandhi's communications minister, replied that telephones were a luxury, not right, and that anyone who was dissatisfied could return the telephone, because there was an eight-year waiting list for this 'broken-down product.'

Along with the general public dissatisfaction with the telephone system, the government was also cognisant of the large import bill from the P&T. Struggling to expand its network through equipment supplied by ITI, particularly into rural India, and the lack of telecom equipment manufacturing capabilities in India, the government had few options but to look at foreign companies for the technology (Taskar, 1981). Projects by the P&T to develop switching technology through its Telecom Research Centre were unsuccessful.

In 1981, the government appointed a Committee on Telecommunications, known popularly as the Sarin Committee, to advise on the P&T. While the main focus on the committee was on internal issues within the P&T, it was widely seen as an attempt to change the existing status quo within the government ministries ('P&T circles worried over Sarin committee appointment,' 1981). The committee recommended that the P&T be split to separate postal services from telecom services. 1981 also saw the entry of Sam Pitroda, an Indian-born US businessman. His access to the Prime Minister Indira Gandhi, and subsequently to the next Prime Minister, Rajiv Gandhi, led to a shift in government attitude towards technology, from being a luxury to an important role in development (Nayak & Maclean, 2013, pp. 11–13). Bypassing the monopoly held by Department of Telecommunications (DoT), Indira Gandhi and, subsequently, Rajiv Gandhi, championed the Department of Electronics (DoE) to promote a wide range of electronics products and services. Pitroda set up the Centre for

Development of Telematics (C-DOT) in 1984 to develop electronic switches for Indian con-ditions. C-DOT was quick to involve Indian private-sector companies, beginning the partial entry of private Indian firms into the equipment industry ('C-DOT vendors talk on digital systems,' 1985).

This period also saw the attempt to privatise the DoT. In 1986, two corporate entities were created, Mahanagar Telephone Nigam Limited (MTNL), to operate telephone services in Mumbai and New Delhi, and Videsh Sanchar Nigam Limited (VSNL), for overseas telephony ('Bombay-Delhi phone corporation,' 1986). The carving out of two lucrative sectors opened up the potential for foreign firm entry. AT&T/Philips, Alcatel/Thompson and NEC made offers to develop the city networks ('Three consortia offer $4B Each,' 1985). However, the govern-ment chose to create MTNL and VSNL as corporate entities, albeit under the control of DoT. The aims of the corporate entities were to operate separately from the ministry and to intro-duce market-oriented and commercial management policies, systems and practices to ena-ble fast growth. It was also seen as a potential model for privatising that could be replicated across India (Athreya, 1996, p. 13). However, the attempt to privatise led to strong opposition and several strikes.

With the convergence of telecom technology with electronics, the DoE was in a position to challenge the P&T's stronghold on manufacture of telephone handsets and other con-sumer facing devices. In 1984, the government marked a shift away from the IPR of 1948, which had excluded private-sector involvement in telecommunications, by allowing a range of new entrants ('Industrial policy change,' 1984). The DoE set up several State-owned Electronic Development Corporations (SEDCs) to manufacture telephone handsets, fax machines, answering machines and other telecom-related equipment. Usha Martin Limited joined with Bihar SEDC to manufacture cables in 1986, collaborating with AEG Kabel from Germany. Himachal Futuristic Communications Limited (HCFL) partnered with the Himachal Pradesh SEDC in 1987 to manufacture cables. They brought in Seiscor Technologies Inc., USA and Philips Kommunikation Industries AG, Germany. Bharti Telecom Limited also started their forays into telecom during this period. They partnered with Siemens AG, Germany, to manufacture push-button handsets in 1985. They also sourced technology for answering machines from Takachiho Corporation, Japan, and cordless telephones from Lucky Goldstar (LG), Korea.

The shift in Industrial Policy in 1984 marks an important, although unanticipated, change in the telecom industry from the point of view of firms. Although telephony and postal services were separated by splitting the P&T, the government still maintained the monopoly over the telephone service by creating the DoT and restricting telecom equipment manu-facturing to ITI. However, the move by DoE to set up SEDCs inadvertently allowed private firms to join the industry. Since consumer facing devices, such as handsets, telex machines and answering machines, were seen as luxury goods, the government opened the door to multiple firms. The SEDCs developed joint ventures with private Indian firms that brought in finance, which in turn brought in foreign firms to provide technology. Crucially, this marked the beginnings of Indian firm–foreign firm capability development in telecom.

Liberalisation (1991–2005)

The 1990s was a highly dynamic period in Indian politics, and this had a clear impact on the ability of the government to formulate a coherent telecoms policy. In the 1980s, the Congress

Table 1. Foreign companies and Indian partners in 1992.

Foreign partner	Indian partner	Bidding company
SFR France, Emtel Mauritius and Talkland UK	Bharti Tele-Ventures	Bharti Cellular
Bell South, USA	Crompton Greaves	Skycell
France Telecom, MaCaw Cellular, US and LCC Inc. US	BPL	BPL Telecom
Hutchinson, Hong Kong	Max	Hutchinson Max
Telecom Malaysia	Usha Martin	Usha Martin Telecom
Telecom Malaysia	Dalmiya	India Telecomp
Alta Telecom, Canada		
OIC Australia	Modi	Indian Telecom Ltd
Vodafone	RPG	Mobile Telecom
Bell Canada Enterprises	Tata	Tata Cellular
Nynex, USA	Modi	Modi Telecom
Singapore Telecommunications	HCl	Mobile Comm
	Essar	Sterling Cellular

Source: Tata Cellular v Union of India.

government was in power, led by Indira Gandhi (1980–1984) until her assassination, and by her son, Rajiv Gandhi (1984–1989). However, the 1990s saw seven prime ministers as the balance of power shifted between various political parties. This is important because the telecommunications industry was a key ingredient in political success and patronage nationally. Changes to the telecommunication industry would impact a large number of employees at DoT and ITI.[5] It was also important internationally, because it enabled powerful ministers and Indian companies to seek patronage from Indian and foreign firms looking to enter the deregulated industry. Furthermore, as an important source of foreign-exchange investment, the telecom ministry was a sought-after position in the various coalition governments in the 1990s. [6]

The creation of MTNL as a separate corporate entity created significant challenges for the DoT and the government. In 1990, MTNL announced bonuses to its staff. This led to protests from the other employees of the DoT. In response to the employee bonus issue, the government set up a Telecom Restructuring Committee (popularly known as the Athreya Committee) to propose a new structure. While the main recommendations for restructuring faced significant political opposition, the government agreed to allow private companies to enter, what were seen as, 'value-added services'. These were electronic mail, voice mail, data services, audio text services, video text services, video conferencing, radio paging and, crucially, cellular mobile telephony. Mobile telephony escaped the political turf-wars because it was seen as a luxury, and that mobile phone calls would be primarily made to fixed-line telephones, thus increasing the traffic to DoTs monopoly. This resulted in a tendering process in 1992 to grant eight licences, two for each city, for New Delhi, Mumbai, Kolkata and Chennai, to set up mobile phone operations. Although licences were granted, this led to a long-drawn legal battle between the rejected bidders and the government. As India did not have a mobile phone industry, the government stipulated that Indian private companies wishing to bid for licences should have a foreign collaborator with experience and funding to set up the infrastructure. The court cases between India Telecomp Ltd v Union of India in 1993 and Tata Cellular v Union of India in 1994 provide initial evidence of various foreign entrants and their Indian partners (see Table 1).

The court cases led to some clarity with respect to foreign company participation, particularly in terms of providing technical and financial expertise.[7] For example, Bharti Cellular's foreign partners were SFR, Emtel and Talkland. The court case argued over the telecom expertise necessary to qualify for the licences, focusing on the scale of operations of the foreign collaborator. The case also illustrated the importance of foreign collaborators providing all the foreign exchange needed to finance the setup costs. It also clarified the number of joint ventures each foreign collaborator could be part of. For example, Telecom Malaysia had partnered with two Indian companies. The case judgement revealed that this was seen unfavourably by the DoT panel in their shortlisting process.

The legal battles delayed the entry of mobile phone companies until 1995. By this time, a National Telecom Policy in 1994 (NTP-94) was created, and another round of bidding was initiated, this time for value-added services such as mobile phone and wired telephone services. The 1995 action brought in new foreign partners, but also led to the exit of some. The companies and their Indian/foreign partners awarded licences to operate in New Delhi, Mumbai, Chennai and Kolkata in 1995 were:

Table 2. Winners of 1995 bids for New Delhi, Mumbai, Kolkata and Chennai.

Foreign partner	Indian partner	Company name
Hutchinson, Hong Kong	Max India	Hutchinson Max
France Telecom	BPL	BPL Telecom
SFR, France	Bharti Tele-Ventures	Bharti Cellular
Cellular Communications International	Essar	Sterling
Malaysia Telecom	Usha Martin	Usha Martin Telecom
Telstra Australia	Modi	Modi Telstra
Bell South, USA	Crompton Greaves	Skycell
Vodafone	RPG	Mobile Telecom

Subsequently, as the licences for other regions in India were auctioned, there were more new foreign company entrants in the bidding process. However, during this period, it is difficult to ascertain if bidding can be seen as entry because the rules for bidding and controversy over the role of government may have persuaded some to exit. For example, several foreign companies, such as Shinawatra, Thailand and Bezeq, Israel, partnered with HCFL to bid for eight licences. Furthermore, the relationship between Vanguard, US and BK Modi, who partnered to bid for six licences, was strained following the issue of licences and led to a fallout over investments (Tewari, 1996). However, it was clear that there was significant interest in bidding for the wider licences across the globe, in terms of bringing in telecom expertise and equity, as well as finance for infrastructure development. Table 3 provides a list of the foreign companies, divided into telecom and finance capabilities.

Between 1999 and 2002, several of the licences were traded, which led to exits and consolidation. For firms, the licences had value irrespective of whether they started operations. This period saw several firms merge and the number of players in the industry reduced. While the challenges of regulatory uncertainty contributed to the consolidations, firms also saw this as an opportunity to value their equity stake in trading their licences. The relationship between foreign entrants and the Indian partners was strained in some joint ventures, owing to differences in strategy (Anand, 1996). The DoT also aimed to strengthen the bargaining power of Indian companies by allowing them to change their foreign collaborators (Pandey, 1995). The consolidation also made sense in terms of business strategy and benefitting from economies of scale.

In terms of actual operations, the first few companies to launch services were Bharti Cellular, Modi Telstra, Usha Martin, Essar, RPG, Skycell, Hutchinson Max and BPL Mobile, who were granted licences for the major cities (see Table 2). In other words, the foreign

Table 3. Major foreign equity investors in cellular companies, circa 1997.

Investor	Country	Stake (%)	Cellular company	Business house
National incumbent				
AT&T	USA	49	Birla AT&T	Birla
NTT	Japan	49	Basic	RP Goenka
Telstra	Australia	47.6	Modi Telstra	Modi
MBT	Malaysia	40	Usha Martin Telecom	Rai
Bell Canada	Canada	39	Tata Teleservices	Tata
PTC	Philippines	34	Koshika	Rai
STET	Italy	33	Bharti Telenet	Bharti
Swiss PTT	Switzerland	30	Aircel Digilink	Sterling
France Telecom	France	26	BPL Mobile	BPL
Other telephone operators				
First Pacific	Hong Kong	49	Escotel	Escorts
Vodafone	UK	49	RPG Cellcom	RP Goenka
Hutchinson	Hong Kong	49	Hutchinson Max	Max
Jasmine	Thailand	49	J.T. Mobile	Parasrampuria
Media One	USA	49	BLP Cellular	BLP
Distacom	Hong Kong	39	Spice	Modi
Shinawatra	Thailand	33	Facel	Maloo-Nahata
BellSouth	USA	24.5	Skycell	Thapar
GMC	USA	22.5	Bharti Cellular	Bharti
Century USA	USA	19.5	Aircel	Sterling
Financiers				
Al Amin	Mauritius	49	Barakhamba	Sterling
AIG	USA	49	Tata Cellular	Tata
Cellfone	Mauritius	46	RPG Cellular	RP Goenka
Asia Pacific Infra	Hong Kong	39	Essar Commvision	Essar
Mobilvest	Mauritius	30	Sterling Cellular	Sterling
Reddington	Singapore	29	Aircel	Sterling
Emtel	Mauritius	17	Bharti Cellular	Bharti
Others				
Hughes Electronics	USA	49	Hughes Ispat	Ispat
Millicom	Luxembourg	24.5	Skycell	Thapar

Source: Desai (2006, p. 99).

collaborators, Hutchinson, France Telecom, SFR, Cellular Communications International, Malaysia Telecom, Telstra Australia, Bell South and Vodafone, provided the foreign exchange capital and their technical expertise in launching services.

In 1999, India revised its National Telecom Policy and produced the NTP-99, which provided greater clarity and certainty for firms. It also created a regulatory body, Telecom Regulatory Authority of India (TRAI) and subsequently further clarified its role in dispute resolution.

Differences in Foreign Firms' Entry Strategies

From the viewpoint of foreign firms, the evolution of Indian telecommunication industry from a national monopoly to a liberalised economy with several private sector companies has posed different strategic questions. By adopting a firm-level perspective, I have focused on the role of firms, and in particular foreign firms. We can see that the pre-liberalisation period was one where the political actors were foregrounded and were the key players in the co-evolution of the telecom industry. The Indian government was the sole actor that foreign firms engaged with to gain access to the Indian market. Financial capabilities and technological capabilities played an important part, but success rested in demonstrating

Table 4. Privatisation of the European telecom industry and liberalisation of their markets.

Domestic market	Year of liberalisation	National operator	Year of privatisation
United Kingdom	1984	British Telecom	1984
Italy	1997	Telecom Italia	1997
Switzerland	1997	Swiss PTT	1997
France	1998	France Telecom	1997

political capabilities and knowledge-transfer capabilities. For example, the French firm, CIT-Alcatel, was the one that was able to engage with technology transfer to India through the Indian public-sector company, ITI. This technology transfer, brokered at the highest political level, enabled CIT-Alcatel to enter the Indian market. The links between CIT-Alcatel and the French government, and diplomatic relations between Indian and France, played an important role in the process of knowledge transfer.

Post-liberalisation, the dynamics within the industry changed dramatically for foreign firms. While the nexus between business and government was still important in terms of understanding the various changes in telecom policy, the main conduit for foreign firms' activities was the Indian private-sector companies. The choices made by foreign firms from different countries and the route they took to enter the Indian telecom sector were different. In terms of choices for market entry, government regulation stipulated that foreign firms could not engage in the sector without local partners. Hence, the only choice open to foreign firms was the joint-venture route. There were two key issues that were pertinent to forming a joint venture: expertise in telecommunications and/or financial clout. Some of the foreign firms that entered the market did so purely in terms of providing finance to their Indian joint venture partner. Others entered with their telecom expertise (see Table 3). Furthermore, the mode of engagement also differed. Some companies chose to adopt a 'hands off' approach, allowing the local partner to manage the operations and the complicated relationship with government officials. Managing the relationship with the DoT and with the regulator was a specialised capability that foreign firms did not have. Hence, they relied on the local partner to bring this capability. This is where a company like Bharti Airtel was very successful. In contrast, Swiss-PPT chose a much more 'hands on' approach, appointing their own senior team and seeking to increase their equity stake. However, this also led to their quick exit from the industry because they lacked the key capability, of managing the relationship with the government, telecom ministry and the regulator, to operate in the industry.

To appreciate the differences between foreign firms that entered India in the post-liberalisation period, I divide the foreign entrant firms into three categories: European firms (including the UK), US firms and others. The European telecom firms' entry into the Indian market needs to be seen in the context of liberalisation and privatisation in their home countries (Clifton et al., 2011; Davids, 2005; Hulsink, 1999; Kornelakis, 2015; McDowell & Lee, 2003). During the 1990s, the monopoly of national telecom operators was dismantled, and the sector faced new entrants into their domestic markets. Table 4 shows the year in which the country liberalised and privatised its telecom operator.

One of the early entrants was the French national company, France Telecom. In 1994, it entered into a joint venture with BPL by taking a 37% stake in BPL Mobile Telecom. The firm won the lucrative Mumbai licence in 1995 and was the leading company, competing against Hutchinson Max. In 2000, France Telecom expanded through a series of acquisitions. One of these was the brand 'Orange', which belonged to Hutchinson. Despite France Telecom owning the brand worldwide, Hutchinson had retained the rights to the brand in India, launching it in 2000. This meant that BPL would be competing with the Orange brand in the Mumbai market. France Telecom tried to increase its stake in BPL. However, it finally exited India in 2004 by selling its stake, unable to consolidate its position in India.

SFR was another early French entrant in 1994. However, they exited early, in 1997, selling their stake to BT. SFR's exit seems to be a result of BT's alliance with Compagnie General Des Eaux (CGE), the owners of SFR ('British Telecom picks up 22.5% in Bharti Cellular', 1997).

Another European early entrant into the Indian market was the Italian national telecom company, Telecom Italia. Using their Dutch subsidiary, STET NV, they partnered with Bharti Airtel by taking a 33% stake in Bharti Telnet and a 20% stake in Bharti Tele-Ventures in 1995/1996. As part of their global strategy and in preparation for privatisation, STET expanded its international operations rapidly, including into India (Hill, 1995).

Telia, Sweden entered the industry through a joint venture with Parasrampuria Group to form J.T. Mobile, which won the licences to operate in three regions (Karnataka, Andhra Pradesh and Punjab) in 1995. However, the significant changes in their home market led to their exit in 2002. During that time, Telia was privatised and merged with the Norwegian company, Sonera, to form TeliaSonera in 2002.

Another early European company to enter the Indian market was Switzerland's national carrier, Swiss PTT, renamed Swisscom after privatisation in 1997. In preparation for competition in its domestic market and the EU in general, Swisscom followed an international strategy and entered several countries in the 1990s, including India. Swisscom partnered with one of the large Indian business houses, Essar, to create Sterling Cellular in 1996. Swisscom invested US$215 m and provided financial guarantees for its 32.5% stake in Sterling (Swisscom, 1997, p. 36). In contrast to the other European companies, Swisscom was keen to have operational control in India. It appointed Swisscom personnel to key positions, including Chief Executive Officer (Jan Erik Boers), Chief Operating Officer (Andreas Schelling), Chief Financial Officer (Neill Quinn) and Head of Marketing (Peter Stock) and attempted to increase its stake in Sterling (Mohan, 1998). However, by 1999, Swisscom had decided to sell its stake in India because of its attempts to focus on 'the Heart of Europe' strategy and the continuing delays and uncertainty in the Indian government's telecom policy.

BT, the UK's former national carrier, was a late entrant into the cellular industry. While it had presence in other industries, such as V-SAT and electronic mail (Malik, 1986), and had bid for cellular licences in 1992, it had not managed to enter the industry. As stated earlier, BT's entry into India was an unexpected outcome of its alliance with CGE whose subsidiary, General Mobile Company (GMC), had a stake in Bharti Cellular ('BT acquires stake in Bharti Cellular', 1997). However, it too exited India in 2001 to focus on its UK strategy and to reduce its debt. During this period, BT had borrowed heavily to bid for the UK 3G licence.

Arguably, the US telecom industry was better placed to enter the Indian market because it had liberalised and privatised its operations earlier. In 1978, the US allowed competition in the sector, and the national carrier, AT&T, was broken up into several independent companies in 1987. Two US communications companies, Hughes Electronic Corporation (HEC) and Alltel Corporation, joined the Indian business house, Ispat, to launch Hughes Ispat Limited (HIL). With HIL as the 51% equity partner, HEC held a 34% stake, and Alltel held 15%. The main strength of this joint venture was the technical expertise brought by HEC and Alltel. HEC had strong capabilities in telecommunication networks, and Alltel had strong operational support capabilities such as systems and software for billing and customer support. The management of HIL was also strongly determined by HEC, who appointed a former HEC executive, Rajendra Patel, as CEO, who brought his vast experience in telecommunications in the US and his Indian-origin credentials to the job.

The US major, AT&T, formed two partnerships in entering India. First, in 1994, it joined A.V. Birla to form AT&T Communications, which won licences for Gujarat and Maharashtra. Subsequently, in 2000, it joined BPL to form BPL Cellular, which won licences for Maharashtra, Goa, Tamil Nadu and Kerala. The partnership with BPL became problematic because BPL/France Telecom had a separate joint venture for Mumbai (see above). However, as with the European markets, AT&T was facing challenges in the US. In 2004, it merged with Cingular Wireless, leading to consolidation in the US market. This refocusing strategy resulted in AT&T's exit from India.

Along with the US/European entrants, there were several Asian firms that participated in joint ventures. The Japanese national carrier's entry choice into India was through the wireline service. In contrast to the interest in cellular operations, NTT chose to partner with RP Goenka in bidding for the wireline licence in Tamil Nadu in 1995. However, disagreements led to this licence being forfeited in 1998.

By far the most successful entry was by Hutchinson, the Hong Kong-based telecom company. Hutchinson Max, the joint venture with Max India, bid for and won the licence for Mumbai. It consolidated its position in India through a series of acquisitions, buying Sterling Cellular, Usha Martin Telecom and Aircel. Globally, Hutchinson has demonstrated the capability to create large telecom businesses and exit. Its strategy in Europe showcased its capability to grow the Orange brand, and subsequently sell off the business to Mannesmann in 2001. Similarly, after building the brand in India, Hutchinson sold the business to Vodafone in 2007.

The entry and exit of Australia's Telstra's followed a similar pattern to the European companies. They initially entered the industry with Modi, and received the licence for Kolkata. As with the European companies, Telstra faced competition in its home market because of deregulation. Similarly, Telstra focused on the Asia-Pacific region and its home market, rather than invest in expanding its operations in India.

Conclusions

The Indian telecommunications industry has transformed remarkably, from the low teledensity, poor connectivity and long waiting lists for telephones, to a thriving and competitive market with advanced technology. While India's liberalisation and the regulatory changes in telecom have played an important part in facilitating this transformation, the Indian and foreign firms have played an important part in achieving this at the ground level. The aim of this article was to provide a firm-level perspective on the changes. Whereas previous research has focused on the regulatory and economic issues, I focused on the role of foreign firms. Focusing on the firm level, we can see that firm capabilities are crucial in delivering the changes. Prior to liberalisation, the main capabilities that foreign firms needed were financial resources, technological expertise and, crucially, political capabilities to enable them to work with the Indian government. They also needed knowledge-transfer capabilities, once they gained entry. Liberalisation led to the need for foreign firms to develop new capabilities. In particular, they needed to form joint ventures with Indian private companies, and provide technical knowledge and capital investment.

For foreign firms, India was one of the international markets that opened up as they faced competitive pressures in their home markets. Success/failure in the Indian market depended not so much on the technical and financial capabilities, but on their ability to manage the joint venture and to deal with the market uncertainties. Equally important were the changes in the foreign firms' home markets and their capabilities of strengthening their positions in their domestic industry. The article shows that firms were able to exercise strategic choice, leading to different approaches to their India entry/exit strategy. The European firms faced significant challenges in their home market, which impacted their India strategy. Several international mergers and alliances also led to different strategic choices made by US firms.

For foreign firms, two key capabilities stand out from their Indian experience. First, foreign firms need political capabilities to understand and influence the institutional setting and understand the 'rules of the game'. Pre-liberalisation, this was orchestrated through their connections with the Indian government, mediated by the home-country government. In contrast, post-liberalisation, firms needed the ability to form and maintain joint ventures with Indian firms. The joint-venture firms' political abilities to navigate the changing regulatory environment played an important part in foreign firms' success. By demonstrating the interplay between financial, technological, joint venture, political and inter-organisational knowledge-transfer capabilities that shaped the participation of foreign firms in the Indian telecommunications success story, I have highlighted the significance of a firm-level perspective. In so doing, I hope to stimulate further empirical research that investigates firm-level issues that drive internationalisation of industries across countries and over time.

Notes

1. Telecom Regulatory Authority of India (TRAI).
2. Given India's large population spread across urban and rural areas, it is instructive to look at the urban/rural difference in teledensity. By mid-2017, urban teledensity was 172.98 and rural teledensity was 57.73. The Indian telecom sector still has a significant challenge in achieving urban/rural parity.
3. While not systematic data collection, I have benefitted from conversation with Ashok Juneja, ex-CEO of Bharti Broadband and part of the Usha Martin Telecom bidding team.
4. Committee of Public Undertakings (COPU).
5. There were a number of strikes at P&T and ITI during this period.
6. Deregulation of the telecom industry is mired in controversy. Two telecom ministers, Sukh Ram (1993–1996), and A Raja (2007–2010), have been prosecuted of corruption. Because the process of granting telecom licences is set by the telecom minister, and firms are looking for information about the policy, it opened up the potential for corruption and bribery.
7. The DoT invited bids for the first licences for the metro cities on 31 March 1992. The DoT announced the winners on 12 December 1992. Four companies filed writ petitions at the Delhi High Court, challenging the decision. On 26 February 1993, the Delhi High Court upheld the challenge from two companies, forcing the DoT to change the companies it granted licences. The resulting changes meant that Tata Cellular lost its licence and, hence, challenged this in the courts. On 26 July 1994, the Supreme Court of India delivered its verdict on the bidding process for the metro licences. The evidence presented in the two cases provided useful data for understand the joint venture partnerships in the bidding process. Since the courts examined and clarified the criteria used for selection, they provided information on the technical and financial capabilities of the foreign partners.

Disclosure statement

No potential conflict of interest was reported by the author.

References

Ahuja, G., & Yayavaram, S. (2011). Perspective—Explaining influence rents: The case for an institutions-based view of strategy. *Organization Science, 22*(6), 1631–1652.

Amit, R., & Schoemaker, P. J. (1993). Strategic assets and organizational rent. *Strategic Management Journal, 14*(1), 33–46.

Anand, S. (1996, March 18). Cracking telecom marraiges on the rise. *The Times of India*.

Anchordoguy, M. (2001). Nippon Telegraph and Telephone Company (NTT) and the building of a telecommunications industry in Japan. *Business History Review, 75*(3), 507–541.

Athreya, M. B. (1996). India's telecommunications policy - A paradigm shift. *Telecommunications Policy, 20*(1), 11–22.

Barkema, H. G., Shenkar, O., Vermeulen, F., & Bell, J. H. (1997). Working abroad, working with others: How firms learn to operate international joint ventures. *Academy of Management Journal, 40*(2), 426–442.

Barney, J. B. (1996). The resource-based theory of the firm. *Organization Science, 7*(5), 469–469.

Baron, D. P., & Diermeier, D. (2007). Strategic activism and nonmarket strategy. *Journal of Economics & Management Strategy, 16*(3), 599–634.

Bhushan, B. (1987, August 9). Controversy over telecom technology. *The Times of India*.

Bombay-Delhi phone corporation. (1986, 4 February). *The Times of India*.

Bonardi, J.-P., Holburn, G. L., & Bergh, R. G. V. (2006). Nonmarket strategy performance: Evidence from US electric utilities. *Academy of Management Journal, 49*(6), 1209–1228.

British Telecom picks up 22.5% in Bharti Cellular. (1997, 11th January). *Business Standard*.

BT acquires stake in Bharti Cellular. (1997, 11th January). *The Times of India*.

C-DOT vendors talk on digital systems. (1985, 16th January). *The Times of India*.

Chowdary, T. H. (1998a). Politics and economics of telecom liberalization in India. *Telecommunications Policy, 22*(1), 9–22.

Chowdary, T. H. (1998b). Telecom liberalization and competition in developing countries. *Telecommunications Policy, 22*(4-5), 259–265.

Chowdary, T. H. (2004). Telecom reforms: A decade on. *Economic and Political Weekly, 39*(21), 22–28.

Clifton, J., Comín, F., & Díaz-Fuentes, D. (2011). From national monopoly to multinational corporation: How regulation shaped the road towards telecommunications internationalisation. *Business History, 53*(5), 761–781.

Collis, D. J. (1994). Research note: How valuable are organizational capabilities? *Strategic Management Journal, 15*(S1), 143–152.

COPU 1975–76. (1975). *Action taken by Government on recommendations contained in 34th Report of committee of public undertakings*. New Delhi: Fifth Lok Sabha.

Corbridge, S., & Harriss, J. (2013). *Reinventing India: Liberalization, Hindu nationalism and popular democracy*. John Wiley & Sons.

Das, G. (2002). *India unbound. Fom independence to the global information age*. New Delhi: Penguin Books.

Davids, M. (2005). The privatisation and liberalisation of dutch telecommunications in the 1980s. *Business History, 47*(2), 219–243.

Desai, A. V. (2006). *India's telecommunication industry: History, analysis, diagnosis*. London: Sage.

Dhanaraj, C., Lyles, M. A., Steensma, H. K., & Tihanyi, L. (2004). Managing tacit and explicit knowledge transfer in IJVs: The role of relational embeddedness and the impact on performance. *Journal of International Business Studies, 35*(5), 428–442.

Doh, J. P., Lawton, T. C., & Rajwani, T. (2012). Advancing nonmarket strategy research: Institutional perspectives in a changing world. *Academy of Management Perspectives, 26*(3), 22–39.

Dokeniya, A. (1999). Re-forming the state: Telecom liberalization in India. *Telecommunications Policy, 23*(2), 105–128.

Dosi, G., Nelson, R., & Winter, S. (Eds.). (2000). *The nature and dynamics of organizational capabilities.* Oxford: Oxford University Press.

Dossani, R. (Ed.). (2002). *Telecommunications reform in India.* Westport: Quorum Books.

Dyer, J. H., & Singh, H. (1998). The relational view: cooperative strategy and sources of interorganizational competitive advantage. *Academy of Management Review, 23*(4), 660–679.

Eisenhardt, K. M., & Schoonhoven, C. B. (1996). Resource-based view of strategic alliance formation: Strategic and social effects in entrepreneurial firms. *Organization Science, 7*(2), 136–150.

Emerson, A. (1989). From Strowger to system X: The history of the Edge Lane plant in Liverpool. Retrieved 2018 from http://www.britishtelephones.com/histatm.htm#chapter9

Ethiraj, S. K., Kale, P., Krishnan, M. S., & Singh, J. V. (2005). Where do capabilities come from and how do they matter? A study in the software services industry. *Strategic Management Journal, 26*(1), 25–45.

French pressure pays off. (1982, March 31). *The Times of India.*

Frynas, J. G., Mellahi, K., & Pigman, G. A. (2006). First mover advantages in international business and firm-specific political resources. *Strategic Management Journal, 27*(4), 321–345.

Grant, R. M. (1996). Toward a knowledge-based theory of the firm. *Strategic Management Journal, 17*, 109–122.

Grant, R. M., & Baden-Fuller, C. (1995). A knowledge-based theory of inter-firm collaboration. *Academy of Management Journal, 1995*(Winter), 17–21.

Gulati, R., Wohlgezogen, F., & Zhelyazkov, P. (2012). The two facets of collaboration: Cooperation and coordination in strategic alliances. *Academy of Management Annals, 6*(1), 531–583.

Henisz, W. J., & Delios, A. (2004). Information or influence? The benefits of experience for managing political uncertainty. *Strategic Organization, 2*(4), 389–421.

Henisz, W. J., & Zelner, B. A. (2005). Legitimacy, interest group pressures, and change in emergent institutions: The case of foreign investors and host country governments. *Academy of Management Review, 30*(2), 361–382.

Hill, A. (1995, December 14). Stet's Line to overseas growth. *The Financial Times.*

Hillman, A. J., & Hitt, M. A. (1999). Corporate political strategy formulation: A model of approach, participation, and strategy decisions. *Academy of Management Review, 24*(4), 825–842.

Holburn, G. L., & Bergh, R. G. V. (2008). Making friends in hostile environments: Political strategy in regulated industries. *Academy of Management Review, 33*(2), 521–540.

Hulsink, W. (1999). *Privatisation and liberalisation in European Telecommunications.* London: Routledge.

Industrial policy change. (1984, 24th March). *The Times of India.*

Ireland, R. D., Hitt, M. A., & Vaidyanath, D. (2002). Alliance management as a source of competitive advantage. *Journal of Management, 28*(3), 413–446.

Jain, R. (2006). Interconnection regulation in India: Lessons for developing countries. *Telecommunications Policy, 30*(3-4), 183–200.

Jamison, M. A. (1998). Emerging patterns in global telecommunications alliances and mergers. *Industrial and Corporate Change, 7*(4), 695–713.

Kornelakis, A. (2015). European market integration and the political economy of corporate adjustment: OTE and Telecom Italia, 1949–2009. *Business History, 57*(6), 885–902.

Lane, P. J., & Lubatkin, M. (1998). Relative absorptive capacity and interorganizational learning. *Strategic Management Journal*, 461–477.

Levi, K. J. B. (2007). *Entry strategies of foreign companies in Indian telecommunications market.* Frankfurt: Deutscher Universitäts-Verlag.

Liu, C., & Jayakar, K. (2012). The evolution of telecommunications policy-making: Comparative analysis of China and India. *Telecommunications Policy, 36*(1), 13–28.

Loo, B. P. (2004). Telecommunications reforms in China: Towards an analytical framework. *Telecommunications Policy, 28*(9-10), 697–714.

Lucas, L. M. (2010). The role of teams, culture, and capacity in the transfer of organizational practices. *The Learning Organization, 17*(5), 419–436.

Malik, N. K. (1986, April 17). Technology acquisition and development: Case of telecom switching equipment. *Economic and Political Weekly.*

Mani, S. (1989). Technology acquisition and development: Case of telecom switching equipment. *Economic and Political Weekly,* M181–M191.

McDowell, S. D. (1997). *Globalization, liberalization and policy change.* Basingstoke: Macmillan Press.

McDowell, S. D., & Lee, J. (2003). India's experiments in mobile licensing. *Telecommunications Policy, 27*(5-6), 371–382.

Meyer, K. E., Estrin, S., Bhaumik, S. K., & Peng, M. W. (2009). Institutions, resources and entry strategies in emerging economies. *Strategic Management Journal, 30*(1), 61–80.

Minutes of the Nineteenth Estimates Committee. (1957).

Mody, B. (1995). State consolidation through liberalization of telecommunications services in India. *Journal of Communication, 45*(4), 107–124.

Mohan, R. (1998, January 16). Swiss PTT to step up stake in sterling cellular stake. *Indian Express.*

Mowery, D. C., Oxley, J. E., & Silverman, B. S. (1996). Strategic alliances and interfirm knowledge transfer. *Strategic Management Journal, 17*(S2), 77–91.

Mukherji, R. (2009). Interests, wireless technology, and institutional change: from government monopoly to regulated competition in indian telecommunications. *The Journal of Asian Studies, 68*(2), 491–517.

Nayak, A., & Maclean, M. (2013). Co-evolution, opportunity seeking and institutional change: Entrepreneurship and the Indian telecommunications industry, 1923-2009. *Business History, 55*(1), 29–52.

Nevalainen, P. (2017). Facing the inevitable? The public telecom monopoly's way of coping with deregulation. *Business History, 59*(3), 362–381.

North, D. C. (1990). *Institutions, institutional change and economic performance.* Cambridge: Cambridge University Press.

Oliver, C., & Holzinger, I. (2008). The effectiveness of strategic political management: A dynamic capabilities framework. *Academy of Management Review, 33*(2), 496–520.

P&T circles worried over Sarin committee appointment. (1981, 2nd June). *The Hindu.*

Panagariya, A. (2008). *India: The emerging giant.* Oxford: Oxford University Press.

Pandey, V. (1995, December 29). DoT policy favours Indian firms. *The Times of India.*

Peng, M. W. (2003). Institutional transitions and strategic choices. *Academy of Management Review, 28*(2), 275–296.

Peng, M. W., Sun, S. L., Pinkham, B., & Chen, H. (2009). The institution-based view as a third leg for a strategy tripod. *Academy of Management Perspectives, 23*(3), 63–81.

Peteraf, M. A. (1993). The cornerstones of competitive advantage: A resource-based view. *Strategic Management Journal, 14*(3), 179–191.

Petrazzini, B. A. (1996). Telecommunications policy in India: The political underpinnings of reform. *Telecommunications Policy, 20*(1), 39–51.

Ramesh, J. (1982, August 18). The Alcatel decision and after. *The Times of India.*

Sarkar, M., Cavusgil, S. T., & Aulakh, P. S. (1999). International expansion of telecommunication carriers: The influence of market structure, network characteristics, and entry imperfections. *Journal of International Business Studies, 30*(2), 361–381.

Schreiner, M., Kale, P., & Corsten, D. (2009). What really is alliance management capability and how does it impact alliance outcomes and success? *Strategic Management Journal, 30*(13), 1395–1419.

Serrano, R. M., Bane, W., & Tunstall, W. B. (1991). Reshaping the global telecom industry. *Telephony, 221*(15), 38–40.

Silverman, B. S., & Ingram, P. (2000). Introduction: The new institutionalism in strategic management. *Advances in Strategic Management, 19*, 1–30.

Singh, J. (2000). The institutional environment and effects of telecommunication privatization and market liberalization in Asia. *Telecommunications Policy, 24*(10-11), 885–906.

Spender, J. C. (1996). Making knowledge the basis of a dynamic theory of the firm. *Strategic Management Journal, 17*(S2), 45–62.

Sridhar, V. (2011). *The telecom revolution in India: Technology, regulation, and policy.* Oxford: Oxford University Press.

Subramanian, D. (2009). The politics of technology and site location: Impact of state interventionism on an Indian public sector firm. *Netcom, 23*(23-3/4), 201–220.

Subramanian, D. (2010). *Telecommunications industry in India: State, business and labour in a global economy.* New Delhi: Social Science Press.

Swisscom. (1997). *Annual Report.* https://www.swisscom.ch/en/about/investors/reports/downloads.html

Taskar, N. T. (1981, July 1). Why telephones do not always work? *The Hindu.*

Tewari, M. S. (1996, January 8). Vanguard won't oblige Modi's with funds or farewell. *The Times of India.*

Thomsen, S. (1997). Recent trends in foreign direct investment. *Financial Market,* p. 67.

Three consortia offer $4B Each. (1985, September 9). *The Economic Times.*

TRAI. (2017). The Indian telecom services performance indicators: April - June, 2017. Retrieved 2018 from http://trai.gov.in/sites/default/files/Performance_Indicator_Reports_28092017.pdf

Wernerfelt, B. (1984). A resource-based view of the firm. *Strategic Management Journal, 5*(2), 171–180.

Internment as a business challenge: Political risk management and German multinationals in Colonial India (1914–1947)

Christina Lubinski ⓘ, Valeria Giacomin and Klara Schnitzer

ABSTRACT

Internment in so-called 'enemy countries' was a frequent occurrence in the twentieth century and created significant obstacles for multinational enterprises (MNEs). This article focuses on German MNEs in India and shows how they addressed the formidable challenge of the internment of their employees in British camps during both the First and the Second World War. It finds that internment impacted business relationships in India well beyond its endpoint and that the First World War internment shaped the subsequent perception of and strategic response to the Second World War experience. It is shown that internment aggravated existing staffing challenges, impacted on the perception of racial lines of distinctions and re-cast the category 'European business'. While internment was perceived and managed as a political risk, the case also shows that it created unexpected networking opportunities, generating a tight community of German businesspeople in India.

1. Introduction

Internment during wartime is a frequent occurrence. As the historical literature shows, it creates major challenges for internees, the governments of belligerent and neutral states, and humanitarian organisations such as the Red Cross (Speed, 1990; Stibbe, 2006). However, it also produces significant obstacles for multinational enterprises (MNEs), which the literature has so far largely ignored. Internment, we argue in this article, is a relevant and frequent form of political risk that historically required MNEs to engage in new strategies to manage operational challenges.

We explore the issue of 'internment management' by focusing on the specific situation of German businesspeople interned in British camps in India during both the First and the Second World War. Given how little has been written about internment as a form of political risk, such an in-depth approach is suitable to identify MNEs' reactions to the issue, the strategies they explored and the subsequent impact of internment on their business in India. By tracing MNE strategies through both world wars, we show the learning effects and the legacy of previous internment experiences. Based on our admittedly limited case study, we seek to identify major issues and questions for future scholarly research on internment.

India is a particularly relevant and under-researched case for the purpose of exploring the issue of internment management. While the group of internees tended to be diverse in most other countries, internment in India was *primarily* a business problem, as the majority of internees were employees of foreign MNEs. Most of them were German and Austrian nationals; during the Second World War some Italians also resided in the camps. Yet, neither Indian history nor business history research has addressed this issue. This is partly because Indian business history focuses strongly on the British–Indian relationship pre-1947 and has given significantly less attention to the fate of MNEs of non-British origin, as Tripathi (2014, p. 6) rightly criticises.

Scholars are slowly starting to fill this void. Japanese historians Kaoru (1990) and Akita (together with White) (2010) trace the relationship between India and Japan, acknowledging the influence of Britain but finding that the economic region also developed independent trading relationships. Arnold (2013), Dejung (2013), Lubinski (2015) and Ramnath (2017) all suggest that India was a free (or almost free) trade area for most of the nineteenth and the early twentieth century. As a consequence, there was competition between British companies and multinationals from Switzerland, Germany, France, Japan and the United States – to name just the countries discussed in the literature so far.

On the issue of MNEs' political risk management, India is certainly a case of great importance. As Austin, Dávila, and Jones (2017) have recently argued, political risk is particularly severe in emerging markets due to their colonial past and institutional inefficiencies. As a result, both local and foreign companies need to design strategies to deal with political turbulence. However, the existing literature on political risk in India mirrors the focus on the British–Indian relationship in Indian business history more generally and focuses on the biggest political concern for British companies: rising Indian nationalism. Other forms of political risk in India have rarely been addressed, even though MNEs in India clearly faced a plethora of different political challenges over the course of the twentieth century, in particular if we take Tripathi's call seriously and include MNEs of non-British origin, as for example Dejung and Zangger (2010) and Arnold (2011, 2013) show.

Howell and Chaddick (1994, p. 71) define political risk as 'the possibility that political decisions, events or conditions in a country … will affect the business environment such that investors will lose money or have a reduced profit margin'. Business historians have empirically shown a variety of responses to political risk in different countries around the world. The results in the existing literature can be loosely grouped into at least three sets of strategies that multinationals engaged in: (i) 'cloaking' strategies, which introduce changes in the organisational structure to camouflage ultimate ownership, (ii) strategies focused on resilience to political change and continuous negotiations with local decision-makers, and (iii) approaches based on maintaining or increasing legitimacy as a protective shield against political risks. Most organisations, over time, employ a combination of these strategies in their attempt to manage political risks.

The first line of research detailing contributions on cloaking, i.e. the art of concealing ownership, is by far the largest. So far, this set of contributions primarily focuses on political risks originating in Nazi Germany during the interwar and Second World War period and deals with organisational responses to these risks. Works by Wubs (2008), Boon and Wubs (2016), Kobrak and Wüstenhagen (2006), Jones and Lubinski (2012), and Aalders and Wiebes

(1996) show that Nazi Germany created risks for both foreign and German MNEs and that companies often responded with a combination of cloaking and decentralisation of their organisational structure. Outside the context of Nazi Germany, MNEs have for long used the same strategy of cloaking and decentralisation to avoid for example taxation or penalising regulation (Donzé & Kurosawa, 2013; Jones & Gomopoulos, 2005; Jones & Storli, 2012).

A second line of research focuses on MNEs dealing with open conflicts with host governments and local decision-makers. For example, White (2012) shows how British companies in post-independence Indonesia survived a series of challenging (albeit temporary) takeovers by trade unions and various government authorities in the early 1960s. Donzé and Kurosawa (2013, p. 1329) detail how a Nestlé executive suggested facing the continuous antagonism of Japanese stakeholders by 'sweat[ing] it out' until the situation normalised. Similarly, van der Eng (2017) finds that Philips handled the risk of asset confiscation, internment and exclusion from government contracts in Australia during the Second World War with a flexible adaptive strategy based on negotiations and resilience. Philips replaced individual employees who were considered a political risk (one of the managers was suspected of being a German spy) and revised production methods to best access government contracts.

Finally, a third group revolves around legitimisation strategies to mitigate the impact of political risks. Smith (2016) shows that maintaining legitimacy with stakeholders in the home market can positively affect company survival in (temporarily) hostile host markets. Bucheli and Salvaj (2013) stress the point that changing political conditions may turn strategies designed to increase legitimacy with local stakeholders into liabilities. Gao, Zuzul, Jones, and Khanna (2017) emphasise reputation as a meta-resource that can help companies survive politically unstable periods in emerging markets and overcome, or even capitalise on, institutional inefficiencies.

None of these previous contributions focuses explicitly on the challenge of internment or explores how MNEs addressed it. This is surprising given the ubiquitous and widespread application of internment in many countries. Numerous MNEs faced the challenge of their employees being incarcerated in camps all over the world. Historians have established that the internment of civilians was very common, in particular since the First World War. Historian Stibbe (2008, p. 5) argues that although there had been detentions during previous conflicts, such as the Spanish war in Cuba (1896–1897), the Boer war in South Africa (1899–1902), and the Balkan wars (1912–1913), it was precisely in the First World War that the internment of civilians became a global phenomenon, undertaken by all belligerent states on all continents. He estimates that overall several hundred thousand civilians were captured and detained during the First World War. Several thousand Germans were held in British colonies and in areas occupied by Britain, including camps in Transvaal, Egypt, Singapore, Palestine and of course India. They joined the thousands of 'enemy aliens' detained in Hong Kong, Australia, New Zealand and, after 1917, in the United States, China, Siam, Cuba, Brazil, Panama and Haiti. A smaller number of Germans were also imprisoned by the French in Morocco, the Cameroons and Togoland (for details on these estimates, see Stibbe, 2006, pp. 7–8).

To analyse internment as a management challenge for German MNEs in India during the twentieth century, we draw primarily on the detailed corporate archives of three German companies: the electrical company Siemens; the chemical company Bayer, which in 1925 merged with other German chemical firms to form IG Farben; and the steel producer Krupp. We selected these three companies because of all German MNEs they employed the largest number of people stationed and consequently interned in India. We complement the material with archival sources from the German Foreign Office, the German Federal Archives and the British Library's Asia, Pacific and Africa Collections.

While we acknowledge that comparative perspectives with other MNEs in India or other countries of the colonial global South are extremely valuable, there is unfortunately very little empirical research that explicitly addresses the issue of internment. We draw on the business history of the Swiss trading house Volkart by Dejung (2013), which offers valuable insights into a Swiss firm in India reacting to the internment of the Germans. Although different in context, Miller's (2015) recent analysis of human resource policies of British MNEs in South America and Sluyterman's (pre-published online 2017) of Dutch MNEs in Indonesia provide details to contextualise some of the decisions German multinationals took in India.

The structure of the article is as follows: Section 2 describes the (sudden and unexpected) internment of German businesspeople in the First World War and gives some background on the prior German business in India. Section 3 focuses on the reconstruction of that business after the war and highlights the problem of recruiting qualified labour. Section 4 deals with the outbreak of the Second World War and the new wave of internment, which the historical actors interpreted within the framework of their previous experience. Section 5 traces the almost immediate reactions from different stakeholders in Germany, including the concerned companies, the larger business community and the German government. Section 6 focuses on the internees in the camps and gives information on their professional and personal backgrounds based on a database of 361 German employees who were interned in India. It then traces the careers of a few selected internees to explore possible long-term consequences of the internment experience. The final section concludes and provides direction for future research.

2. German–Indian business in the First World War

The First World War came suddenly and unexpectedly for the German business community. At the outbreak of the war, German assets in India were expropriated under the Trading with the Enemy Act. Several different ordinances and orders addressed the enemy trading issue, stipulating that all hostile foreigners or firms should cease to trade unless licensed by the Government of India. The definition of a hostile firm was comprehensive, including 'any company, firm, association, or body of individuals incorporated or not, of which any member or officer is a hostile foreigner' (Government of India Legislative Department, 1915).

Both Siemens and Bayer bore the devastating consequences of this law. Bayer had had a wholly owned subsidiary in India since 1896, which was fully expropriated (Bayer, 1918). Siemens conducted most of its business with India from Great Britain, where all its manufacturing facilities were equally seized. As a consequence, the India business came to a complete halt. Moreover, both companies lost important patents and trademarks, which damaged their pre-war competitive position (IG Farben, 1939).

Shortly after the outbreak of the First World War, German nationals in India were gathered in internment camps. The internment camp system of the British Empire operated at both the national and imperial level, with prisoners frequently being transferred between different locations and across national borders (Panayi, 2014, p. 15). The largest internment camps were in New Zealand, Hong Kong, Singapore and India (Proctor, 2010, p. 79, n13). The largest Indian internment camp was situated at Ahmednagar, a city in the state of Maharashtra in

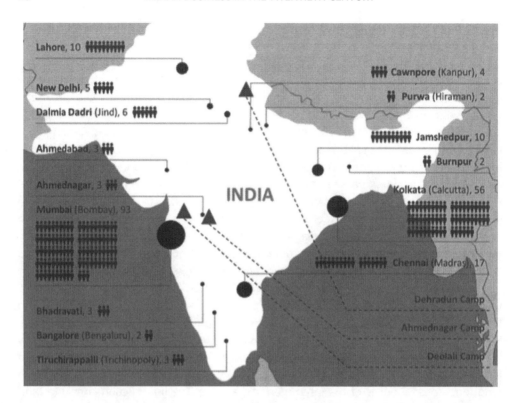

Figure 1. Places with more than one German businessperson residing prior to 1939. Database by the authors. Three major internment camps (depicted by triangles): Dehra Dun, Ahmednagar and Deolali.

the western part of India, about 120 km (75 miles) north-east of Pune and 250 km (155 miles) east of Bombay (see Figure 1). Camp Ahmednagar had a history as a prisoner-of-war camp. During the Boer war in South Africa (1899–1902) the British shipped around 9000 prisoners from Africa to Ahmednagar (Great Britain War Office, Maurice, & Grant, 1906, vol. 4, appendix 20). In the First World War, it was once again used as internment camp for enemy aliens.

By March 1917, the camp held 1621 men, primarily Germans and Austrians. Of those, 452 (28%) were prisoners of war, predominantly captured on German ships. The remaining 1169 (72%) were civilians, mostly businesspeople or missionaries. When a Red Cross Committee visited the camp in early 1917, it commented on the previous lifestyle of the internees:

> Most of them had been several years in India, engaged in business, managing prosperous commercial firms or enjoying well-paid employment. They had become used to the free, comfortable Indian life.... To have to leave their pretty bungalows for the internment camp, give up business, see their future compromised and their interests endangered, was truly hard to endure. (International Committee of the Red Cross & Thormeyer, 1917, p. 12)

The Committee also reported that the British Government had initially allowed the firm liquidators of German and Austrian businesses to pay former employees 80 to 120 Indian rupees (INR), equalling c.5.3 to 8 GBP,[1] per month. This permission was withdrawn in August 1916, leading to a sudden decline of liquidity in the camp (International Committee of the Red Cross & Thormeyer, 1917, p. 33).

The prisoners were accommodated in old stone barracks and newly constructed huts made of corrugated iron. The camp was surrounded by barbed-wire fences and British and

Indian soldiers kept guard. Internees were not forced to do physical labour, but some worked in the kitchen for pay. Most spent their time learning foreign languages (reports indicated classes in Hindi, Arabic, English, French and Spanish taught by internees) or engaged in theatre, sports or studies in the camp library. Courses were organised by the internees in stenography, mathematics, chemistry, biology, macroeconomics and theology (International Committee of the Red Cross & Thormeyer, 1917, pp. 32–33; Probst, 1917, p. 59). In retrospect, the internees argued that the desire for meaningful occupation was essential to fight the boredom, in particular for the 'fresh young men' who had taken on qualified positions overseas to broaden their horizons. However, the longer the internment lasted, the more infrequent the courses became (Probst, 1917, pp. 92–93).

Wives and children were held at a different internment location in Belgaum, 400 kilometres (248 miles) south of Ahmednagar. In March 1916, after several petitions, the British authorities turned Belgaum into a family camp and held couples and families together (International Committee of the Red Cross & Thormeyer, 1917, pp. 35–39). Unlike the men, the women were allowed to keep indigenous servants, which became an important marker of status in the colonial society.

The internment experience fundamentally changed the (perceived) status of Germans in India – both in the eyes of outside observers and in the eyes of the Germans themselves. While the Germans had previously felt themselves part of the 'white Western elite' in India, they struggled with the new line of distinction based on nationality rather than race. In his report, N. O. Tera (1939), who had gone to India for a Hamburg-based rubber company, argued that the day of the internment was when 'the British destroyed the "Schicksalsgemeinschaft" [community of fate] of the Europeans vis-à-vis the coloured races of the world. Here is when for the first time the British destroyed the fiction of the superiority of the white race.' Similarly, the missionary Hans Georg Probst (1917, p. 11) remembered the good old times when 'there still was a feeling of community between the Europeans vis-à-vis the Blacks'. Similar to Hyslop's (2006) findings on the white working class before the First World War, among western businesspeople in India, nationality had been secondary to race in attributing privilege and status. Before the war German businessmen had shared with their British peers European clubs, which Sinha (2001) describes as vehicles for a 'political mobilization of whiteness' (p. 505). These clubs consolidated the racially exclusive colonial elite in India and at the same time served important business functions, such as information exchange, conflict mediation and networking. With the outbreak of the war, Germans and Austrians were expelled from these clubs and the doors remained closed to them even after the war (Consulate Calcutta, 1930).

Some internees resisted the perceived loss of status and actively fought for their belonging to the colonial elite, for example by insisting on a European diet and engaging in recreational activities that highlighted their belonging to this privileged class. At the Ahmednagar camp, a group of affluent internees even built two tennis courts, an activity criticised by others as unpatriotic because tennis was considered a typical pastime of the British upper class (Probst, 1917, p. 61). The conflict between the internees illustrates the change in the interpretation of the category 'European' and the new lines of distinction based on nationality rather than race. While the internment conditions in India were overall rather favourable in terms of nutrition, health and control over personal time, the German internees' major affliction was their exclusion from the privileged community of western businesspeople.

On 19 November 1918, the armistice marked the end of the armed conflict. The Versailles Treaty was signed on 28 June 1919. It took another six months before the internees were released from Ahmednagar camp on 27 December 1919. German–Indian business relations had dissolved. A travel ban prohibited Germans from traveling to or residing in India. It remained in place until 1925.

3. Staffing problems while reconstructing the India trade

Despite the travel ban, after the end of the war German firms were eager to access the Indian market once again, not least because it was one of the few foreign markets that remained accessible to them. While France, Britain and the United States introduced protectionist policies against foreign MNEs and had expropriated German patents and trademarks during the war to favour domestic companies, India remained a free-trade country with open competition between different western MNEs.

While German MNEs aimed to expand in foreign markets, in her growing ambitions for independence India sought trade partners that could deliver products it could not yet manufacture. Thanks to this particular alignment of interests, Indians took the initiative and went to Germany in search of an alternative to firms associated with their colonial overseer. As early as 1921, Bayer hosted J. C. Das Gupta, a representative of several Calcutta-based companies eager to negotiate with the Germans as a substitute for British trade. According to an internal memo, Das Gupta tried 'to lay the ground for the many Indians who now arrive daily in Hamburg' (Bayer Archives, 1921). Other businesspeople reported Sikh buyers roaming the country to purchase much-needed goods for sale in India (Lohmann, 1934, p. 43).

Indians turned to Germany because they saw a potential partner with similar anti-British feelings; and Germans looked to India as a promising accessible market, which was open to German engagement. In this environment, both Siemens and Bayer were swift in rebuilding their business. To circumvent the travel ban, both companies started working and cooperating with the Italian company Gorio Ltd, which had offices in Bombay and Calcutta as well as initially in Karachi and had tight connections with the local colonial administration (Siemens, 1922). In addition, Siemens sent the non-German engineer Eduard de Rziha to India to supervise the new business (De Rziha, 1923). By the end of 1924, Siemens founded Siemens (India) Limited, a British-Indian corporation with a capital of 200,000 INR (c.13,334 GBP) (Siemens (India) Ltd, undated). Siemens (India) had a contractual agreement with Siemens Berlin describing its representation of Siemens' interests in India (Siemens Archives, 1925). Over the following years, it opened offices in Rangoon (1925) and Lahore (1926) and hired agents for the United Provinces, Delhi, Madras (now Chennai) and Ceylon (now Sri Lanka).[2]

In 1925, Bayer merged with five other German chemical companies to form the 'Interessen-Gemeinschaft Farbenindustrie AG', or IG Farben.[3] The massive conglomerate had a total workforce of 100,000 people worldwide (Tammen, 1978, p. 195). To conceal ultimate ownership, IG Farben engaged in a secret contract with a Dutch cover firm, Havero, which conducted the business with British India, Burma and Ceylon. It was not until 1938 that IG Farben founded wholly-owned and locally incorporated subsidiaries in India again.

One of the biggest challenges for both Siemens and IG Farben was finding and controlling qualified staff. After the First World War and the internment in India, most German businesspeople with experience in India had returned home. 'Only few of the old India experts have found their way back here', reported the German consul in Bombay, Karl Kapp, in 1927 (German Federal Archives, 1927). Work in India came with great responsibility. The tasks that managers abroad had to cope with were hard to standardise and changed frequently. As communication and transport were slow and often unreliable, it was hard to supervise these faraway agents. In 1924, Hermann Reyss (1924), head of Siemens' overseas administration, stressed the need for independently acting employees in overseas offices: 'The management of an overseas office requires extraordinary independence and initiative. We cannot guide these gentlemen via regulations and circular letters, and even the men in second and third row must possess similar qualities.' That this was not an easy task is shown by the example of the Siemens India office, for which top manager de Rziha complained in 1926 that 'the performance is not such as can be expected in all fairness'. In the future, he suggested, employees should have the opportunity to work in a variety of fields before being sent abroad (De Rziha, 1926).

Recognising the challenge of labour management, Siemens' overseas administration had its own human resource department before the 1920s (Siemens Archives, undated). Suitable candidates for India had to prove themselves in Germany or in another European country before being sent overseas. Siemens managers were well aware that the wrong choices could only be corrected after a lengthy period of time and were thus very costly. Good candidates needed both technical expertise and an awareness of the corporate culture. Siemens' overseas department required that they had 'to be familiar with the spirit and the business conduct ["Geschäftsgebarung', CL] of our house [of Siemens]" (Siemens Archives, undated).

Those employees that were sent to India had an initial contract for three or five years, similar to what Miller (2015, p. 162) reports regarding British business in South America in the immediate post-war period. Siemens paid for their relocation and travel. For higher-ranking officials it was standard to grant at least one business trip back to Germany during a five-year period. When it came to recruitment, Siemens HR managers frequently pointed out that the best experience was achieved with those young men who had started their career with Siemens as apprentices (Siemens Archives, undated).

Initially, German MNEs were reluctant to employ locals. They were afraid of opportunistic behaviour and wanted to keep tight control on their offices. Racial prejudices aggravated the situation. These challenges were not unique to the Germans in India. Miller (2015, pp. 162–163) reports a similar setup for the staffing policy of British companies (especially banks and trading houses) in Latin America. They employed shorter contracts for their expats and were generally averse to recruiting or training local managers, which resulted in chronic shortages of skilled staff. Dejung's (2013, p. 239) detailed analysis of the Swiss trading company Volkart in India similarly shows the unequal treatment of Indian and European employees, including differences in working conditions, medical coverage (Indian employees did not receive financial support), and travel reimbursements (Europeans travelled first class, while Indians were supposed to get cheaper tickets).

However, these practices increasingly came under pressure. The Swiss company Volkart introduced bonus payments for its Indian employees around the turn of the century, and from 1916 offered old-age pensions (Dejung, 2013, pp. 210–221). Siemens manager Eduard Beha was called out for not hiring Indian engineers and clerks during a visit to the Lahore office in 1931. He admitted to having been hesitant in the past but stressed that 'good engineers and managers, independently if Europeans or Indians, should always have the best

Table 1. Siemens (India) sales, total and as a percentage of all overseas branches, 1928–1939.

	Sales Siemens (India) (in 1000 RM)	Sales of all overseas branches (in 1000 RM)	India as % of all overseas branches
1928/29	4461	88,000	5.1
1931/32	4167	59,083	7.1
1932/33	n/a	32,000	n/a
1933/34	3064	25,577	12.0
1934/35	4085	32,684	12.5
1935/36	4296	37,326	11.5
1936/37	5458	44,000	12.4
1937/38	8082	44,867	18.0
1938/39	7508	54,707	13.7

Note: 25 LG 136; 8136 and 4286, all SAA. The category 'overseas' includes Siemens' subsidiaries in: Argentina, Brazil, British India, Chile, China, Dutch East Indies, Egypt, Japan, Mexico, South Africa and Sri Lanka.

Table 2. IG Farben Sales in India, total and as percentage of exports 1926–1937.

Year	Sales IG Farben (India) (in 1000 RM)	Export sales IG Farben (in 1000 RM)	India as % of all export sales
1926	28,620		
1927	n/a		
1928	n/a	813,500	
1929	28,980	781,600	3.71
1930	29,760	577,900	5.15
1931	32,189	534,600	6.02
1932	28,316	473,200	5.98
1933	27,069	452,000	5.99
1934	26,420	418,200	6.32
1935	31,528	451,100	6.98
1936	28,374	450,000	6.31
1937	27,770	488,400	5.69
1938	n/a		

Note: 4 b 14 3 6 Dye market British India; 330/1267 Files of IG Farben; 1113 British India; 420 Sales dyes. 82/1 Situation of the Indian Rupee, all BA.

prospects in our company' (Siemens (India) Ltd, 1931). Siemens was not alone in its initial reluctance to consider locals for higher qualified jobs. Although labour was numerically abundant in India, skilled labourers were hard to find. The British Trade Commissioner for India (1919, p. 19) highlighted the lack of skilled mechanics and pointed out that 'industrial success will be in spite of, rather than on account of, the low paid labour'. The high cost of skilled labour has even been interpreted as one reason why India remained inclined to small-scale traditional manufacturing during the first half of the twentieth century (Roy, 2006, pp. 235–237).

The increasing and unmet demand triggered slow and moderate changes, which were reinforced by the improving political and cultural relations between India and Germany (Manjapra, 2014). In the context of rising sales numbers for both Siemens and IG Farben in the mid-1930s (see Tables 1 and 2), hiring Indians for qualified posts slowly became more common. In particular Indian engineers could exploit new opportunities (Overseas HR Department, 1934, 1935, 1936, 1937, 1938). All Indian employees – even the much-needed engineers – received significantly lower salaries than expatriates. While the salaries of Siemens' and IG Farben's Indian employees only survived in fragments in the archives, the third largest German employer Krupp kept detailed records. These records show the wage gap between expatriates and Indians but also a slow but steady increase in the salaries of

Table 3. Value of 100 Indian Rupees in German (Reichs-)Mark, 1914–1938.

	100 Indian rupees in German (Reichs-)Mark	Change in %
1914	133	
1928–1931	150	+12.8
1931 (Jan.–Sept.)	150	0
1931 (Sept.–Dec.)	123	−18
1932	111	−9.8
1933	105	−5.4
1934	95	−9.5
1935	92	−3.2
1936	93	+1
1937	93	0
1938	92	−1

Note: Based on BA 82/1 The situation of the Indian rupee, 1938.

Indian staff. Top-level managers at Krupp (India) received 1500 to 2500 INR (or 112.5 to 187.5 GBP) monthly, which is slightly higher than the base pay at Siemens. However, Siemens worked with bonus and commission payments. The lowest paid European staff were three women working as typists with salaries between 150 and 190 INR (11.25 to 14.25 GBP) in the mid- to late 1930s. At the same time, the highest paid Indian engineers received 200 INR (15 GBP) and a typical Indian typist between 60 and 85 INR (4.5 to 6.38 GBP). The lowest paid Indians were apprentices, coolies and sweepers who made 20 INR (1.5 GBP) or less. In the late 1930s Indian engineers, in particular, could increase their salaries to up to 250 INR (18.75 GBP). However, still in 1939, the German General Manager of Krupp (India) reported with a great sense of urgency that other MNEs paid higher salaries to their Indian engineers and that competitors had successfully poached qualified engineers from Krupp (Steffens, 1939a, 1939b).[4]

The shortage of high-skilled talent was further reinforced by the instability of the international monetary system since the 1930s, which made relocation less attractive for German engineers. In 1931, the British pound departed from the gold standard, while the German Reichsmark remained pegged to gold. Consequently, the Indian rupee depreciated relative to the Reichsmark (see Table 3). Employees overseas were paid in the local currency. Siemens' overseas human resource department reported that due to the fact that overseas employees could no longer accumulate substantial savings, which had been common practice for many of the young Germans working in India, engineers showed little interest in relocating (Overseas HR Department, 1938). Throughout the interwar years, staffing challenges dominated the managerial agenda of German MNEs in India, thus creating a context in which any employment issue, in particular one as severe as internment, had to be taken very seriously.

4. Outbreak of the Second World War and a new wave of internment

The Second World War began with the German invasion of Poland on 1 September 1939. Two days later Britain and France declared war on Germany. That very night German nationals in India were interned as enemy aliens once again, 25 years after the the First World War internment (Overseas HR Department, undated). In most parts of India all male Germans were arrested, even if they were beyond military age or were Jews who had previously fled to India to escape persecution in Germany. The only exception was the province of Calcutta, where Jews remained free for the time being (Schoberth, 1940). Approximately 900 men were arrested and deported either directly to camp Ahmednagar, or via smaller camps, such as Fort Williams in Calcutta (Pazze, 1939; Schoberth, 1940; Weingarten, 1939). In hindsight, one observer remarked: 'The comfortable and secured life of these people changed abruptly on the day of the internment' (Urchs, 1948, p. 181).

Women and children were not among these prisoners of the first hour. The police expropriated their cars, radios, cameras and binoculars; other private property remained untouched. The women were allowed to sell those assets to cover their living expenses (Luitpold, 1940). Moreover, the Indian government paid them 80 INR (*c*.6 GBP) per woman and 30 INR (*c*.2.25 GBP) per child. However, the internees complained that this was not sufficient for survival and argued that approximately 400 INR (*c*.30 GBP) per family and 100 INR (*c*.7.5 GBP) for internees were needed (Luitpold, 1940). Indeed, household budgets were much depleted for the women and children that remained outside internment camps. German managers had previously received 1500 to 2500 INR (or 112.5 to 187.5 GBP) monthly, as reported before. Making ends meet on 140 INR (*c*.10.5 GBP) for a woman with two children would have required significant changes in lifestyle.

The legal basis for internment was the Registration of Foreigners Act, 1939, in combination with the Foreigners Order and Enemy Foreigners Order (UNHCR, 1939/2018). The first internment camp was situated once again in Ahmednagar. Given the previous history of this camp during both the Boer War and the First World War, some Germans experienced a déjà-vu upon arrival 'at the exact same spot where the old German prisoners of war were held 25 years ago' (Luitpold, 1940). While all Germans interned during the First World War had returned to Germany after the war, some later went back to India to engage once more in business there. The most unfortunate individuals – for example Sydney Schüder (born 1893)[5] who went to India for Schering – were interned twice at Ahmednagar, once during the First World War and again during the Second World War.

The Germans were taken to Ahmednagar by train. Upon arrival, they had to walk from the railway station to the camp – a distance of approximately 8 kilometres (4.9 miles), which became one of the most reported traumatic events of the internment experience. Similar to the First World War, some internees again highlighted the embarrassment of being supervised by 'coloured' (Sikh) soldiers. Otto Zimmer (1939), the commercial attaché and Nazi Party supporter, stressed that 'in the Indian context this [being supervised by Sikhs] is a massive humiliation for the Europeans'. Drawings, which selected internees made during their internment, emphasised the race difference between the white German businessmen, often depicted as slightly overweight and oddly misplaced in the camp, and their darkskinned guards in a tropical environment (Figures 2 and 3).

5. Reactions in Germany

Unlike during the First World War, German multinationals reacted swiftly to the new internment situation. Both Siemens and IG Farben collected information on their internees, stayed in close contact with their families and shared all available eye-witness reports with them as well as with other companies and the Foreign Office. First reports came from those employees of the German companies who were not German nationals, such as the Italian citizen

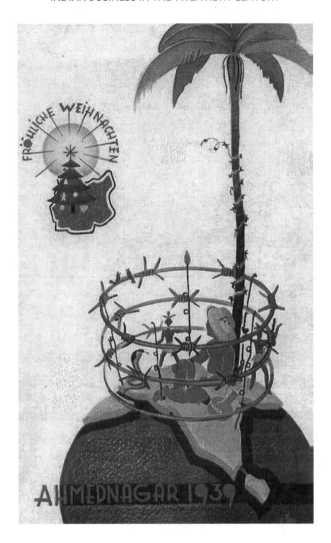

Figure 2. Christmas Card from camp Ahmednagar, December 1939. Private collection Gaebler (http://www.gaebler.info/), copyright owner unknown.

Pazze (1939), a representative of Continental in Bombay, or the Swiss national Schoberth (1940) of Siemens, who were able to return to Germany.

As early as September 1939, German business coordinated its support activities in a 'Special Committee for the Assistance of Interned German Nationals in British India' in close cooperation with the Foreign Office and the Nazi Party's 'Auslandsorganisation [Overseas Organisation]' (Bayer Archives, 1944; Orient Verein, 1939a). The Committee was part of the 'Deutscher Orient Verein [German Orient Association]' and was headed by Hermann Waibel, management board member of IG Farben since 1928 and an expert on East Asian trade (Orient Verein, 1939d). The committee's first meeting was on 29 September 1939 in Berlin and included representatives of the Foreign Office and the companies IG Farben, Siemens, AEG, Krupp, Schering-Kahlbaum and Hansa India. They discussed a support scheme and decided to distinguish the employees of German companies from 'other' German nationals

Figure 3. Drawing of internee, undated. Private collection Gaebler (http://www.gaebler.info/), copyright owner unknown.

in internment, who would receive less or no support (Orient Verein, 1939a). They also planned for a letter to be sent to all German firms with business in India to collect financial aid. The letter highlighted that the support scheme had nothing to do with charity but rather would guarantee that employees were available to reconstruct German business in India after the war, highlighting the need for a long-term strategy that could bridge politically turbulent times (Orient Verein, 1939e).

Finally, Waibel was assigned the task to request special permission to send money to India, in the context of Germany's strict foreign exchange controls (for context, see Tooze, 2007, pp. 71–86). This required complicated negotiations with the German authorities, despite the general support of the Foreign Office for the assistance of internees. It was not until March 1941 that the initiative finally achieved a payment of 10 Reichsmark per month (*c.*11 INR or 0.825 GBP) to all internees, a much more moderate sum than the initially envisioned 50 Reichsmark (*c.*54 INR or 4.05 GBP) (Orient Verein, 1941). In light of the fact that internees claimed to be needing 100 INR (*c.*7.5 GBP) for themselves and 400 INR (*c.*30 GBP) for their families, the sum has to be considered symbolic. Eventually, the Foreign Office came up with a scheme in which more affluent internees were asked to pay an additional 30 Reichsmark (c.33 INR or 2.475 GBP) monthly to internees in need, which the Special Committee promised to reimburse after the end of the war (Bayer Archives, 1941; Orient Verein, 1940b).

While the affected companies in Germany debated possible support schemes, business-people who had experienced internment in India during the First World War lobbied for more engagement. C. W. Kuehns (1939) of the Hamburg-based rubber company Phoenix addressed Hermann Waibel directly and expressed his hope 'that one learned from previous events'. Reflecting on the entire quarter-century since the last internment he argued:

> It has been hard enough after the previous war to get back onto foreign markets, and if we don't show our employees abroad a warm heart, we later won't find anyone anymore who is willing to go abroad to represent German interests. (Kuehns, 1939)

Comparative perspectives were plentiful. One of Kuehns' biggest worries was the fact that at the outbreak of the First World War many older and relatively affluent businesspeople ended up in internment and were able to take some of their private money. 'This time it is a very young colony with young assistants who do not have large financial reserves' (Kuehns, 1939). Due to similar concerns, AEG had paid out three months' salary to all unmarried employees and six months' salary to married ones just before the war broke out. By November, the Special Committee had identified 236 employees as being interned (Bayer Archives, 1944; Orient Verein, 1939c). Their average age was 34.45 years. Some 86 (36 %) of them were 30 years old or younger.

To lobby for more systematic support, C. W. Kuehns, together with two other previous internees in India, Hans E. B. Kruse[6] and C. Mensendieck, wrote an official letter to the Foreign Office appealing to the MNEs' long-term strategy:

> Again, as in 1914, after 25 years, German managers, engineers, chemists, and technicians are interned as prisoners of war in Ahmednagar.... We all want that after the victorious war, patriotic, courageous young Germans go abroad again as commercial pioneers. How can we ever count on precious men to take this risk, if their home country cannot support them in times of need. (Mensendieck, Kruse, & Kuehns, 1940)

They also asked the Special Committee to include at least one former internee in its meetings to rely on his local knowledge and experience. The committee appointed Wolf Sthamer from Hamburg, who was interned at Ahmednagar in the First World War, and a nephew of the former German ambassador in England (Waibel, 1940).

6. The community of internees and its legacy

Based on archival sources from different corporate and German government archives, we built a database with basic information on 361 Second World War internees who had worked for German companies in India, and collected information on their age, education, position in the company, marital status and careers.[7] The total number of internees in Indian camps varied quite considerably, between c.900 (at the first internment in September 1939) to 324 (according to the Swiss authorities' list in May 1940, after the temporary release of most Jews and missionaries) and 604 (according to a German Foreign Office report of August 1941, including a number of newly captured German sailors and the re-interned Jews and missionaries that had remained in India) (German Foreign Office, 1941b; Sauvage, 1942). We cross-checked our database against individual lists of German companies and the German Foreign Office as well as address lists of internees, which were used to remain in touch after the war.

Information on age was available for 236 (65%) of the 361 internees with the average being 34.45 years, as reported earlier. Marital status could be identified for 229 (63%). The group splits fairly evenly between husbands (111, 48.5%) and bachelors (118, 51.5%). The internees worked for a variety of German companies (see Table 4). The biggest employers were IG Farben (51 internees) and Siemens (36). Of the 236 internees for whom an educational background or position was mentioned in the sources, the vast majority were sales people (88) and engineers (48), followed by technicians and mechanics (18).

Most German nationals resided in Bombay (93) and Calcutta (56) followed by Madras (17), Jamshedpur (10) – where the Tata Iron and Steel Company was located – and Lahore (10). While concentration in the big commercial centres of India is not surprising, it is interesting to note that German businesspeople did not exclusively live in these areas but, rather, were spread out over the vast Indian subcontinent, with one or two representatives of German firms present in many smaller cities in India (see Table 5 and Figure 1). For 183 internees (50.7%), the sources reveal when they first arrived in India. On average they had spent 3.78 years in the country prior to their internment. The veteran was the technician Otto Engelmann of IG Farben (born 1902) who first went to India in 1924. A total of 41 businesspeople had arrived only a few months prior to being arrested.

The internees also varied according to political leaning, which was reflected in the structure of the internment camp. The camp was divided into A and B camps. At the A camp, prisoners paid 3 INR (c.0.23 GBP) daily for better food and accommodation (Osten, 1940; Schoberth, 1940). Internally, the B camp was considered the 'Nazi camp', with the argument that not paying any money to the British was a contribution to Germany's war efforts. The camp was commanded by a British Colonel named Quale and the guards were Sikhs. In each camp, the internees elected one camp supervisor. At the A camp an internee called Schneider represented the group. For the B camp Oswald Urchs was chosen. Urchs (born 1895 in Pilsen, then part of Austria-Hungary) was a medical doctor by profession, who went to India in 1927 in the services of IG Farben. He had previously lived in Dutch Guyana (1923–1926) and was an expert on malaria research. Before the war Urchs had acted as the head of the local Nazi club in Bombay, which, in his own words, 'must make every German abroad an ambassador of the National Socialist movement' (Oswald Urchs, directly quoted in 'Spreading Nazism Abroad', *Singapore Free Press and Mercantile Advertiser*, 8 September 1937, p. 2). The Nazi Party's Foreign Organisation had an extensive network of local clubs around the world and gave out centralised guidelines on how to mobilise Germans abroad (Jacobsen, 1968, p. 44).

The most frequent complaints about the camp conditions focused on nutrition. However, they were not addressing quantity but rather quality, based on the argument that the kitchen staff was Indian. The German internees rejected their cooking and eventually took over the preparing of the meals themselves (Bayer Archives, 1944; Orient Verein, 1939b). Like the attempts during the First World War to sustain an elite European identity and distinguish themselves from the local population, the complaints over food preparation can be interpreted as a set of efforts to maintain (some) racial distinction from the Indian staff.

German women were not interned but had to live within much more moderate means. They started combining households to cut down on living expenses (Orient Verein, 1940a). They lived off their savings, some support money and the earnings from selling furniture

Table 4. Companies for which German internees worked.

Company	Number of internees
IG Farben	51
Siemens	36
Krupp	14
Polysius AG	12
AEG	10
Voith	8
Hansa India	6
Lohmann & Co.	6
Schering AG	6
Robert Bosch GmbH	5
Dr C. Otto & Co. GmbH	4
MAN	4
Maschinenfabrik Sack GmbH	4
Carl Zeiss	3
Christian Poggensee	3
Daimler Benz	3
Damag AG	3
Deutsche Dampfschiff Ges. Hansa	3
Fritz Haeuser AG	3
Himalaja Expedition	3
Maschinenfabrik Buckau	3
Merck	3
Miag	3
Allianz	2
Auto-Union	2
Continental	2
Deutsche Akademie in Muenchen	2
Hugo Schneider AG	2
L. & C. Steinmueller	2
Lederfabrik Max Schneider	2
Maschinenfabrik Wagner-Doerries	2
Mannesmann	2
Tata Iron Steel	2
Bamag-Meguin	1
Beiersdorf	1
Boehme Fettchemie	1
Bombay Talkies	1
C. F. Boehringer & Sohn GmbH	1
D.O.V. Eildienst	1
Deutsches Kali-Syndikat	1
Dr Madaus & Co.	1
Elektrizitaetsgesellschaft Sanitas	1
F. H. Schule GmbH	1
Francke-Werke	1
H. C. Mueller & Co.	1
Hallesche Maschinenfabrik	1
Kistenmacher & Co.	1
Klein, Schanzlin & Becker AG	1
Maschinenbau & Bahnbedarf	1
Rheinmetall Borsig	1
Salge-Buehler GmbH	1
Schimmel & Co.	1
Stahlunion Export	1
Times of India	1
Total	237

Note: Database compiled by the authors.

and household items (Kopp, 1940). The British-Indian intelligence bureau, jointly run by the India Office and the Government of India, suspected some of them of engaging in espionage and spreading propaganda: 'with the internment of their men-folk, German women in this

Table 5. Places where German internees last resided.

City	Number of internees with last residence in this city
Bombay	93
Calcutta	56
Madras	17
Jamshedpur	10
Lahore	10
Dalmia Dadri	6
Delhi	5
Cawnpore	4
Ahmedabad	3
Ahmednagar	3
Bhadravati	3
Rangoon	3
Trichinopoly	3
Bangalore	2
Burnpur	2
Himalaya	2
Purwa Hiraman	2
Bhavnagar/Kathiawar	1
Bhopal	1
Chetak	1
Coimbatore	1
Curaru	1
Funalur	1
Karachi	1
Karur Taluk	1
Kevachi	1
Sagauli	1
Senares	1
Total	235

Note: Database compiled by the authors.

country are finding scope for intelligence work' (Public & Judicial Department, 1939a, p. 184; on propaganda see also Public & Judicial Department, 1939b, p. 201). In particular, Oswald Urchs' wife was said to exercise control over other German women and collect information on the political leanings of their husbands, which she reported back to her husband in internment (Public & Judicial Department, 1939a, p. 184).

At the camp, a commission of British officials started interrogating each individual internee to determine their level of support for the Nazi government. As a consequence, between December 1939 and March 1940, approximately 600 Jews were released from internment (Schoberth, 1940). The Jewish Relief Association, founded in 1934 in Bombay, had lobbied the Government of India to free the Jewish internees and also provided them with support during internment (Public and Judicial Department, 1944; Tucher, 1980, p. 108). By May 1940, the official list of the Swiss authorities numbered 324 internees, of whom 220 had been identified by German companies as their employees (Sauvage, 1942). Some observers speculated that the Commission's additional purpose was to identify the links between German businesspeople and Indian nationalist circles (Anonymous, 1941; Tucher, 1980, p. 113). By the end of May and in early June, as the war intensified, the British authorities re-interned many of those previously released and put women and children under house arrest. By September, the number of German nationals in Ahmednagar rose again to 505. In February 1941, German internees were transferred from Ahmednagar to the interim camp Deolali, 150 kilometres (93 miles) east of Bombay (see Figure 1). The conditions in the much smaller camp Deolali were significantly worse than in Ahmednagar and, as Oswald Urchs reported in hindsight, the camp and the move 'were seen as a humiliation, an abasement' (Urchs, 1948, p. 187). As a consequence, the internees went on a hunger strike, which lasted 112 hours (Urchs, 1948, p. 188).

In October 1941, and in response to their protests and complaints by the Swiss and German authorities, the internees were transferred once more to the newly established central internment camp Dehra Dun, 200 kilometres (124 miles) north-east of New Delhi, near the Himalayas (see Figure 1). In January 1942, approximately 2000 internees from the Dutch East Indies joined the group at the Dehra Dun camp, increasing the overall number of prisoners by approximately a factor of five.

Throughout the entire internment period (with the exception of the first months in Deolali) the prisoners reported that they were held under favourable conditions. They were not forced to work but could engage in activities such as theatre, educational course work, gardening and even mountaineering, for which internees could leave the camp for up to nine hours and hike in the surrounding areas (Urchs, 1948, pp. 194–204). Prisoners explicitly discouraged parties at home from sending packages with food or hygiene articles, arguing that they had adequate access to these items. However, books were highly appreciated and were used for self-studies at the camp (see letters and reports in German Foreign Office, 1941). As during the First World War, regular classes were organised by the internees for internees (Rolshoven, 1944). The longer the internment lasted, the more psychologically challenging it became. In July 1942, internee Grauthoff (1942) expressed the 'bitter thought of having been forgotten' and worried that German companies at home may have lost interest in them given that they were experts for countries that might no longer be accessible after the war.

The Second World War in India officially ended on 7 May 1945, with the surrender of the Nazis in Europe. However, the internees in British India were not released until November 1946, when they travelled back to Germany, reaching Hamburg on 26 December 1946. From there, they were immediately moved to a transit camp at the location of the former concentration camp Neuengamme, where they were interrogated about their political leanings and past activities. A few were held back at Neuengamme for their track record of having supported the Nazi party (Tucher, 1980, pp. 486–500).

The camp experience – while psychologically and physically challenging – also provided a unique opportunity for German businesspeople to network. The 300 to 400 German businessmen in India had close social ties as a comparatively small expat community. The internment experience (and the financial support scheme organised by the companies and the German government) reinforced those ties. Due to the tight currency restrictions, the support scheme relied partly on well-off internees supporting their fellow compatriots, which required both trust in the company back home to reimburse these expenses and close personal ties. Wives and children, who initially remained free, for some time shared households to make ends meet and thus built very close relationships with each other.

Interestingly, internment in India also created inter-generational ties beyond the group of people sharing the barracks at the same time. Internees from the First World War, when hearing about the renewed internment in India, organised and lobbied for support both German employers and the German authorities. They stressed the importance of ongoing company support in particular in India, where skilled labour was so scarce.

The social networks created at the camp did not dissolve after the internees returned to Germany. Many of them stayed in touch. Medical doctor Oswald Urchs was able to do a follow-up study on his former malaria patients. Of 172 patients whom he examined during the camp time, he managed to reconnect with 71 in the years 1954/55, to re-examine them and analyse long-term problems after a malaria episode (Urchs, 1958). Several internees collected address lists among themselves and circulated their written memoirs of the internment experience after the war had ended. In this way, they created a community of businesspeople with experience in India, which survived well into the post-war era.

Anecdotal evidence shows how internees profited from the social network, for example for finding new positions or receiving recommendations from fellow internees. Some internees leveraged their country experience and were hired by the Foreign Office for postings in India or Pakistan. Ernst Kunisch, a former Siemens employee, became an assistant to the German Trade Commissioner in Bombay in 1952. Walter Knips, also a former Siemens employee, took over as Trade Commissioner in Karachi, Pakistan (1952–1957), after the partition of India and Pakistan. Knips was considered for this position thanks to the recommendation of Mrs Geisse, the wife of the late Reinhard Geisse, who was interned with Knips but died in November 1941 at the Dehra Dun camp. Other former internees capitalised on their India experience by positioning themselves as experts for the British Empire. Rolf Magener of IG Farben became famous for his escape from Dehra Dun together with a group of professional mountaineers of a Himalayan expedition. He published his escape narrative after the war (Magener, 1954). Once returned, he started working for BASF and became an executive for the chemical company in London in 1957. Beginning in 1962, he was a member of the Managing Board of BASF. His experience in India qualified him for a high-ranking position in Britain, as he was seen as an expert for the British Empire. These experiences resonate with Sluyterman's (pre-published online 2017) account of the role that the Dutch expats' network played in the process of decolonisation and transition to local management for MNEs in Indonesia.

Finally, there was a group of Germans that lobbied to stay in India after the Second World War. Of the 14 former Krupp employees, six remained in India after being released from internment and started working for Indian companies (Steffens, 1946).[8] One of the leading managers of Krupp (India), Otto-Zeno Steffens, first went back to Germany but reported to Krupp in 1947 that he would return to India as soon as he received a permit. Two large Indian companies (Tata and Godrej & Boyce) lobbied on his behalf with the Indian government and made him lucrative employment offers (Steffens, 1947).

7. Conclusion

Indian business history has a strong focus on British–Indian business and political relations before Indian independence in 1947. This scholarship studied selected industries and topics, for which the British–Indian relationship is of greatest significance. However, India as a market and trading partner was also attractive to multinationals beyond the British Empire. Their experience in India not only complements existing accounts of corporate strategies in India but helps us better understand Indian business within the wider world economy, addressing new topics such as political risk. As we show in this paper, the threat of internment was one such risk.

India was politically a high-risk country. MNEs of all origins saw their business being affected by Indian government policies, e.g. tariffs, taxation and nationalism. Across the period we see German MNEs adopting a mix of political risk-management strategies to ensure long-term survival in India. In line with results of the previous political risk literature, they engaged in concealing ownership, negotiating with governments, and developing legitimacy and resilience.

During wartime, companies from enemy countries were particularly challenged by property expropriations and the internment of their expatriate employees. So far, the experience of businesspeople in internment is a gap in international business history, in India and elsewhere. The First World War and the first wave of civilian internment was a turning point, which triggered corporate strategies for dealing with this challenge. In India, the problem was not so much the material deprivation that internment entailed. Prisoners were in fact relatively well treated, especially when compared with the experience of internment elsewhere in the historical record. However, internment impacted on business relationships in India well beyond its endpoint, in at least three ways.

First, it aggravated the broader problems and risks that MNEs faced when it came to staffing their operations abroad. In India in particular, talent was scarce and German MNEs worried about the long-term effects of internment on their ability to recruit and retain European nationals for their business. These facts explain the swift reaction by German MNEs in the Second World War and the immediate rise of a public–private partnership between companies and the German government. The relationship between staffing challenges and political risk is an important issue that is less explored so far and requires further research by international business historians.

Second, the internment of German businesspeople was crucial for understanding the development of German–Indian business relations in the interwar and post-war period. Specifically, it was the symbolic and political importance that internment represented which mattered. For many Germans, the humiliating internment experience first challenged the idea of a cohesive 'western white community' in India. In the colonial society, Germans had previously understood themselves as part of this community. With the outbreak of the First World War, however, the categories of 'nationality' and 'enemy alien' trumped racial belonging, drawing a new line of distinction between German and British businesspeople.

On the flipside, the outbreak of the two world wars and the public internment of German expats signalled to Indian nationalists that there was no homogeneous western interest and that the Germans could be seen as victims of British power as well. Indians actively sought German partners, who had similar levels of technical expertise to the British but came with less political 'baggage'.

Internment thus helped to disintegrate the conception of a white business elite in India, not by eliminating racial prejudices among the Germans but by signalling to Indian observers that the 'European' business community was more diverse than previously assumed. It shattered the belief in a cohesive white western community in India, creating new lines of division and belonging in the relationship between Germany, India and Great Britain. As the article shows, internment was a major blow to Germans' own sense of status vis-à-vis the British because it broke apart the idea of a cohesive western whiteness of status. Even more importantly it opened the eyes of Indians to the possibility of seeing the Germans as fellow victims of British aggression.

Finally, the challenge of internment created unexpected learning and networking opportunities within the German business community, which research has so far ignored. In India, the centralised internment camps provided a framework for a community of businessmen to establish dense social links. Interestingly, the emotional and memorable internment experience even created inter-generational connections between individuals who were not interned at the same time. The generation of First World War internees spoke up for the internees during the Second World War, lobbying the German government to become more involved. The exploratory study of German business in British India shows that the internment episodes in the First World War and the Second World War have to be analysed together to understand actors' perceptions of this particular challenge. German First World War internees provided a frame of reference for the interpretations during the Second World War, and were indeed employed by the German government as consultants. Only the full sequence of events allows us to see the emerging community of internees, bound together by an asynchronous experience.

The case of the German business community in India is but one example of internment as a management issue; follow-on studies for other geographies and time periods will be required to explore the issue of internment more broadly and engage in much needed comparative perspectives. Highlighting the strategies of a non-British business community, moreover, stresses that MNEs' experience in India differed significantly depending on country of origin, questioning the widely used category 'European business' and instead pleading for a more nuanced analysis.

Notes

1. 1 INR equalled 16 pence or 1/15 GBP. For details see Roy (2006).
2. General Electric Trading Co. acted as agent for the United Provinces and Delhi, Chari & Chari Ltd. for Madras, Messrs. Freudenberg & Co. for Ceylon.
3. BASF (27.4% of equity capital), Bayer (27.4%), Hoechst including Cassella and Chemische Fabrik Kalle (27.4%), Agfa (9.0%), Chemische Fabrik Griesheim-Elektron (6.9%) and Chemische Fabrik vorm. Weiler Ter Meer (1.9%).
4. Salary numbers are based on a series of documents in the Krupp Archives (Krupp, undated). Between 1927 and 1947, 1 INR equalled approximately 18 pence or 0.075 GBP. For details see Roy (2006).
5. Schüder spent 1916 to 1920 under internment at Ahmednagar and was arrested again in 1939 (Office Waibel, 1941; Schüder, 1939).
6. Hans E. B. Kruse went for Wiechers & Helm to Karachi in 1913 and was interned at the outbreak of the First World War. He spent five years behind barbed wire (Kruse, 2006, pp. 10–11).
7. The data collected were based on various sources (Orient Verein & Waibel, 1939; Kaufmaennischer Ausschuss, 1940; Bayer Archives, 1940; Orient Verein, 1940c; German Foreign Office, 1941a; Siemens HR Department, 1940; Office Waibel, 1941; German Foreign Office, 1941b).
8. Heinrich Klein, Hans Fuchs, Heinrich Hendricks, Helmut Scharbau, (first name unknown) Duckstein, and W. Rutenberg.

Acknowledgements

The authors would like to thank Dr Frank Wittendorfer of Siemens Corporate Archives, Ruediger Borstel of Bayer Corporate Archives, and Dr Ralf Stremmel and Simone Snyders of Krupp Corporate Archives. The authors are particularly grateful to Christoph Gaebler, Bremen, who shared his extensive research with them. His website (http://www.gaebler.info/) is a rich collection of visual material and reports concerning the internment experience in India.

Disclosure statement

No potential conflict of interest was reported by the authors.

ORCID

Christina Lubinski (iD) http://orcid.org/0000-0001-9150-3284

Bibliography

Archival collections

Bayer Archives, Leverkusen (BA).
British Library's Asia, Pacific and Africa Collections (BL).
Bundesarchiv Deutschland [Federal Archives of Germany], Berlin (BArch).
Krupp Archives, Essen (KA).
Politisches Archiv des Auswärtigen Amtes [German Foreign Office Archives], Berlin (PA).
Siemens Archives, Munich, now Berlin (SAA).

Quoted archival files

Anonymous. (1941). Anonymous report enclosed to letter Kuehns to Waibel, 25 March 1941, Southeast Asia Internees, BA 330-596.
Bayer. (1918). Report on activities after the Versailles Peace Treaty, March and July 1918, BA 202/16.
Bayer Archives (1921). Visit Das Gupta, BA 9 K 1.
Bayer Archives (1940). List of confirmed payments for support scheme with number of internees per firm, [undated, c.Febr. 1940], total: 232 internees, BA 330–596.
Bayer Archives (1941). Correspondence and notes, 1941, Office Waibel, German Internees in the Far East, BA 330–443.
Bayer Archives (1944). Note for files, 10 Jan. 1944, Southeast Asia Internees, BA 330-596.
Consulate Calcutta (1930). Letter Consulate Calcutta to Foreign Office Berlin, 29 July 1930, BArch R3101-02664.
De Rziha, E. (1923). *"Letter de Rziha to Reyss", 4 April 1923* (p. 8106). SAA: Siemen in the Middle East.
De Rziha, E. (1926). Letter de Rziha to Reyss, 4 Oct. 1926, Siemen in the Middle East, SAA 8106.

German Federal Archives (1927). Report on the question of representatives in British India, 30 June 1927, BArch R 3101/21030.

German Foreign Office (1941a). Third Report about the Conditions of Germans in British-India and Ceylon, Jan. 1941, total: 505 (Sept 1940), German Civil Internees in British India, PA R 14820.

German Foreign Office (1941b). Fourth Report about the Conditions of Germans in British-India and Ceylon, Sept. 1941, total: 604 (11 August 1941), German Civil Internees in British India, PA R 14821.

Grauthoff (1942). Letter to his wife, 16 July 1942, Office Waibel, BA 330-443.

IG Farben (1939). World Dyestuff Production, 8 June 1939, BA 4/B 14.3.6.

Kaufmaennischer Ausschuss (1940). I. G. Farben employees in enemy countries, 29 Jan. 1940, Office of the "Kaufmaennische Ausschuss" Berlin NW 7, Southeast Asia Internees, BA 330–596.

Kopp (1940). Report Mrs. Kopp (Siemens), in letter by Foreign Office to Waibel, 9 May 1940, Southeast Asia Internees, BA 330-596.

Krupp (undated). Development of Krupp India Trading Co., vol. 1, 1932-1939, salary statements, KA WA 51-5060.

Kuehns (1939). Letter Kuehns to Waibel, 13 Sept. 1939, BA 330–596.

Luitpold (1940). Letter, 15 Sept. 1940, Southeast Asia Internees, BA 330-596.

Mensendieck, C., Kruse, H., & Kuehns, C. (1940). Letter by C. Mensendieck, Hans E.B. Kruse and C. W. Kuehns to the Foreign Office Berlin, 22 Febr. 1940, Germans in enemy countries, reports by internees, British India, PA R 127689.

Office Waibel (1941). List of internees in British India, 3 July 1941, and enclosed list of all internees in British India who receive Orient Verein support, total: 243, German Internees in the Far East, BA 330-443.

Orient Verein (1939a). Minutes of Orient Verein meeting re support for internees in India, 29 Sept. 1939, Office Waibel, German Internees in the Far East, BA 330-443.

Orient Verein (1939b). Minutes of Orient Verein meeting, 1 Nov. 1939, Southeast Asia Internees, BA 330-596.

Orient Verein (1939c). Minutes of Orient Verein meeting, 10 Nov. 1939, BA 330–596.

Orient Verein (1939d). Account statement of the Orient Verein, PA R 61364.

Orient Verein (1939e). Letter Orient Verein to German firms, 30 Sept. 1939, PA R 41819.

Orient Verein (1940a). Letter Orient Verein (recipient undisclosed), 29 January 1940, Office Waibel, German Internees in the Far East, BA 330-443.

Orient Verein (1940b). Letter Orient Verein to participants of the support scheme, 18 March 1940, Office Waibel, German Internees in the Far East, BA 330-443.

Orient Verein (1940c). Letter to members of the Special Committee, 3 April 1941, and enclosed list of internees in British-India as identified by Foreign Office (14 May 1940), total: 324, BA 330–596.

Orient Verein (1941). Minutes of Orient Verein meeting, 20 Aug. 1941, Southeast Asia Internees, BA 330-596.

Orient Verein and Waibel (1939). "Letter to Foreign Office (Kundt), 7 Oct. 1939, and enclosed list of confirmed payments for support scheme with number of internees per firm, total: 102.

Osten (1940). Report, 29 April 1940, Southeast Asia Internees, BA 330-596.

Overseas HR Department (1934). Annual Report of the Overseas HR Department, 1933/34, 1934, SAA 8149.

Overseas HR Department (1935). Annual Report of the Overseas HR Department, 1934/35, 1935, SAA 8149.

Overseas HR Department (1936). Annual Report of the Overseas HR Department, 1935/36, 1936, SAA 8149.

Overseas HR Department (1937). Annual Report of the Overseas HR Department, 1936/37, 1937, SAA 8110.

Overseas HR Department (1938). Annual Report of the Overseas HR Department, 1937/38, 1938, SAA 8110.

Overseas HR Department (undated). Report on Employees Abroad, SAA 8149.

Pazze (1939). Report, 24 Oct. 1939, BA 330–596.

Public and Judicial Department (1939a). Survey No. 30 of 1939 for the week ending 9th December, 1939, IOR/L/PJ/12 1913-1947, British Library.

Public and Judicial Department (1939b). Survey No. 32 of 1939 for the week ending 30th December, 1939, IOR/L/PJ/12 1913-1947, British Library.
Public and Judicial Department (1944). Survey of Foreign Intelligence Activities directed against Indian security dated 14th August, 1944, No. 44/27, IOR/L/PJ/12 1913-1947, British Library.
Reyss (1924). Speech by Reyss about his Asia trip, SAA 8185.
Rolshoven (1944). Report. Nov. 1944, Office Waibel, German Internees in the Far East, BA 330–443.
Sauvage, P. (1942). Letter Paul Sauvage dated 26 June 1942, 26 June 1942. *Office Waibel, German Internees in the Far East, BA,* 330–443.
Schoberth, G. (1940). Report about living conditions of Germans in Calcutta during the first nine month of the war, 5 Nov. 1940, BA 330–596.
Schüder (1939). Letter [recipient undisclosed], 17 Nov. 1939, Southeast Asia Internees, BA 330-596.
Siemens (1922). Memorandum of Association, 8 Nov. 1922, Siemens Abroad 1913-40, SAA 8156.
Siemens (India) Ltd (1931). Letter Siemens (India) to Headquarter, 24 Jan. 1931, HR Calcutta, 1925-36, SAA 9470.
Siemens (India) Ltd (undated). Organization of Siemens (India) Ltd, Siemen Abroad 1913-1940, SAA 8156.
Siemens Archives (1925) Memorandum of Agreement, 1 Oct.1924/25 March 1925, Siemens Abroad 1913-40, SAA 8156.
Siemens Archives (undated). Historical development of the overseas business [undated, before 1914]", in: "Note for Mr. Wegner, dated 15.5.1952, SAA 8188.
Siemens HR Department (1940). Report 'Our Internees overseas', 10 Febr. 1940, and list of Siemens internees, 15 January 1941, total: 43, HR Statistics, SAA 8149.
Steffens, O. Z. (1939a). Development of Krupp India Trading Co., vol. 1, 1932-1939, letters Steffens to Krupp, 24 Jan. 1939, KA WA 51-5060.
Steffens, O. Z. (1939b). Development of Krupp India Trading Co., vol. 1, 1932-1939, letters Steffens to Krupp, 8 May 1939, KA WA 51-5060.
Steffens, O. Z. (1946). letter Steffens to Krupp, 11 Dec. 1946, Personnel files about Otto Zeno Steffens, KA WA 51-5036.
Steffens, O. Z. (1947). Letter Steffens to Hobrecker, 20 May 1947. *Krupp Archives, WA,* 131–2668.
Tera, N. O. (1939). Report; attachment to letter from Kuehns to Waibel, 6 Dec. 1939, BA 330–596.
Waibel (1940). Letter Waibel to Sthamer, 4 April 1940, BA 330–596.
Weingarten (1939). German Internees in the Far East, 24 Oct. 1939, Office Waibel, BA 330–443.
Zimmer (1939). Report by Otto Zimmer about the events in Bombay since outbreak of the war, received 7 Nov. 1939, 7 Nov. 1939, German Civil Internees in India, PA R 41819.

References

Aalders, G., & Wiebes, C. (1996). *The art of cloaking ownership: The secret collaboration and protection of the German war industry by the neutrals: The case of Sweden.* Amsterdam: Amsterdam University Press.
Akita, S. & White, N. (Eds.). (2010). *The international order of Asia in the 1930s and 1950s.* Farmham, UK; Burlington, VT: Ashgate.
Arnold, D. (2011). Global goods and local usages: The small world of the Indian sewing machine, 1875–1952. *Journal of Global History, 6*(3), 407–429.
Arnold, D. (2013). *Everyday technology: Machines and the making of India's modernity.* Chicago, IL: University of Chicago Press.
Austin, G., Dávila, C., & Jones, G. (2017). The alternative business history: Business in emerging markets. *Business History Review, 91*(3), 537–569. doi:10.1017/S0007680517001052. Retrieved from https://www.cambridge.org/core/article/alternative-business-history-business-in-emerging-markets/DC9B665E89B4AF5C7990C8E357E93A22
Boon, M., & Wubs, B. (2016). Property, control and room for manoeuvre: Royal Dutch Shell and Nazi Germany, 1933–1945. *Business History,* 1–20. doi:10.1080/00076791.2016.1205034 Retrieved from https://doi.org/10.1080/00076791.2016.1205034
Bucheli, M., & Salvaj, E. (2013). Reputation and political legitimacy ITT in Chile, 1927-1972. [Article]. *Business History Review, 87*(4), 729–756. doi:10.1017/S0007680513001116 Retrieved from http://

esc-web.lib.cbs.dk/login?url=http://search.ebscohost.com/login.aspx?direct=true&db=afh&AN=9
3404722&site=ehost-live&scope=site

Dejung, C. (2013). *Die Faeden des globalen Marktes: Eine Sozial- und Kulturgeschichte des Welthandels am Beispiel der Handelsfirma Gebrüder Volkart 1851–1999*. Köln: Böhlau.

Dejung, C., & Zangger, A. (2010). British wartime protectionism and Swiss trading firms in Asia during the First World War. *Past & Present, 207*(1), 181–213.

Donzé, P.-Y., & Kurosawa, T. (2013). Nestlé coping with Japanese nationalism: Political risk and the strategy of a foreign multinational enterprise in Japan, 1913–45. *Business History, 55*(8), 1318–1338. doi:10.1080/00076791.2012.745065 Retrieved from doi:10.1080/00076791.2012.745065

Gao, C., Zuzul, T., Jones, G., & Khanna, T. (2017). Overcoming institutional voids: A reputation-based view of long-run survival. *Strategic Management Journal, 38*(11), 2147–2167. doi:10.1002/smj.2649 Retrieved from doi:10.1002/smj.2649

Government of India Legislative Department. (1915). *Legislation and orders relating to the war* (3rd ed.). Delhi: Superintendent Government Printing, India.

Great Britain Trade Commissioner for India. (1919). *Trade of India: Report on the conditions and prospects of British trade in India, at the close of the war, by his majesty's senior trade commissioner in India and Ceylon*. London: H. M. Stationery off. printed by Eyre and Spottiswoode.

Great Britain War Office, Maurice, J. F., & Grant, M. H. (1906). *History of the war in South Africa, 1899-1902*. London: Hurst and Blackett limited.

Howell, L. D., & Chaddick, B. (1994). Models of political risk for foreign investment and trade. *The Columbia Journal of World Business, 29*(3), 70–91. doi:10.1016/0022-5428(94)90,048-5 Retrieved from http://www.sciencedirect.com/science/article/pii/0022542894900485

Hyslop, J. (2006). The World Voyage of James Keir Hardie: Indian Nationalism, Zulu Insurgency and the British Labour Diaspora 1907–1908. *Journal of Global History, 1*(3), 343–362. doi:10.1017/S1740022806003032 Retrieved from https://www.cambridge.org/core/article/world-voyage-of-james-keir-hardie-indian-nationalism-zulu-insurgency-and-the-british-labour-diaspora-19071908/C1D276123E7B48516E1CA585C28F1645

International Committee of the Red Cross, & Thormeyer, F. (1917). *Reports on British prison-camps in India and Burma, visited by the International Red cross committee in February, March and April, 1917*. London: T.F. Unwin Ltd.

Jacobsen, H. A. (1968). *Nationalsozialistische Aussenpolitik, 1933–1938*. Frankfurt, Main: A. Metzner.

Jones, G., & Gomopoulos, P. (2005). Aristotle Onassis and the Greek Shipping Industry. *Harvard Business School Case 805-141, May 2005. (Revised December 2015.)*

Jones, G., & Lubinski, C. (2012). Managing political risk in global business: Beiersdorf 1914-1990. *Enterprise & Society, 13*(1), 85–119.

Jones, G., & Storli, E. (2012). Marc rich and global commodity trading. *Harvard Business School Case 813-020, June 2012. (Revised March 2014.)*

Kaoru, S. (1990). Japan as an engine of the Asian international economy, c. 1880–1936. *Japan Forum, 2*(1), 127–145. doi:10.1080/09555809008721383 Retrieved from doi:10.1080/09555809008721383

Kobrak, C., & Wüstenhagen, J. (2006). International investment and Nazi Politics: The cloaking of German assets abroad: 1936-1945. *Business History, 48*(3), 399–427.

Kruse, H. (2006). *Wagen und Winnen. Ein hanseatisches Kaufmannsleben im 20. Jahrhundert*. Hamburg: Die Hanse / EVA.

Lohmann, H. C. (1934). *Die Ausfuhr Solinger Stahlwaren nach Britisch-Indien, Burma una Ceylon*. Würzburg: Mayr.

Lubinski, C. (2015). Global trade and Indian Politics: The German Dye business in India before 1947. *Business History Review, 89*(3), 503–530.

Magener, R. (1954). *Die Chance war null*. Vienna: Ullstein.

Manjapra, K. (2014). *Age of entanglement: German and Indian intellectuals across empire Cambridge*. MA: Harvard University Press.

Miller, R. M. (2015). Staffing and management in British MNEs in Argentina and Chile, 1930-1970. In G. Jones & A. Lluch (Eds.), *The impact of globalization on Argentina and Chile: Business enterprises and entrepreneurship* (pp. 152–181). Cheltenham: Edward Elgar.

Panayi, P. (Ed.). (2014). *Germans as minorities during the First World War: Global comparative perspective.* Burlington, VT: Ashgate.

Probst, H. G. (1917). *Unter indischer Sonne: 19 Monate englischer Kriegsgefangenschaft in Ahmednagar.* Herborn: Oranienverlag.

Proctor, T. M. (2010). *Civilians in a world at war, 1914–1918.* New York, NY: New York University Press.

Ramnath, A. (2017). *The Birth of an Indian Profession: Engineers, Industry, and the State, 1900–47.* New Delhi: Oxford University Press.

Roy, T. (2006). *The economic history of India, 1857–1947.* New Delhi: Oxford University Press.

Sinha, M. (2001). Britishness, clubbability, and the colonial public sphere: The Genealogy of an imperial institution in colonial India. *Journal of British Studies, 40*(4), 489–521. doi:10.2307/3,070,745 Retrieved from http://www.jstor.org/stable/3070745

Sluyterman, K. (prepublished online 2017). Decolonisation and the organisation of the international workforce: Dutch multinationals in Indonesia, 1945–1967. *Business Historydoi.* doi:10.1080/000767 91.2017.1350170 Retrieved from doi: 10.1080/00076791.2017.1350170

Smith, A. D. A. (2016). A LBV perspective on political risk management in a multinational bank during the First World War. *Multinational Business Review, 24*(1). doi:10.1108/MBR-09-2015-0045 Retrieved from http://www.emeraldinsight.com/doi/abs/10.1108/MBR-09-2015-0045

Speed, R. B. (1990). *Prisoners, diplomats, and the great war: A study in the diplomacy of captivity.* New York, NY: Greenwood Press.

Stibbe, M. (2006). The internment of civilians by belligerent states during the the First World War and the response of the international committee of the red cross. *Journal of Contemporary History, 41*(1), 5–19.

Stibbe, M. (2008). *British civilian internees in Germany: The Ruhleben Camp, 1914–1918 Manchester.* New York, NY: Manchester University Press.

Tammen, H. (1978). *Die I. G. Farbenindustrie Aktiengesellschaft (1925-1933): Ein Chemiekonzern in der Weimarer Republik.* Berlin: H. Tammen.

Tooze, J. A. (2007). *The wages of destruction: The making and breaking of the Nazi economy.* New York, NY: Viking.

Tripathi, D. (2014). Business, networks, and the state in India: Introduction. *Business History Review, 88*(1), 3–8. doi:10.1017/S0007680513001396

Tucher, P. H. V. (1980). *Nationalism, case and crisis in missions: German missions in British India, 1939-1946.* Erlangen: P. Tucher.

UNHCR. (1939/2018). India: Act No. 16 of 1939, Registration of Foreigners Act, 1939, 8 April 1939. Retrieved 20 February 2018, from http://www.refworld.org/docid/3ae6b52fc.html

Urchs, O. (1948). Beobachtungen eines Lagerarztes ueber Psycho-Neurotische Reaktionen waehrend einer ueber sieben Jahre dauerndes Internierung in Britisch Indien. *Psyche, 11*(2), 181–210.

Urchs, O. (1958). Zur Frage der Spaetschaeden nach Kriegs-Malaria. *Muenchner Medizinische Wochenschrift, 100*(18), 710–713.

van der Eng, P. (2017). Managing political imperatives in war time: Strategic responses of Philips in Australia, 1939–1945. *Business History, 59*(5), 645–666. doi:10.1080/00076791.2016.1259311 Retrieved from doi:10.1080/00076791.2016.1259311

White, N. (2012). Surviving Sukarno: British Business in Post-Colonial Indonesia, 1950-67. *Modern Asian Studies, 46*(5), 1277–1315.

Wubs, B. (2008). *International business and national war interests: Unilever between Reich and Empire, 1939–45 London.* New York, NY: Routledge.

Ambiguous decolonisation: a postcolonial reading of the IHRM strategy of the Burmah Oil Company

Neveen Abdelrehim, Aparajith Ramnath, Andrew Smith ⓘD and Andrew Popp

ABSTRACT
This article uses the lens of postcolonial theory to determine the extent to which colonial features persisted in the organisational culture of the Burmah Oil Company (BOC) after decolonisation in South Asia. It does this through an examination of the evolving staffing strategies of the BOC and its South Asian (especially Indian) subsidiaries before and after 1947. Through an analysis of archival material and company literature, we demonstrate that the BOC switched from an ethnocentric to a polycentric-staffing strategy very gradually, with senior managerial positions being occupied by British managers into the 1970s, well after other British MNEs operating in India had already made this transition. We suggest that this persistence of colonial modes of organisation contributed to the BOC's tense relations with the Indian government, and the latter's decision to nationalise the firm.

Introduction

There is a growing body of historiography on the impact of colonialism and imperialism on the evolution of business in Asia (Benedict, 2011; Horesh, 2014; Lubinski, 2014; Misra, 1999; Mollan, 2012; Smith, 2016; Webster et al., 2015; White, 2004; Yacob and White, 2010). This research has documented the manifold ways in which Western imperialism shaped firm strategies in the colonised and semi-colonised countries of Asia. During the era of empire, the power imbalance between Westerners and so-called 'natives' of this region influenced the behaviour of European multinationals and, crucially, the Westerners who managed these firms. As Geoffrey Jones has noted, a 'surprising number' of the multinational firms founded in the institutional context of colonialism were able to survive decolonisation and are still extant. Their numbers include such important companies as HSBC and Unilever. In contrast, other European multinationals were unable to adapt to the end of empire and the system of attitudes that went with it (Jones, 2015, p. 129). The rise of Asian economies has prompted some academics and journalists to announce the end of Western global economic and cultural primacy (Rachman, 2016). These writers suggest that Western imperialism is now just 'ancient history', a backstory with limited relevance to understanding how multinationals operate in the present. The implication of this position is that colonialism ended a very long time ago and we need not refer to it when seeking to understand present-day multinational firms. In contrast, our reading stresses continuities and the persistence of colonialist attitudes long after the end of formal imperialism.

This article, a study of the Burmah Oil Company's subsidiaries on the Indian sub-continent before and after 1947 (Bamberg, 2000), seeks to determine the extent to which the organisational culture of the BOC became less colonial after political independence.[1] We do so by examining the extent to which staffing policy changed in the wake of decolonisation. Although the article refers briefly to BOC's experience in Pakistan, Burma, and East Pakistan/Bangladesh, its focus is on its subsidiary in the Republic of India. This article was determined by the nature of the surviving primary sources. The article shows that the process of promoting local people to positions of real authority in the firm's India subsidiaries was a complicated one that was driven largely by pressure from local governments rather than being something that was embarked on with willingness by the firm's headquarters. Our article is not primarily about how the firm interacted with the British state in the period surrounding decolonisation. Nor is this another account of how a British firm lobbied in Whitehall and Westminster to protect its interest once it saw that decolonisation was inevitable. Instead, our focus is on the internal dynamics of the firm and the question of the extent to which Western employees should have to share power and resources with local managers and technical experts within the firm.

Drawing on postcolonial theory, this article will help us to construct a new system of historical periodisation for thinking about the transition from coloniality to postcoloniality in British international business. The account shows that the BOC did not rapidly shed its colonialist features when India and Pakistan became independent in 1947. Instead, the process was very gradual and undertaken only grudgingly by the firm in the face of considerable political pressure. As late as the 1970s, the senior managerial positions were still occupied by British expatriates. We contrast the slow pace of change at BOC with the more rapid changes at Unilever's Indian subsidiary in the same approximate period: between the late 1930s to the early 1960s, Unilever successfully switched from an ethnocentric to polycentric staffing strategy in India. We show that BOC failed to do so and likely suffered as a result. Although BOC did make some moves in the direction of a more polycentric strategy, its efforts were ultimately too little, too late. We suggest that the persistence of colonial attitudes in BOC likely exacerbated the firm's tense relations with the Indian government. We suggest, somewhat more speculatively, that the failure to appease local nationalist sentiment via an accelerated Indianisation of the subsidiary's senior management team may have contributed to the Indian government's decision to nationalise the firm.

Literature review

We begin by presenting a multi-part literature review. We consider first mainstream approaches to the study of International Human Resource Management (IHRM), before providing, in contrast, an introduction to Postcolonial Theory. Thereafter we move through the historiography of business in India, the historiography of the impact of decolonisation on the IHRM practices of British firms in India, and, finally, the historiography of BOC.

Table 1. Nationalities employed in oil industry.

Nationality	BOC (All operations)		BOC (Refinery staff)	
	year (1904)	%	year (1913)	%
European and Eurasians	205	3	233	3
Burmese	1,091	14	503	6
Indians	6,334	83	7,363	91
Total		100		100

Source.
compiled from Corley, T. A. B. (1988). A history of the Burmah Oil Company:1924–1966.

IHRM Research

Academic research on International Human Resource Management (IHRM) originated in the 1960s, when researchers began to notice dramatic shifts in the way multinational firms were staffing their global operations. The key text was a 1969 paper by Howard Perlmutter that noted that US and European multinationals were becoming less ethnocentric about whom they appointed to managerial positions in their overseas subsidiaries (Perlmutter, 1969). Prior to that point, multinationals had, in general, exclusively used home-country nationals to manage their overseas operations, particularly in developing countries. These firms would employ local workers to perform manual labour and other menial tasks, but technical and managerial functions were reserved for people of the same nationality and ethnicity as the directors of the firm. Subsequently, Perlmutter developed a typology of four main strategies that MNCs adopt in managing their workforces: ethnocentric, polycentric, regiocentric and geocentric (Heenan & Perlmutter, 1979; Perlmutter, 1968). Perlmutter's terminology and his conceptual framework continues to be debated and refined by researchers in international management and strategy (Michailova et al., in press).

Empirical research on IHRM has explored the costs and benefits of each of these strategies. An ethnocentric IHRM strategy has some advantages, as it helps to ensure the perspective of the overseas subsidiary is aligned with that of the home country managers. It also eliminates language and cultural barriers, at least at managerial levels. An ethnocentric IHRM strategy may also make sense when a firm's subsidiaries are located in countries with under-developed education systems in which few locals are qualified to fill technical and managerial roles. The downsides of this approach include the loss of valuable local contextual knowledge, the greater cost of sending expatriates and their families overseas, and, crucially, antagonising local nationalist sentiment. As we show below, BOC continued to use an ethnocentric IHRM strategy long after the Indian subcontinent achieved independence in 1947. We also show that its relations with the Indian government deteriorated steadily, a process that culminated with the nationalisation of its main assets in 1976.

Similarly, a polycentric IHRM strategy has both upsides and downsides. The upsides include benefits that come from the knowledge and political connections of the locally hired managers, but there is also the risk that these managers will begin to run the subsidiary in their own interests, rather than those of the parent corporation. A regiocentric IHRM strategy is broadly similarly to a polycentric one, except that managers are moved around between neighbouring countries, thereby sharing knowledge of best practice and allowing for greater regional coordination. While such a strategy may be appropriate when relations between neighbouring countries are generally good (as in the European Union), it can be

Table 2. Nationalities employed in oil industry.

Nationality	All oil companies (Refinery staff)		All oil companies (Fields staff)	
	year (1921)	%	year (1921)	%
European and Eurasians	741	2	24	2
Burmese	9,475	29	831	73
Indians	22,867	69	279	25
Total		100		100

Source.
compiled from Corley, T. A. B. (1988). A history of the Burmah Oil Company:1924–1966.

inappropriate when tensions within a region complicate the exchange of goods and people between nations, as was the case in the Indian subcontinent after partition. IHRM theory would predict that BOC would not develop a regiocentric staffing strategy in its subsidiaries in the Indian sub-continent and this prediction is entirely consistent with our reading of the primary sources, which revealed no evidence of any moves towards a regiocentric strategy after 1947.

A geocentric IHRM strategy involves taking the best and the brightest locally hired man-agers and moving them around the firm, including into posts in the global head office. This approach allows the firm to take advantage of a global talent pool without worrying about an individual's nationality. This strategy can promote a global mind-set among a firm's cadre of top managers and can improve morale in foreign subsidiaries. Unfortunately, this strategy is particularly expensive to execute well, especially when communications costs are high (Lakshman et al., 2017). The high costs associated with the geocentric strategy help to explain why it was only adopted relatively recently (after 1980). Geocentric IHRM strategies were first used by US multinationals and were adopted later, and with apparently greater reluc-tance, by European and then Japanese multinationals, which retained ethnocentric staffing policies for longer (Kopp, 1994). Data published in 1982 show that US MNCs in developing countries were much more likely to hire local citizens for senior positions than were European multinationals operating in the same region (Tung, 1982, Table 2).

Postcolonial theory

IHRM theory is interested, then, in inter-country and inter-regional differences. However, it typically does not situate those differences in terms of international structures of power, or the cultural and ideological systems that underpin and maintain those structures. In contrast, postcolonial researchers in other areas of social science are interested in the persistence of the ideas that Westerners created to legitimate their political, military, and economic inter-ventions in countries in the non-Western world. Deriving inspiration from Edward Said, Gayatri Spivak, and Derek Gregory, postcolonial scholars are interested in establishing when, or rather if, colonialism ended. Many strands of postcolonialist theory argue that colonialist modes of thought remained long after the attainment of political independence. Around the year 2000, management academics began to call for the application of postcolonial theory to the study of international business (Banerjee & Linstead, 2004; Prasad, 2003). A key text here was the manifesto by Robert Westwood and Gavin Jack (2007).

In response to such calls, postcolonial management academics have applied postcolonial thought in researching the contemporary operations of multinational firms and in documenting the colonialist origins of contemporary management theory and practice (Banerjee & Prasad, 2008; Boussebaa & Brown, 2017; Boussebaa & Morgan, 2014; Boussebaa et al., 2014; Decker, 2010; Frenkel & Shenhav, 2006; Prasad & Qureshi, 2017).

By showing that colonial attitudes and practices have persisted into the present, or at least long after the end of formal European colonial rule, postcolonial management scholars have contributed to our understanding of the thorny issues of historical periodisation relating to the end of the European colonial empires. Postcolonial management research suggests that the end of coloniality in multinational firms was gradual. For scholars of international business history, this reframing of the chronology of decolonisation raises the question of when British MNEs operating in Commonwealth countries ceased to be colonialist.

We propose that postcolonial theory would interpret the fact that European multinationals, many of which were headquartered in countries that had formerly ruled colonial empires, were slow to abandon the ethnocentric IHRM model as due to the persistence of colonialist modes of thought in the cultures of these nations and firms. The evolution of the IHRM system of BOC, a British company, is consistent with this broader pattern and argument. The company's move away from ethnocentric IHRM strategy towards a more polycentric one was extremely gradual, never entirely complete and, apparently, grudging. Our reading of the primary sources suggests that to the extent that BOC began to fill senior technical and managerial posts with Indians, this decision was motivated by the desire to placate India's nationalist government rather than other considerations, such as an appreciation of the improving quality of Indian engineering and management graduates. Moreover, while the firm moved in the direction of the polycentric IHRM strategy in the 1950s and 1960s, none of the changes in its staffing policy suggest that it considered adopting anything resembling a geocentric IHRM strategy.

Historiography of Indian business

IHRM strategies unfold in specific national contexts. We study BOC's IHRM strategy in the context of South Asia and India specifically. The field of Indian business history is rapidly growing in terms of the number of scholars active in it. The field, previously dominated by commissioned and corporate histories, is increasingly characterised by serious academic research. The primary focus of historians of Indian business remains the country's large firms. Large firms active on the subcontinent either side of 1947 fall into three main categories: (a) British managing agencies, (b) Indian-owned and managed firms, and (c) the subsidiaries of foreign MNEs, British or otherwise. Firms in the first category have received the greatest attention from economic and business historians. These scholars have published a series of studies that show that these managing agencies dominated the organised economy for much of the colonial period (Aldous, 2015; Kling, 1966; Oonk, 2001; Ray, 1982). Indian-owned and managed firms have also attracted the attention of Indian business historians, and their evolution in the period between Independence and the liberalisation of the Indian economy in 1991 has been discussed in a variety of works including popular histories and biographies of industrial leaders (Lala, 1981; Piramal, 1998a, 1998b).

Unfortunately, the Indian subsidiaries of foreign multinationals have received far less attention from Indian business historians, notwithstanding the fact that they played a very important part in the Indian economy from the interwar period through to the 1970s. They have been seen as a modernising influence in terms of their business strategies and willing-ness to invest in technology, in contrast to the more conservative, mercantile approach of the managing agencies (Misra, 1999). One of the few historians to discuss these firms at any length is Maria Misra. She argues that the Indian subsidiaries of some MNEs in this period had a relatively progressive approach to staffing: some of these firms, including Burmah-Shell, the Indian trading representative of the Burmah Oil Company, understood the impor-tance of Indianisation (at least in the interests of 'political expediency') even before Independence. To a certain extent, she contrasts the willingness of the MNCs to promote Indians to positions of authority and expertise with the more conservative attitude of the British managing agencies. Yet, as Misra notes, '[o]ne should not exaggerate the differences between the agency houses and the multinationals' in this respect (Misra, p. 206). The present study shows that, leaving aside the comparison with the managing agencies, there were important continuities in the staffing policy of the Burmah Oil Company and its subsidiaries before and after Independence.

Historiography of the impact of decolonisation/indigenisation on the IHRM strategies of British MNEs

Building on the preceding discussion, we note that business historians with an interest in the workforces of British MNEs have written about the transition from colonialism to post-colonialism in MNEs that were established in the heyday of the British Empire and that are still in operation today. These researchers are interested in the process by which the firms went from having ethnocentric IHRM strategies to less overtly colonialist and discriminatory approaches that correspond to the regiocentric, polycentric, or geocentric strategies iden-tified by IHRM scholars. Their studies of different countries, regions, and industries suggest that the transition from colonial to postcolonial IHRM took place at different points in the case of each company but broadly within the period from the late 1930s to the early 1980s. These research outputs differ considerably in terms of the disciplinary backgrounds of their authors and the research methods used. However, it is possible to come to some general conclusions about the nature of the shift from coloniality to postcoloniality in British MNEs based on these studies. A common theme is that the shift from coloniality to postcoloniality in IHRM was gradual, marked by considerable resistance within firms, and rarely if ever coincided with political Independence.

This is the lesson one can take away from Jones (1995), a monograph-length study of British multinational banking from 1830 to 1990. Jones is a methodologically conservative business historian who does not directly engage with postcolonial theory; nonetheless he examines the various forces, particularly political ones, that have influenced British global banks. Much of the book deals with British banks in Asia, since many of Britain's banking multinationals have their origins in that area during the era of Empire and colonialism. Tracking the cultural shifts that paralleled the end of empire, Jones grapples with the issue of the transition to postcoloniality in the sections of the book about human resource man-agement policy in British banking multinationals. He shows that until c. 1935 all British banking multinationals pursued policies that were uniformly ethnocentric, with all execu-tive-level positions reserved for white British men. Jones notes that the first tentative moves to raise the status of indigenous staff in the British multinational banks took place in the inter-war period.

After 1945, 'nationalist criticism of foreign banks and competition from local banks suggested that the British banks needed to assume stronger local identities' by hiring and promoting more locals (Jones, 1995, p.315). Jones uses internal records to show that proposals for such reforms were often contentious within banks. He observes that 'among the Eastern Exchange banks' there were marked differences 'in the speed they moved on changing the status of local staff. The Mercantile Bank of India had begun to recruit Asians to executive positions in the mid-1930s' but this move was resisted for longer in the other banks, such as HSBC (Jones, 1995 p.316; Smith, 2016). Jones' narrative shows that the transition towards a less colonial staffing policy took decades to complete and was frequently controversial. Jones' work points to a system of periodisation that blurs the lines between the colonial and postcolonial eras.

The lines between colonial and postcolonial eras are also blurred in a very different study by postcolonial theorist Nidhi Srinivas focused on Prakash Tandon (1911–2004), the first indigenous chief executive of Lever Brothers India, the subsidiary of the Anglo-Dutch MNE Unilever. Srinivas is interested in determining when the culture of the British-controlled Indian subsidiary of this Anglo-Dutch company ceased being colonialist. Unilever grew out of Lever Brothers, a British soap-making company that expanded to many countries, including India, after the 1880s. Manufacturing began in India in 1931. Until the late 1930s, however, its managerial workforce in India was exclusively white and British. Prakash Tandon joined the company as a management-track trainee in 1937. He recalled that when he arrived the other junior executive assumed he was a tea server. Srinivas quotes the sections of Tandon's autobiography in which Tandon deals with the cultural legacies of Empire and uses this evidence to suggest that the true end of the culture of colonialism in Hindustan Lever came when Tandon, who had come under the growing influence of US managerial ideologies during his time at Harvard Business School, became the chief executive of the company in 1961. For example, Tandon promoted the ideology of scientific management as a way of undercutting colonial-era ethnic hierarchies. In his narrative, 1961, not 1947, the year in which Indian gained independence, is the key temporal marker distinguishing the colonial from the postcolonial era, at least within this firm (Srinivas, 2013). A recent historical study of Unilever in post-Independence India depicts 1956, the year the subsidiary listed on the Bombay Stock Exchange, as marking the effective end of coloniality within that firm (Pant & Ramachandran, 2017).

Andrew Smith's study of the end of ethnocentric IHRM practices at the Hongkong and Shanghai Banking Corporation (HSBC) again shows that this process was very gradual, characterised by resistance from some white executives, and driven by a host of technological and cultural factors that were separate from political decolonisation. Indeed Hong Kong, the firm's most important market in the 1960s, was still a British colony at that time and was expected to remain in British hands into the future. In Smith's narrative, HSBC's ethnocentric IHRM strategy was abandoned very gradually and over a long period from the 1950s up to the late 1970s. His contribution connects this change to both computerisation in the 1960s and to the marked shift in attitudes towards racial and ethnic discrimination that occurred in the capitalist world in the 1960s, an era in which the Civil Rights Movement made major gains in the United States, raising the global profile of civil rights issues (Smith, 2016).

Broadly similar conclusions about the timing of the abandonment of the IHRM strategy can be derived from the studies of how Barclays DCO responded to decolonisation in Africa by Africanising its workforce. Decker (2005) and Morris (2016) reveal that the firm's promotion of Black Africans to positions of real authority was not driven by a single decision taken at the firm's headquarters in response to the imminent end of the British Empire, but was rather the result of a series of piecemeal decisions taken by management throughout the firm at various points from the 1950s to the 1970s. Decker (2010) suggests that the process of Africanisation in the very different political context of South Africa is still an ongoing project. Uche (2012), a study of the indigenisation of foreign (largely British) businesses in Nigeria, suggests that the turning point was in the 1970s, long after Nigeria's political independence, which was granted in 1960.

Readers should derive one key lesson from our survey of the business-historical research on the evolution on IHRM in the era of decolonisation: that there is significant disagreement about when British business in Asia actually ceased to operate in a colonialist-imperialist fashion suggests that the institutional cultures of these firms changed very gradually. This survey provides the context against which we can consider developments at BOC.

Historiography of BOC

Any researcher studying BOC owes a considerable debt to T.A.B. Corley's two volume *History of the Burmah Oil Company*, which appeared in 1983 and 1988, at a time when the firm's identity as a separate organisation was ending due to its integration into the BP Group. Professor Corley's scholarly research into the history of British multinational enterprise was informed by his previous career in banking, which included a period working in the Central Bank of Iraq from 1953 to 1955. Corley's books thus combined a degree of insider knowledge of the politics of oil with the research methods of a traditional historian. To the extent Corley's study engaged with theory, it referenced the work of Mark Casson, an economist of international business. Corley's research questions were, therefore, quite different from ours, which are informed by postcolonial theory.

Corley said relatively little about staffing within the firm. He briefly explained the similarity in background and mentality of the British civil servants who governed India and the top managers of the firm, noting that the senior management cadres, who bore the title 'executive assistant' were 'graduates of British universities [who] were similar in background and in attitude to their British ICS counterparts' and had been selected, in part, based on their sporting abilities (Corley, 1988, p. 310).

Newer research by Verma and Abdelrehim (2016) is somewhat closer to our approach in that these authors apply postcolonial theory to understanding the development of foreign oil companies in India after 1947. The postcolonial theory on hybridity to understand the operations of BOC's relationship with the government of India after 1947. Abdelrehim et al. (2017) use Durkheimian theory to understand the firm's painful restructuring in the wake of the 1973 oil shock. This restructuring was supervised by the Bank of England, which supported this iconic British company but with strict conditions designed to limit the firm's potential burden on the British state. The focus of the aforementioned authors is clearly on the relations between this oil company and national governments rather than the internal life of the firm. In this sense, it is similar to the bulk of the vast literature on the history of the oil industry, which has long been preoccupied with the theme of state-business relations and has paid comparatively little attention to staffing (Bradley, 1996; Bucheli, 2008, 2010; Bud-Frierman, Godley, and Wale, 2010; Jones, 1981; Taylor, 2015). Yergin (2011); Duran & Bucheli (2017), a best-selling yet scholarly historical study of the geopolitics of oil, exemplifies this approach. While we certainly understand the reasons why previous historians of the oil industry have focused on the relations between governments and the oil majors, we believe that it is time to build on this research by writing histories of staffing systems in oil companies that draw on postcolonial theory.

Overview of company history: the Burmah Oil Company, 1886–2000

From its inception, Burmah Oil Company's strategy was closely connected to British military and political power in India. The company was founded in Glasgow in 1886 by David Cargill, a Scottish merchant who had prospected for oil in Upper Burma, a territory that was added to the British Empire that year (Corley, 2006). It should be explained that the oil industry was then barely a quarter of a century old, as the start of modern oil production is conventionally located in Pennsylvania in 1859 (Black, 2014). In 1876, Cargill had bought the Rangoon Oil Company Ltd, a Glasgow firm that had failed in its efforts to exploit oil in Upper Burma due to the actions of the territory's independent ruler (Corley, 1988). As already noted, the annexation of the territory by the British dramatically changed the prospects of the firm and led to the creation of the Burmah Oil Company in 1886 (Corley, 2006). The BOC grew rapidly, developing oil fields in the Central Burma Basin, building a large refinery, and creating a distribution network to bring lamp oil to consumers throughout India and Burma. The firm also profitably marketed by-products such as wax in Britain (Corley, 1988, p. 2). In 1905, BOC signed a long-term agreement to supply fuel oil to the British navy's new oil-burning ships (Corley, 1988, p. 2). The BOC's increasingly close relationship with the British government resulted in BOC's expansion into oil production in Persia, a nominally independent country over which the British were attempting to exert influence (Corley, 1988, p. 5). In 1909, BOC established a subsidiary called the Anglo-Persian Oil Company (APOC), which subsequently played an important role in Iranian political history (Abdelrehim & Toms, 2017; Marsh, 2007; Vassiliou, 2009; Venn, 2016).

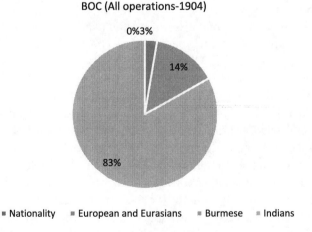

Figure 1. Nationalities employed in BOC in 1904. Source: compiled from Corley, T. A. B. (1988). A history of the Burmah Oil Company:1924–1966.

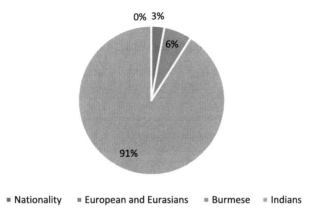

Figure 2. Nationalities employed in BOC in 1913. Source: compiled from Corley, T. A. B. (1988). A history of the Burmah Oil Company:1924–1966.

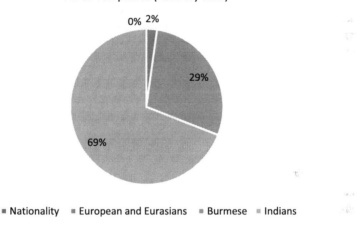

Figure 3. Nationalities employed (refinery staff) in oil industry in 1921. Source: compiled from Corley, T. A. B. (1988). A history of the Burmah Oil Company:1924–1966.

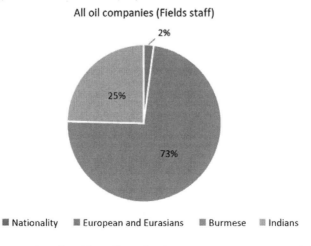

Figure 4. Nationalities employed (Fields staff) in oil industry in 1921. Source: compiled from Corley, T. A. B. (1988). A history of the Burmah Oil Company:1924–1966.

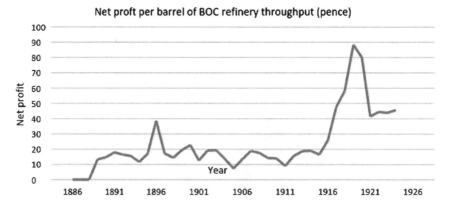

Figure 5. Net profit of BOC refinery throughput. Source: Compiled from Corley, T. A. B. (1988). A history of the Burmah Oil Company:1924–1966, p. 320–321.

In the interwar period, intensifying competition among the major oil producers prompted BOC to attempt to negotiate a variety of anti-competitive agreements with rival firms such as Shell. In 1928, BOC negotiated the Burmah-Shell agreement, which provided for the establishment of a joint distribution system in India of that name (Bamberg, 1994, p. 107; Corley, 1988, pp. 5–8).

The Second World War an produced an existential threat to BOC. One of Japan's motivations for entering the war in December 1941 had been to secure oil supplies (Black, 2014, p. 136). Not surprisingly, control of BOC's Burmese fields was important to both sides in the conflict (Corley, 1988, p. 112). In early 1942, as Japanese forces pushed through Burma, the British military destroyed BOC's Burmese production facilities so as to deny them to the enemy (Evans, 1946).

As illustrated in Tables 1 and 2; and Figures 1, 2, 3, 4 and 5, the post-war period, India remained the main source of BOC's oil net profit contributing 50% in 1949 and 54% in 1955 respectively, despite the coming of Indian independence in 1947. BOC's focus remained on the Indian subcontinent as late as 1955, with sales of lubricants, wax, and other products in European markets representing a mere 10 per cent of revenues, as shown in Figures 6 and 7.

At independence in 1947, foreign firms in India did not know what to expect from the new government (Tyson, 1947). The BOC's Annual Report for 1948 observed that 'The constitutional changes in India, Pakistan and Burma have affected all residents in those countries in some degree, and particularly in Burma where our employees have had to live and work in an atmosphere of disturbance and uncertainty' (BOC Annual Report, 1948, p. 10). In 1948, W.E.V. Abraham, the Managing Director of BOC, travelled to India and Pakistan to try to ascertain the stances of the two governments with respect to foreign enterprises (Abraham, 1948). The initial signals from the Indian government were, however, largely positive. As a 1952 investigation by London's India, Pakistan and Burma Association reported, T.T. Krishnamachari, the Minister for Commerce and Industry, had declared that the government did not want to take over foreign-owned enterprises. The report also noted that G.L. Mehta, the Indian ambassador to the United States, was in favour of 'foreign capital … subject to qualifying conditions, and the right to select'. Moreover, C.D. Deshmukh, Minister of Finance, had told his compatriots in the context of oil refineries 'that there are some things in the

Sources of Burmah oil net profit (1949)

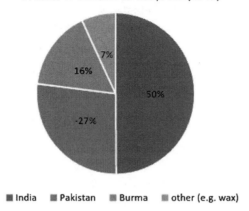

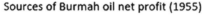

Figure 6. Sources of Burmah oil net profit (1949). Source: Compiled from Corley, T. A. B. (1988). A history of the Burmah Oil Company:1924–1966, p. 398.

Sources of Burmah oil net profit (1955)

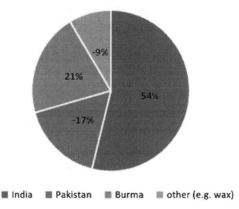

Figure 7. Sources of Burmah oil net profit (1955). Source: Compiled from Corley, T. A. B. (1988). A history of the Burmah Oil Company:1924–1966, p. 398.

world which they cannot expect to get on their own terms' (Basu, 2001, p. 138; India, Pakistan and Burma Association, 1952). In the period between independence in 1947 and 1956, Nehru's government sought to remain on good terms with BOC and other foreign oil companies and actively encouraged them to continue investing in India.

In the middle of the 1950s, however, there was an apparent shift in the political climate, for the BOC's annual report of 1954 stated that: 'It is becoming increasingly difficult to be sure just how welcome private enterprise is in the India of to-day' (BOC Annual Report, 1954, pp. 19–20) . Around this time, the rise within the Congress party of Keshav Dev Malaviya, a strident Indian nationalist, threatened the hitherto largely amicable relations between the BOC and Nehru's government. In 1956, Malaviya established an Oil and Natural Gas Commission to investigate how the government could nurture an India-owned industry using technology supplied by the Soviet bloc (Bamberg, 2000, p. 257; Economist, 1961). In subsequent years, the Indian government began the process of constructing an integrated, Indian-owned oil firm (Verma & Abdelrehim, 2016). In the 1960s, the Indian government began to impose various regulations on Burmah-Shell, which were clearly designed to redistribute market share away from Burmah-Shell towards the Indian government's own company. The most onerous of these regulations took the form of restrictions on the company's freedom to import crude oil from its preferred suppliers, thereby reducing the efficiency of its refineries (The Economist, 1970). Other regulations, such as price controls and restrictions on the firm's ability to hire and fire, also eroded profits (Burmah-Shell, 1974). The rules imposed by the Port of Bombay also hurt the bottom line of the firm, since they prevented the importation of Middle Eastern crude in the most modern ships and also complicated Burmah-Shell's extensive coastwise trade (Patwardhan, 1974).

Many of these regulations represented a form of 'creeping nationalisation' that reduced the efficiency of Burmah-Shell's refineries and thus the value of the subsidiary to the parent company. The value of BOC's Indian assets was also likely reduced by the fact that Burmah-Shell's refining and marketing distribution activities were performed by legally separate firms. Aware of the benefits of full integration, executives sought advice in 1964 from a Bombay law firm about the complex legal and taxation implications of a takeover of Burmah Shell Marketing by Burmah Shell Refinery Ltd (Jones, 1964; Mehra, 1964). However, these firms remained separate entities as late as 1975, as the agreement selling Burmah-Shell to the Indian government shows (Patwardhan, 1975b).

After the oil industry was nationalised in Burma in 1963, BOC encountered an increasingly difficult market with increased government involvement in the activities of the company. The company therefore looked to expand activities in other parts of the world, even as a freshly established government company (later the Myanmar Oil and Gas Enterprise, or MOGE) took charge in Burma (Thornton, 2015). In 1957, BOC chairman William Eadie initiated a major change in the strategy of the company that involved shifting away from the politically troubled Indian subcontinent towards more promising markets in the Western Hemisphere (Canada, the United States, Peru, and Ecuador) as well as Australia. The company also acquired two specialist oil refineries in England that allowed it to capitalise on its expertise in lubricants. In 1963, a business journalist observed that the company had evolved into a 'rather eclectic' enterprise that included its 'traditional' business in India and Pakistan as well as newer ventures in Canada (The Economist, 1963).

In 1966, Burmah Oil merged with Castrol, the United Kingdom's leading producer of lubricants. The Burmah Group also began investing in North Sea oil production, started acquiring petrol stations in the United Kingdom, and further diversified into the sale of non-petroleum products to motorists (Corley, 1988, p. 66; BOC Annual Report for 1966, p.19; BOC Annual Report for 1968, p.12). In 1973, the Burmah Group used loans from a syndicate of banks to acquire Signal Oil and Gas of Houston, a move that was interpreted by contemporaries as a sign that the firm was planning to create a vertically integrated US subsidiary that could challenge the US oil majors in their home market (Financial Times, 1974). Burmah Group further increased its debt levels in the course of acquiring a large fleet of tankers designed to connect its refinery in the Bahamas with ports in the south-eastern US (Burmah Group Annual Report for 1974, p.5). All of these changes meant that the relative importance of the firm's operations in India and Pakistan was rapidly declining even before the 1973 oil shock forced the firm to further contract operations on the Indian subcontinent.

The shift in the firm's strategic focus away from India was accompanied by the grant of much greater autonomy to the firm's Indian subsidiary. Prior to January 1967, the CEO of the subsidiary, A.J.W.S Leonard, had extremely limited freedom of action, as a wide range of decisions had to be approved by Burmah-Shell's London Office. In 1967, the London office was closed and this intensive micro-management was replaced by 'management by exception,' a system whereby the parent company's role is reduced to the examination of the main financial and operational results of the subsidiary, only intervening with the subsidiary's managers when there is a failure to meet targets. In the case of Burmah-Shell, there was, however, an important exclusion to the principle of management by exception, for executives in the UK remained responsible for 'Personnel matters ie Recruitment, Career Planning, Training, Employee Relations, and Services to Personnel' in the 'Lettered' or senior manager category. Moreover, these managers retained control of the firm's on-going efforts to train Indians for technical and managerial posts, doing so via the administration of scholarship schemes for Indian nationals, liaison with Loughborough College and Birmingham University, and maintaining contact with Indian trainees during their time in the UK (BOC, 1966).

In the early 1970s, the political pressures on Burmah-Shell increased as Indira Gandhi's government increasingly turned away from the West and towards the Soviet Union. In 1971, the 25th amendment to the Indian constitution was ratified, which removed the requirement that 'adequate compensation' be paid to the owners of companies that were nationalised (Anjara, 1975). Burmah-Shell refused to refine shipments of Soviet crude, a decision that offended the Indian authorities. In the face of mounting hostility, Burmah-Shell took actions to generate goodwill in India. The company assisted the Indian government during the 1971 war against Pakistan, supplied technical expertise to a fertiliser production programme, and funded a highly visible road safety campaign, documenting all of these efforts in a full-colour pamphlet it issued in 1972 (BOC, 1972). In the same year, the BOC appointed M.S. Patwardhan as the Indian subsidiary's first Indian Chief Executive (Kilbey, 1974). In his autobiography, Patwardhan recalled that 'virtually the whole of the Management team had Indian nationality' by the 1970s (Patwardhan, 1986, p.97) and that his appointment was thus the logical outcome of a 'conscious decision' made in the post-war period to 'Indianise the officer cadre progressively … over a number of years' (Patwardhan, 1986, p.86, p. 92).

However, the attacks on the firm continued and there were increasingly strident calls in the Indian press and parliament for government 'participation' in the ownership of all oil companies. In May 1973, an obviously alarmed Patwardhan cabled Burmah-Shell's office in Swindon to report that certain ministers in the government had come out in favour of vaguely defined state participation in the Indian subsidiary of Esso, a US-owned competitor. An executive in Swindon circled the word 'participation' and asked for more information over what type of government equity stake that term implied: '51%? 60%? 75%? 100%' (Patwardhan, 1973). On a visit to India in March 1974, a Burmah-Shell executive found that the subsidiary's top management team, which by then consisted entirely of Indian nationals, was demoralised by the uncertainty over their professional futures. The lack of clarity since the late 1950s over whether foreign oil companies would have a future in India had discouraged a generation of young Indians from joining the firm. The result was that 'the staff has been aging together while a continuous process of contraction has been going on'. The executive also reported that Burmah-Shell 'is now down to 3,400 retail sites, 5 main port installations, 160 depots, two lubricating oil blending plants, and a little over 5000 men' (Trenear-Thomas, 1974).

Unlike Shell, which had engaged in scenario planning related to a possible increase in the world price of oil (Corneluis et al., 2005), the Burmah Oil Group was completely unprepared for the oil shock that followed the 1973 Arab-Israeli War. The firm, which had borrowed extensively to finance its expansion spree, found itself unable to service its debts and was financially supported by the Bank of England, which made the appointment as CEO of Alastair Down, the former head of British Petroleum (BP), a condition of continued financial support. Under Down's leadership, the Burmah Group rationalised its operations and sold off overseas assets so as to focus on the firm's core competences, which were now clearly in the area of lubricants (McCosh & Earl, 1978). Fortuitously for the company, Down's drive to sell overseas assets coincided with the agenda of Indian Prime Minister Indira Gandhi, who had decided that India's oil industry should be under Indian government ownership. This sale took place during the period known as the Emergency (1975–77), when India's democratic institutions and freedom of the press were temporarily suspended (Guha, 2011).

Correspondence in the BP Archive suggests that the decision by the Indian government to seek 100 per cent of Burmah-Shell's Indian assets, rather than merely an equity stake, appears to have been taken rather suddenly in October 1975. In the immediate aftermath of Gandhi's imposition of the Emergency on 26 June 1975, Burmah-Shell executives seem to have been moderately sanguine about the likely impact of the suspension of civil liberties on both India's economic prospects and the outlook for the firm in 1976. A memorandum prepared in early October remarked that while it was unfortunate that Gandhi had jailed opposition politicians, most Indians supported the Emergency as they prioritised economic growth (Burmah Shell Oil Storage and Distributing Company, 1975). On 7 October 1975, M.S. Patwardhan gave a presentation in Swindon that briefly referenced the on-going partnership negotiations with the Indian government but focused mainly on the firm's prospect for 1976. He named the pro-business ministers in the government and approvingly noted the Gandhi government's law and order agenda and observed that Gandhi now 'frowned upon' strikes. He also reported that Gandhi was moving to de-regulate parts of the economy by lifting price controls for certain commodities, 'although not yet oil'. His generally upbeat presentation included a discussion of the likely impact of the recent monsoon season, which had been good, and the 'mildly Bullish' view taken by India's stock exchanges (Patwardhan, 1975a).

The fact that Patwardhan gave such a detailed forecast for 1976 to 12 British colleagues suggests that the executives in Swindon believed that Burmah-Shell would continue to operate in India for at least another year, if not much longer. However, by late October, the company had been plunged into discussions about the complete nationalisation of its Indian assets at prices it considered to be unfair. During these acrimonious discussions, the firm enlisted the support of the British High Commissioner and Dutch Ambassador in New Delhi to help secure an improved valuation of its assets. During the negotiations, Burmah-Shell complained that the Indian government's method of valuing its assets was less generous than that used when the Indian subsidiary of Esso was nationalised. After a compressed period of bargaining, the two parties arrived at an agreement that was tolerable to both (Patwardhan, 1975c). The sale agreement was concluded in November 1975 and by January 1976, most of Burmah-Shell's Indian assets were in the hands of Bharat Petroleum Corporation Limited or BPCL (Finlay, 1975). BOC's holdings in oil-producing refineries in north-east India were sold to the Indian government in 1981 The Economist, 1981; Economic Times, 2017a; Economic Times, 2017b.

By the early 1980s, therefore, BOC's operations on the Indian subcontinent were vestigial and relatively unimportant in the overall strategy of the firm. We would note here that while BOC's subsidiary in Pakistan survived up to the end of the twentieth century, it was a relatively small operation that contributed little to the parent company's overall revenues. In the period after 1947, references to BOC's operations in Pakistan appeared considerably less frequently in the firm's annual reports than did material about the subsidiary in the Republic of India. This pattern suggests that these operations were less important to the parent company. Relatively few primary sources related to BOC in post-1947 Pakistan are available. However, the picture that emerges from the surviving sources suggests that the company's relationship with the government of Pakistan was more harmonious than its relationship with the Indian governments led by Jawaharlal Nehru and Indira Gandhi. In November 1967, BOC executives made plans to list shares of the Pakistani subsidiary on the Karachi and Dacca stock exchanges, which is a sign that they were confident that Pakistan would remained a vibrantly capitalist economy (Burmah-Shell, Pakistan, 1967).

This confidence is understandable, as Pakistan's government was more consistently pro-Western and pro-capitalist than that of India during the Cold War. During the brief period in the 1970s when Pakistan was led by Zulfikar Ali Bhutto, the country experimented with socialist economic policies and improved relations with the Soviet Union. For most of its post-Independence history, however, Pakistan welcomed Western firms. Indeed, Bhutto made it clear in 1974 that Western firms were still welcome and would not be nationalised. Pakistan's largely pro-Western orientation was confirmed in 1977 when conservative military officers overthrew Bhutto in a military coup (Talbot, 2012). As a result of this relatively favourable political environment, BOC was able to continue operating in Pakistan even as it was forced to wind down its operations in India. Burmah Oil Company Pakistan Ltd continued to trade in Pakistan until 2005, selling lubricants in partnership with Pakistan State Oil (Burmah Oil of Pakistan, 2004; Corley, 1988, p. 329).

By the 1970s, BOC's annual reports were referring less and less frequently to the company's operations on the Indian subcontinent, which were now peripheral to the group. While they report in detail on workforce issues in the UK and other parts of the world, the reports cease to be a source of information about the firm's workforce in its vestigial Indian operations. BOC ceased to exist as a separate firm in 2000, when, as part of the corporate merger wave the late 1990s (Evenett, 2003), Burmah-Castrol was purchased by BP Amoco, a firm that had been formed recently by the merger of BP and Amoco. The Castrol brand remained in use, but BOC was no longer an independent entity (Grace's Guide Ltd, 2017). In 2016, just six of BP's 123 subsidiaries continue to bear the name Burmah Oil (BP plc, 2016, p. 232). None of these subsidiaries has any apparent connection to the Indian subcontinent.

These various developments across the history of the firm were reflected in production figures. Figure 8 shows that BOC crude oil production and refinery throughput increased from 1886 until 1942 when denial took place by the British forces. Following that, from 1943 till 1956, BOC was moving towards the reconstruction of the fields and refineries, and production started to increase gradually up to 1956. Figure 9 illustrates that BOC refinery throughput from Burma exceeded the throughput from India during the period 1929–1961.

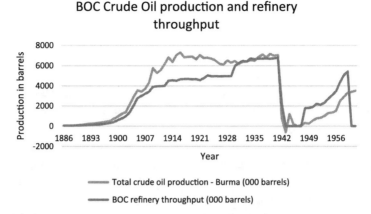

Figure 8. Crude oil production and refinery throughput data. Source: Compiled from Corley, the history of BOC volume 2, 1924–1966, p.398.

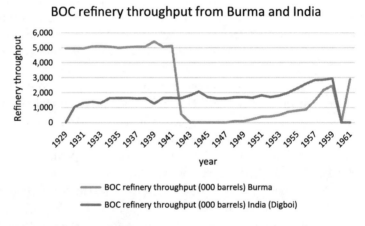

Figure 9. BOC refinery throughput from Burma and India. Source: Compiled from Corley, the history of BOC volume 2, 1924–1966, p.398.

The changing IHRM strategies of BOC, 1920–1980

This section discusses how the Burmah Oil Company (along with its associated companies) approached its policy on personnel in the mid-twentieth century, with particular emphasis on the transition between the periods before and after 1947–8, when South Asia was formally decolonised.

A key question regarding personnel in the years after World War I was that of replacing expatriate British staff with local employees. Initially, in this case, that meant Burmese and Indian nationals, and additionally, after independence and partition in 1947, Pakistanis. In interwar India, the debate on appointing more locals, generally referred to by the term 'Indianisation', was relatively advanced in the context of government services. But pressures for Indianisation were not restricted to the government services: it was also an important consideration in private firms, who implemented the policy to varying degrees (Ramnath, 2016, 2017).

How then, did the BOC go about 'localisation' in the years after 1947? More generally, how did its work culture and the role envisaged for its expatriate (mostly British) staff evolve as a postcolonial identity began to gain definition in the countries of South Asia?

Pre-1947

In the offices, as in the oilfields, the British and American officers formed a numerical minority but had a virtual monopoly of the managerial and expert technical positions. A photograph of the 'Main Office Staff' in Yenangyaung (likely dating from the 1930s) shows a row of about thirty white expatriate staff in the front, and some six rows of Burmese and Indians behind them (Bowlby, 1962, photograph adjacent to p. 26, and Appendices).

A defining feature of British oil companies in colonial South Asia was their close association with the colonial state. Their organisation and culture also mirrored those of the colonial government services. Life was centred on townships developed at or near the oilfields, comparable in many ways to the subcontinent's railway townships (Bear, 1994). These townships were often geographically remote, which inevitably shaped the social life and culture of these expatriate communities. The memoirs of British oilmen in pre-independence Burma give a flavour of the life they led and the work cultures they built and inhabited.

Arriving in 1919 in Rangoon, H.S. Bowlby joined the Burmah Oil Company as Office Assistant, and then rose through the ranks to the post of General Manager. In his 1962 memoirs Bowlby describes how he enjoyed a lifestyle supported by a large number of Indian servants (Bowlby, 1962, p. 3). Inexpensive and plentiful domestic help gave BOC's expatriates ample free time for such pastimes as tennis, golf, sniping, and polo, aristocratic activities that were considered suitably 'pukka' or appropriate to this class (Bowlby, 1962, p. 5). Relations between locals and expatriates were, if not segregated, then certainly hierarchical.

BOC employees were virtually a part of the colonial establishment. As they rose in the ranks, they took on duties outside the company. As General Manager in Rangoon, Bowlby sat on various bodies and meetings, including the Burma Chamber of Commerce, the Burma Railways, the Red Cross, and the Rangoon Golf Club (Bowlby, 1962, p. 28).

The social clubs in Burma's oil-producing region were exclusively for the expatriate employees, which parallels the system in colonial Indian settlements (Grindle, 1997b). The Indians and Burmese, on the other hand, lived austere lives. British oil companies in India did provide some housing facilities for the Indian and some Burmese workers, though food and travel were not paid for (Grindle, 1997a, p. 45). In 1938, Indian as well as Burmese workers of the BOC and British Burma Petroleum Company (BBPC) in the Chauk oilfield went on strike (Grindle, 1997a, p. 71). G.A.F. Grindle, a manager at BBPC, conceded that these workers had legitimate grievances: in addition to the conditions mentioned above, the Indian workers 'lived in barracks, plain unfurnished quarters of about sixty feet by twenty ... None had their families with them and the majority stayed for two or three years before returning to India'. Until the shifts for drilling crews were reduced to 8 hours in the late 1930s, the 'native drilling staff of BOC and BBPC appear to have worked twelve-hour shifts' (Grindle, 1997a, p.72). Despite growing pressure for Indianisation in the inter-war years, as well as evidence of real progress in Indianisation of the Indian civil service, BOC remained entirely ethnocentric in its IHRM practices.

Highly ethnocentric attitudes were revealed in the way in which BOC reported on the casualties suffered by its workforce during the Second World War, when Japanese forces invaded Burma (BOC Annual Reports, 1940s; Corley, 1988), with the firm's annual reports evincing more concern for the smaller number of British casualties than the much larger number of Burmese and Indian workers who were killed or unaccounted for. For example, the Chairman informed the shareholders of the company in 1942 that 'It is with great regret that I have to report the addition of a further seven fatal casualties from acts of War to the six intimated last year among our employees. These were again men of UK origin, but, with one exception, normally serving with us in the East. Four more of this category have been reported prisoners of War' (BOC Annual Report for 1942, p.3). The same report discussed, in passing, the 257 deaths amongst its Indian staff in Burma, as well as noting that almost all its Burmese staff had remained in that country, where 'we have no news of their welfare' (BOC Annual Report for 1942, p.3).

1947 and beyond

After 1945, as operations recommenced in both India and Burma, staff were again thanked for their unstinting efforts, not least as 'especially where they have had to start rebuilding on the ruins of our former properties in Burma conditions have been far from easy' (BOC Annual Report for 1946, p. 8). In the BOC annual report for 1946, which was published when Indian independence was imminent, the chairman of the board claimed that the firm had long-favoured independence for India. The report declared that the company's 'unshaken confidence … in the future of Burma and India and in a square deal – not least for those like ourselves who have served them in the past efficiently and well in their nation building efforts – has been appreciatively commented on in these countries' (BOC Annual Report for 1946, pp.7–8). He also declared that 'this attitude of ours is merely one expression of the good will and good wishes felt generally here for peoples with whom we have lived for so long not in the manner of conquerors but as friends'. The chairman reported that like others in Britain, the company were 'happy that' these countries 'have now achieved that democratic manhood and complete independence which is our own heritage and which has been our long wished gift for them' (BOC Annual Report for 1946, pp.7–8).

Thus, as the company began to look to a postcolonial future, it also attempted to recast its own colonial past as one in which it had played the role of friend and partner. The past was not to be easily thrown off however. The annual report of 1947 welcomed independence for Burma, India and Pakistan, noting how 'To all three countries we wish peace and progress in the evolution of their new independence', but also acknowledged the terrible violence that had accompanied partition. Nonetheless, 'It has been a matter for relief and satisfaction that our staff, British and Asiatic, all came through safely' (BOC Annual Report for 1947, pp. 5–8). Though perhaps unconscious the language used here – particularly in the epithet 'Asiatic' – bears the unmistakeable hallmarks of a colonial mind-set.

However, despite the relatively optimistic tone set in 1946 and 1947, by 1955 the BOC Chairman was wondering 'what room there will be for foreign capital and *expertise* in the Petroleum Industry' of India (BOC Annual Report for 1955, p. 19). Possibly the management was anxious that they would not be allowed to employ as many expatriates in specialist and supervisory positions as had been their normal practice. Nonetheless, it was clear that some localisation was necessary, and 'Asianisation programmes' were inaugurated to train local employees for other than blue-collar positions (BOC Annual Report for 1955, p. 24).

A company brochure reported that as of 1955, Burmah-Shell had 15,364 employees in India, of whom 1,217 were in 'Supervisory' positions. It is not clear what fraction of these 1,217 white-collar employees were Indians, but some institutional efforts were being made to enable localisation. The company had staff training centres in the four metropolitan cities where it had its branch offices. One of them, in Bombay, was residential, and catered to Burmah-Shell staff and those of 'associated companies in other countries'. Some of the Indian staff were sent for 'special courses in the UK'. The company also sponsored a number of scholarships for Indian students of mechanical engineering who wished to study at Loughborough and Birmingham, two universities in the UK (Background to Burmah-Shell, 1956; Malcolm, 1966). There was indeed a conscious 'policy' which dictated that '[w]hen operating and trading in overseas territories we employ nationals where possible' (BOC Annual Report for 1957, p. 23).

The company's annual reports in the late 1950s and early 1960s contain frequent references to progress on Indianisation. Occasionally, though, there was a hint of reluctance. Locals would replace expatriate employees 'as and when suitable men [became] available', but there was a potential trade-off: 'difficulties are encountered in certain cases when we are expected to accelerate matters to an extent which would prove detrimental to efficiency'. The company would probably not, of its own accord, have pursued localisation at the same pace; the impetus was external. Tellingly, they reported that their localisation drive was able to '[meet] the full requirements of the respective governments'. There was also a need to mollify potentially sceptical shareholders and the company reported that its 'confidence in' the emerging (Asian) white-collar staff '[had] been fully justified' (BOC Annual Report for 1959, p. 24). Still, there were limits to how high an Asian employee could rise, even in his own country. As of 1970, not a single Asian name appeared among the Divisional Directors and Chief Representatives of the company and its subsidiaries anywhere in the world. The Chief Representatives for India, Pakistan and 'South-East Asia and the Far East' (J.C. Finlay, M.C.; K.F.D. Wilson; V.W. Good) appear to have been Britons (BOC Annual Report for 1970, p. 44).

There was, of course, another side to the human resource practices of the BOC and its South Asian subsidiaries. This was their policy with respect to the Overseas (ie British) staff who continued to go out to these countries, and the work culture they were socialised into. Whether or not these men had the swagger of their colonial predecessors, there were elements of continuity in the way they approached their jobs abroad. Company instructions to Britons newly recruited to the Overseas Service as of c. 1961 continued to use the diffuse term 'the East' to refer to India, West and East Pakistan, and Burma (Burmah Oil Company, 1961). 'The East' was still presented in somewhat Orientalist terms. New recruits were advised to secure the required 'kit' for their time there (Burmah Oil Company, 1961, p. 19), and to prepare for the weather thus: 'You will have to think in terms of 'cold, hot, wet', rather than 'spring, summer, winter' (Burmah Oil Company, 1961, p. 23). Other colonial-era traditions continued. Expatriates received a special addition to their pay called 'Overseas Differential' (Burmah Oil Company, 1961, p. 7); their conditions of service included various clauses about 'passages' back to the UK (Burmah Oil Company, 1961, p. 9); employees on 'local leave' could travel at the company's expense to the 'nearest approved hill-station' (Burmah Oil Company, 1961, p. 11). The old lifestyle had, of course, to be tempered in some ways: recruits were warned that 'regulations about the carrying and possession of fire-arms in the East are usually very strict. If you intend to take a gun with you, you must ensure that these regulations are known to you and obeyed' (Burmah Oil Company, 1961, p. 25).

Pre- and post-nationalisation

The final period to consider is that immediately before and after the company was nationalised by the Indian government in 1976. Did this event lead to an accelerated programme of 'Indianisation', suggesting that the slow progress hitherto made was largely rooted in company culture and a persistent colonial mind-set? In fact, the process of Indianisation can be considered substantially completed by 1976. The most significant marker was the appointment of M.S. Patwardhan as the company's first Indian Chief Executive in 1972.

Nonetheless, Indianisation was about more than mere headcounts, as attitudes were also manifested in less quantifiable ways. For example, even as lower managerial levels were progressively Indianised in the 1950s, social segregation along effectively racial lines, manifested in features such as separate toilets and dining facilities for members of the company's nationwide and regional cadres, persisted. It was only from the late 1950s that a more unified or unitary managerial cadre, stratified by role hierarchy, began to emerge (Patwardhan, 1986, p. 90). Moreover, the type of Indian picked for inclusion in the managerial cadre reflected a strong desire to hire highly Anglicised Indians. Patwardhan's testimony suggests that the BOC, in recruiting Indians, had traditionally preferred candidates who at least somewhat fitted the model of a 'clubbable' young Englishman; literally a 'club-going Indian with an interest in and preferably aptitude for outdoor sports. If he had an English education, so much the better since his thought processes would follow familiar patterns, communication would be simpler and mutual trust more quickly established'. Indian managers, particularly at the All-India Assistant level, had to conform to a model based on the 'expatriate majority' (Patwardhan, 1986, p. 87). The persistence of colonial-era status hierarchies within BOC also manifested themselves in subtle ways, particularly when British and Indian executives socialised. For instance, Patwardhan recalled in 1991 a dinner party in the 1960s when it had been assumed that the British individual was the guest of honour and was thus entitled to eat first (Patwardhan, 1991, p. 39). In our view, the changes that had been made did not necessarily leave the firm well prepared for the challenges of the 1970s, including the threat of nationalisation.

Analysis: The persistence of coloniality

The process of Indianisation at BOC was slow and halting. The company's move away from an ethnocentric IHRM strategy towards a polycentric one was extremely gradual, never entirely complete, and, apparently, grudging. To the extent that BOC began to fill senior technical and managerial posts with Indians, this decision was significantly motivated by the desire to placate India's nationalist government rather than some other consideration, such as an appreciation of the improving quality of Indian engineering and management graduates. Moreover, while the firm moved in the direction of the polycentric IHRM strategy in the 1950s and 1960s, none of the changes in its staffing policy suggest that it considered adopting anything resembling a geocentric IHRM strategy and senior posts in the Indian subsidiary were held by white British expatriates as late as the early 1970s. In contrast, Unilever India's subsidiary had an Indian CEO, Prakash Tandon, as early as 1961. Postcolonial theory would attribute the fact that BOC was slow to abandon the ethnocentric IHRM model to the persistence of colonialist modes of thought in the cultures of the firm.

We also show that BOC's relations with the Indian government deteriorated steadily, a process that culminated with the nationalisation of its main assets in 1976. From the late 1950s onwards, the firm was attacked by nationalist politicians in India as a relic of oppressive British colonial rule. This pattern raises the counterfactual question of whether BOC could have prevented the deterioration of its relationship with the Indian government – and eventual nationalisation – had it moved more swiftly after 1947 to replace its ethnocentric IHRM system with one more functional in the new political environment?

Providing a conclusive answer to this question is difficult, especially in light of the fact that several non-British multinationals, including Coca-Cola and two US oil companies, were also pushed out of India by the government (Gopinath & Prasad, 2013; Patwardhan, 1986, p. 84). Nonetheless, promoting Indians to high-visibility posts in the company would likely have helped to improve relations with the Indian government. BOC seems to have been aware of this possibility, for Patwardhan testifies that it was believed that a policy of progressive Indianisation, 'culminating in the appointment of an Indian Chief Executive', could 'help to break the log-jam and start an easier relationship, leading eventually to a mutually beneficial partnership' with the Indian Government. Indeed, when appointed Chief Executive in 1972, Patwardhan himself 'saw one of his principal tasks as being the reconciliation of company objectives with national goals' (Patwardhan, 1986, p. 82). Reflecting in 1991 on why Burmah-Shell had been unable to escape nationalisation in 1976, he observed that the 'step of appointing an Indian Chief Executive' in 1972 had 'by itself proved to be inadequate for ensuring Burmah-Shell's survival'. He speculated that 'possibly both parties were the prisoners of the historical evolution of their relationship and the change in personalities came too late to turn the clock back' (Patwardhan, 1991, p. 71).

We therefore face the question why BOC did not Indianise Burmah-Shell's senior management team at an earlier time. As we have argued, postcolonial theory would suggest that it would have been difficult for the individuals who were making strategy at this firm to have conceptualised, let alone implemented, such a strategy for rapid change after 1947 because they were embedded in a culture that remained deeply colonialist in its attitudes towards individuals from the Indian subcontinent and other parts of the non-Western world. However, we have to be cautious in making this argument. Executives in Unilever's global headquarters, who were British and Dutch individuals with cultural backgrounds similar to those of the BOC's leaders, were able to promote Indians to positions of authority in their Indian subsidiary in a swifter fashion, the process being essentially complete with the appointment of Prakash Tandon as chief executive in 1961. The precise reasons for why BOC was slower to accomplish the same transition remain unclear and may have related to some feature of their respective industries, oil versus branded consumer goods, or to subtle differences in mind-set and organisational culture between BOC and Unilever executives.

We would suggest that another possible part of the explanation for why BOC was relatively slow to Indianise its senior management team relates to the dearth of Indians who were qualified to assume technical and managerial positions in its marketing and, a fortiori, refining subsidiaries. As we show above, by the late 1960s BOC was investing extensively in an effort designed to remedy this problem. This investment certainly did not take the form of a positive discrimination programme to put Indian nationals into positions before they were qualified. Instead, it involved a somewhat slower process that involved paying for the training in the UK of promising Indian nationals, who would then be qualified to take over senior roles. As we have mentioned, this training was done at company expense at the universities of Birmingham and Loughborough. With the benefit of hindsight, we can say it may have been advisable for the BOC to have begun investing in such training efforts at an earlier date, perhaps when Indian independence was imminent. However, we cannot conclusively determine whether the more rapid Indianisation of the firm after 1947 would have improved relations with the Indian government enough to have prevented nationalisation, the ultimate fate of BOC's Indian subsidiaries. Moreover, the available primary sources do not allow us to determine whether any features of BOC's organisational culture contributed to the relative slowness with which Indian executives and technicians were trained so that they could replace British personnel.

As this article has argued, multinational firms such as BOC make strategy in a cultural context that includes the legacies of empire. The so-called cultural or linguistic turn in business history in recent years has led to a greater emphasis on language, representations, and meaning (Rowlinson & Delahaye, 2009). Annual reports can be considered a genre and those published by the BOC certainly displayed distinct and consistent stylistic elements. Those of the 1940s and 1950s in particular were marked by a 'clubbability' that would have felt familiar to and reflected the culture of the majority of the senior management and, most probably, many of the shareholders. Moreover, the language deployed in the annual reports displays the clear persistence of a degree of coloniality within the culture and practices of the BOC. Categorisations of staff were made along blunt racial lines that collapsed all non-UK employees into a single category containing a very wide range of nationalities and ethnicities. Striking in the annual reports is the longevity of such terms as 'the East', 'Asian', 'Asianisation', and, most unsettling, 'Asiatic'. Similarly, when the 1956 annual report commented that '[t]he East is no longer "unchanging"'. it was playing on very old Orientalist tropes that saw 'the East' as mysterious, backward, and constrained by inflexible conservatism, in contrast to the modernity and innovativeness of the West (BOC Annual Report for 1956, p. 21). The language of the reports carries out, then, a kind of 'othering' of indigenous employees. Whether conscious or not, this language was not incidental but rather betrayed assumptions and stereotypes held by the firm's management: assumptions and stereotypes that were in turn reflected in the persistence of stratified, hierarchical-staffing practices that were as slow to disappear as the language used. Meanwhile, Patwardhan, the company's first Indian Chief Executive, admits that some individuals within the firm 'might be suspected by an unsympathetic observer to have suffered from delusions of imperial superiority'. In the end, he concludes, by 'history, Burmah-Shell was a somewhat inward-looking society and natural shyness and reserve were often confused by outsiders with arrogance' (Patwardhan 1986, p. 84, p. 78). It appears that in the case of this firm, at least, the persistence of colonial-era attitudes was reinforced by organisational insularity. Coloniality is not then either present or not present in the multinational firms of any given colonial or Imperial nation. Rather we have to attend to the histories of the cultures of both home nations and individual firms.

If this reading of the evidence is correct, we could conclude that the firm's managers were prisoners of the colonialist cultural environment in which they had matured and that their unwillingness to move swiftly to replace its ethnocentric IHRM system with one that was more appropriate ultimately impacted the firm's bottom line. BOC's Indian operations were hampered by a series of regulations that the increasingly hostile Indian government imposed in the 1960s. These regulations, which were clearly designed to redistribute market share away from Burmah-Shell towards the Indian government's own company, represent a form of 'creeping nationalisation' that reduced the value of BOC's Indian subsidiary. This course of action culminated with the coerced sale of the Indian subsidiary to the Indian government in 1976. Quantifying the cost to BOC's shareholders of the ethnocentric staffing policies pursued by BOC executives after 1947 is difficult, since it is unclear to what extent the discounted price paid by the Indian government in 1976 reflected Indian government dissatisfaction with the slow pace of Indianisation at BOC as opposed to the government's other reasons for resenting the firm.

Readers who are familiar with the principal-agent problem might be inclined to suspect that the slowness with which BOC localised its Indian management team was connected to the personal self-interest of the white British managers who had previously dominated managerial posts in BOC's Indian subsidiaries. However, our review of the relevant material in the BP Archive did not turn up any evidence that BOC's white British managers resisted instructions to Indianise that had emanated from BOC's headquarters in the UK. While agency theory may indeed be helpful in explaining why other European multinationals were slow to hire and promote local managers following decolonisation, this dynamic does not appear to have been at work in this firm.

Conclusions

This study has demonstrated that the process of Indianisation was gradual and undertaken by the BOC in the face of considerable political pressure from the Government of India. Although some efforts were made to train Indians and put them into positions of authority and expertise, this process appears to have been slower than in Hindustan Lever, Unilever's Indian subsidiary. BOC's Indian operations continued to operate using an ethnocentric IHRM strategy until the 1970s, the last decade of the subsidiary's existence. While the ultimate source of BOC's greater cultural and institutional rigidity as compared to Unilever is not clear to us, we are reasonably certain that the slow pace of Indianisation in its Indian subsidiary contributed to the hostility of the Indian government, which was evident in the creeping nationalisation of the 1960s and then outright nationalisation in 1976.

Our article points to directions for future research. As noted above, the response of Western multinationals to the Indian government's demands for Indianisation varied considerably, with Unilever completing the process at a relatively early date, and BOC being a relative laggard. We acknowledge that we do not know the precise reasons for the greater institutional rigidity of BOC, but future research projects comparing how a number of multinationals changed in their IHRM systems in the decades after 1945 might shed light on this subject. The cultural turn in business history has also prompted an interest in the experiential dimensions of business life and culture in the past and it would certainly be interesting to track the extent to which the linguistic conventions displayed in the BOC annual reports were merely habitual or did in fact reflect the reality of working for the company, for all grades of staff and all nationalities. How did it feel to be an Indian engineer or junior executive enmeshed within an ethnocentric culture? Did staff variously feel emotions of superiority or of inferiority, of power or powerlessness? Biographies and memoirs give some access to the voice of the white expatriate manager, but the so-called subaltern voice is largely lost. More research to answer these questions is required.

Note

1. We thank the archivists in London and at the Universities of Warwick and Cambridge who enabled us to research this article.

Acknowledgment

Aparajith Ramnath is grateful to the Indian Institute of Management Kozhikode and the University of Liverpool for enabling him to take up the Liverpool India Fellowship in 2017.

Disclosure statement

No potential conflict of interest was reported by the authors.

ORCID

Andrew Smith (iD) http://orcid.org/0000-0002-8589-7608

References

Materials in the BP plc Archives, University of Warwick.

About Ourselves. Information booklet 'About Ourselves in BP Archive ' BP Archive ArcRef: 141869
Anjara, M.R. (1975). Anjara, Legal and Taxation Manager, to Chief Executive, 18 Sept 1975.BP Archive ArcRef:181916
Answers to Indian Government's Second Questionnaire on Participation BP Archive BP Archive ArcRef:232373; B H Trenear -Thomas, March 1974, Visit to India, Ecuador, Peru in BP Archive, ArcRef: 137805.

Trenear –Thomas, B. H., March 1974. Visit to India, Ecuador, Peru. BP Archive ArcRef:137805
BOC annual reports
Burmah Oil Company (Pakistan Trading) Ltd. Full accounts made up to 31 December 2004.
BP plc Archive, University of Warwick. ARC, BOC Report of directors and balance sheets, 1940-1980.
BP plc. *Annual Report* for 2016.
Burmah-Shell. (1974). Answers to Indian Government's Second Questionnaire on Participation BP
    Archive BP Archive ArcRef: 232373;
Burmah Shell Oil Storage and Distributing Company. Memorandum by unknown executive dated 2
    October 1975, BP Archive ArcRef: 181916
Burmah Oil Company (Pakistan Trading) Ltd. Full accounts made up to 31 December 2004.Burmah-Shell
    Pakistan. (1967). "Burmah-Shell Rupee Oil Marketing Company" Checklist dated Karachi, 8 November
    1967 in BP Archive ArcRef: 181491
"Burmah-Shell Rupee Oil Marketing Company" Checklist dated Karachi, 8 November 1967 in BP Archive
    ArcRef: 181491
Finlay, J.C. (1975) Finlay, Chief Secretary, Burmah Group of Companies, to
Shri M. Ramaswami, Joint Secretary, Ministry of Petroleum and Chemicals, 26 November 1975 BP
    Archive ArcRef:181916
Information booklet 'About Ourselves in BP Archive ' BP Archive ArcRef: 141869
Jones, H.M. (1964). Jones to Malcolm 29 December 1964, in BP Archive, ArcRef:181491
Kilbey, R.H. (1974). Kilbey to M.A. Cooke in Swindon, 2 October 1974 BP Archive ArcRef: 180831
Malcolm, B.W. (1966). Malcolm to A.J.W.S Leonard in New Delhi, 18 November 1966 in BP Archive, BP
    Archive ArcRef: 181923.
Memorandum dated 2 October 1975, BP Archive ArcRef: 181916
Mehra, G.D. (1964). Mehra to N.A. Palkhivala, Esq 10 November 1964, in BP Archive, ArcRef: 181491
Patwardhan, M.S. (1973). Cable to Cage and Kilsey. 15 May 1973 in BP Archive BP Archive ArcRef: 182055
Patwardhan, M.S. (1974). Patwardhan to Shell International Petroluem Chemicals, Ltd 21 June 1974,
    in BP Archive ArrcRef: 180692
Patwardhan, M.S. (1975a). Text of presentation in BP Archive ArcRef: 181916
Patwardhan, M.S. (1975b). M.S. Patwardhan to Secretary, Government of India, Ministry of Petroleum
    and Chemicals. 18 September 1975.BP Archive ArcRef: 181916
Patwardhan, M.S. (1975c). Patwardhan, to Kilbey, 29 October 1975. BP Archive ArcRef: 181916
Trenear -Thomas, B H. (1974) Visit to India, Ecuador, Peru in BP Archive, ArcRef: 137805. Dated March
    1974.

Cambridge University, Centre of South Asia Studies Archives

Bowlby, H.S. (1962). *Random Reminiscences: B.O.C. 1919-1940.* Unpublished typescript. Cambridge
    University, Centre of South Asia Studies Archives: H.S. Bowlby Papers.

Materials in the British Library, Asia, Pacific and Africa Collections (APAC)

Abraham, W.E.V. (1948). "Position of British Oil Companies in India and Pakistan: Notes by W.E.V.
    Abraham, Managing Director of the Burmah Oil Company, on his visit to India and Pakistan". APAC
    [Asia, Pacific and Africa Collections], British Library: IOR/L/E/8/6220.
Background to Burmah-Shell (1956). Bombay: Burmah-Shell Oil Storage & Distributing Co. of India Ltd.
    British Library shelfmark: Asia, Pacific & Africa W 7697(a).
Burmah Oil Company. (1947). Letter to Secretary, India Office, London, 30 Sep 1947. APAC, British
    Library: IOR/L/PJ/7/11837.
Burmah Oil Company. (n,d. [1961]). *Notes for those joining the Overseas Service of the Burmah Group of
    Companies.* In Burmah Oil Company, [Miscellaneous publications], British Library: General Reference
    Collection 8292.dd.10.
Grindle, G. (1997a). "Fun is Where You Find it." Handwritten memoir (photocopies). In G.A.F. Grindle
    Papers, APAC, British Library: Mss Eur C800.

Grindle, G. (1997b) Letter to Blake, 22 March 1997. In G.A.F. Grindle Papers, APAC, British Library: Mss Eur C800.

India, Pakistan and Burma Association. (1952). "Industry Development: XXIV-Nationalisation", pasted in "Confidential Report on India", Aug 1952, IPBA [India, Pakistan and Burma Association] Papers, Folio 291. APAC, British Library: Mss Eur F158/172.

Tyson, G. (1947). Speech at the Manchester Chamber of Commerce. In File on Geoffrey Tyson, Folio 5 ff, IPBA [India, Pakistan and Burma Association] Papers. APAC, British Library: Mss Eur F158/1062.

Printed Sources

Abdelrehim, N., Linsley, P., & Verma, S. (2017). Understanding risk disclosures as a function of social organisation: A neo-Durkheimian institutional theory-based study of Burmah Oil Company 1971–1976. *The British Accounting Review, 49*(1), 103–116.

Abdelrehim, N., & Toms, S. (2017). The obsolescing bargain model and oil: The Anglo-Iranian Oil Company 1933–1951. *Business History, 59*(4), 554–571.

Aldous, M. (2015). Avoiding negligence and profusion: The failure of the joint-stock form in the anglo-indian tea trade, 1840-1870. *Enterprise & Society, 16*(3), 648–685.

Bamberg, J. H. (1994). *The history of the british petroleum company*, Vol. 2. Cambridge: Cambridge University Press.

Bamberg, J. (2000). *British petroleum and global oil, 1950–1975.* Cambridge: Cambridge University Press.

Banerjee, S., & Linstead, S. (2004). Masking subversion: Neocolonial embeddedness in anthropological accounts of indigenous management. *Human Relations, 57*(2), 221–247.

Banerjee, S., & Prasad, A. (2008). Introduction to the special issue on 'Critical reflections on management and organizations: A postcolonial perspective'. *Critical Perspectives on International Business, 4*(2/3), 90–98.

Basu, A. (2001). *G.L. Mehta: A many splendoured man.* New Delhi: Concept Publishing Company.

Bear, L. (1994). Miscegenations of modernity: Constructing European respectability and race in the Indian railway colony, 1857-1931. *Women's History Review, 3*(4), 531–548.

Benedict, C. (2011). *Golden-Silk smoke: A history of tobacco in China, 1550–2010.* Berkeley, Los Angeles and London: University of California Press.

Black, B. C. (2014). *Crude reality: petroleum in world history.* Rowman & Littlefield, Plymouth, UK.

Boussebaa, M., & Brown, A. D. (2017). Englishization, identity regulation and imperialism. *Organization Studies, 38*(1), 7–29.

Boussebaa, M., & Morgan, G. (2014). Pushing the frontiers of critical international business studies: The multinational as a neo-imperial space. *Critical Perspectives on International Business, 10*(1/2), 96–106.

Boussebaa, M., Sinha, S., & Gabriel, Y. (2014). Englishization in offshore call centers: A postcolonial perspective. *Journal of International Business Studies, 45*(9), 1152–1169.

Bradley, R. L. (1996). *Oil, gas & government: The US experience.* Vol. 2. Lanham, Md., and Washington, DC: Rowman and Littlefield Publishers and the Cato Institute.

Bucheli, M. (2008). Negotiating under the Monroe Doctrine: Weetman Pearson and the origins of US control of Colombian oil. *Business History Review, 82*(03), 529–553.

Bucheli, M. (2010). Major trends in the historiography of the Latin American oil industry. *Business History Review, 84*(2), 339–362.

Bud-Frierman, L., Godley, A., & Wale, J. (2010). Weetman Pearson in Mexico and the emergence of a British oil major, 1901–1919. *Business History Review, 84*(02), 275–300.

Corley, T. A. B. (1988). *A history of the Burmah Oil Company:1924–66,* Vol. 2. London: Heinemann.

Corley, T.A.B. (2006). Cargill, David Sime (1826–1904). In *Oxford dictionary of national biography.* Oxford: Oxford University Press. Retrieved June 8, 2017, from http://www.oxforddnb.com/view/article/47989

Cornelius, P., Van de Putte, A., & Romani, M. (2005). Three decades of scenario planning in shell. *California Management Review, 48*(1), 92–109.

Decker, S. (2005). Decolonising Barclays Bank DCO? corporate Africanisation in Nigeria, 1945–69. *The Journal of Imperial and Commonwealth History, 33*(3), 419–440.

Decker, S. (2010). Postcolonial transitions in Africa: Decolonization in West Africa and present day South Africa. *Journal of Management Studies, 47*(5), 791–813.

Duran, X., & Bucheli, M. (2017). Holding up the empire: Colombia, American oil interests, and the 1921 Urrutia-Thomson Treaty. *The Journal of Economic History, 77*(1), 251–284.

Evans, P. (1946). The oilfields of India and Burma. *Journal of the Royal Society of Arts, 94*(4717), 369–379.

Economic Times. (2017a). Bharat Petroleum Corporation Ltd. Retrieved June 10, 2017, from http:// economictimes.indiatimes.com/oil-india-ltd/infocompanyhistory/companyid-11941.cms

Economic Times. (2017b). Oil India Ltd. Retrieved June 10, 2017, from http://economictimes.indiatimes. com/oil-india-ltd/infocompanyhistory/companyid-4547.cms.

Evenett, S. J. (2003). *The cross border mergers and acquisitions wave of the late 1990s.* NBER working paper. Cambridge, MA: NBER.

Financial Times. (1974). Burmah oil completes signal purchase, January 29, 24.

Frenkel, M., & Shenhav, Y. (2006). From binarism back to hybridity: A postcolonial reading of management and organization studies. *Organization Studies, 27*(6), 855–876.

Gopinath, C., & Prasad, A. (2013). Toward a critical framework for understanding MNE operations: Revisiting Coca-Cola's exit from India. *Organization, 20*(2), 212–232.

Grace's Guide Ltd. (2017). 'BP', Grace's Guide to British industrial history. Retrieved June 9, 2017, from http://www.gracesguide.co.uk/BP

Guha, R. (2011). *India after Gandhi: The history of the world's largest democracy.* London: Pan.

Heenan, D. A., & Perlmutter, H. V. (1979). *Multinational organizational development: A social architectural approach.* Reading, Massachusetts: Addison-Wesley.

Horesh, N. (2014). *Shanghai's bund and beyond: British banks, banknote issuance, and monetary policy in China, 1842–1937.* New Haven, Conn: Yale University Press.

Jones, G. (1981). *State and the emergence of the british oil industry.* Palgrave Macmillan, London.

Jones, G. (1995). *British multinational banking, 1830–1990.* Oxford: Oxford University Press.

Jones, G. (2015). *Multinationals and global capitalism: From the nineteenth to the twenty first century.* Oxford: OUP Press.

Kling, B. B. (1966). The origin of the managing agency system in India. *Journal of Asian Studies, 26*(1), 37–47.

Kopp, R. (1994). International human resource policies and practices in Japanese, European, and United States multinationals. *Human Resource Management, 33*(4), 581–599.

Lala, R. M. (1981). *The creation of wealth: The Tata story* (paperback ed.). Bombay: IBH.

Lakshman, S., Lakshman, C., & Estay, C. (2017). The relationship between MNCs' strategies and executive staffing. *International Journal of Organizational Analysis, 25*(2), 233–250.

Lubinski, C. (2014). Liability of foreignness in historical context: German business in preindependence India (1880–1940). *Enterprise & Society, 15*(4), 722–758.

Marsh, S. (2007). Anglo-American crude diplomacy: Multinational oil and the iranian oil crisis, 1951–53. *Contemporary British History, 21*(1), 25–53.

McCosh, A.M., & Earl, M. J. (1978). Burmah Oil Company. In *Accounting control and financial strategy.* London: Palgrave Macmillan.

Michailova, S., Piekkari, R., Storgaard, M., & Tienari, J. (in press). Rethinking ethnocentrism in international business research. *Global Strategy Journal, 7* (4), 335-353.

Misra, M. (1999). *Business, race, and politics in British India, c. 1850-1960.* Oxford: Clarendon.

Mollan, S. (2012). International correspondent networks: Asian and British banks in the twentieth century. In S. Nishimura, T. Suzuki, & R. Michie (Eds.), *The origins of international banking in Asia: The nineteenth and twentieth centuries* (pp. 217–229). Oxford: Oxford University Press.

Morris, J. (2016). 'Cultivating the African': Barclays DCO and the decolonisation of business strategy in Kenya, 1950–78. *Journal of Imperial and Commonwealth History, 44*(4), 649–671.

Oonk, G. (2001). Motor or millstone? The managing agency system in Bombay and Ahmedabad, 1850-1930. *Indian Economic and Social History Review, 38*(4), 419–452.

Pant, A., & Ramachandran, J. (2017). Navigating identity duality in multinational subsidiaries: A paradox lens on identity claims at Hindustan Unilever 1959–2015. *Journal of International Business Studies, 48*(6), 664–692.

Patwardhan, M. S. (1986). *Oil and other multinationals in India.* Bombay: Popular Prakashan.

Patwardhan, M. S. (1991). *Cameos from a manager's life and times.* Bombay: Bombay Management Association.

Perlmutter, H. V. (1968). Social architectural problems of the multinational firm. *International Executive, 10*, 14–16.

Perlmutter, H. V. (1969). The tortuous evolution of the multinational corporation. *Columbia Journal of World Business, 4*(1), 9–18.

Piramal, G. (1998a). *Business legends.* New Delhi: Viking.

Piramal, G. (1998b). *Business Maharajas.* London: Penguin.

Prasad, A., & Qureshi, T. (2017). Race and racism in an elite postcolonial context: Reflections from investment banking. *Work, employment and society, 31*(2), 352–362.

Prasad, A. (2003). *Postcolonial theory and organizational analysis: A critical engagement.* New York, NY: Palgrave Macmillan US.

Rachman, G. (2016). *Easternisation: War and peace in the Asian century.* New York, NY: Random House.

Ramnath, A. (2016). Industrial Experts in the Age of Indianisation: The European Engineering Firms of Calcutta, 1914-47. Working paper presented at Delhi, as part of the mid-term workshop of the project "ENGIND", supported by the French National Research Agency.

Ramnath, A. (2017). *The birth of an Indian profession: Engineers, industry, and the state, 1900–47.* Delhi: Oxford University Press.

Ray, R. K. (1982 [1979]). *Industrialization in India: Growth and conflict in the private corporate sector 1914-47.* Delhi: Oxford University Press.

Rowlinson, M., & Delahaye, A. (2009). The cultural turn in business history. *Entreprises et histoire, 2,* 90–110.

Smith, A. (2016). The winds of change and the end of the Comprador System in the Hongkong and Shanghai Banking Corporation. *Business History, 58*(2), 179–206.

Srinivas, N. (2013). Could a subaltern manage? Identity work and habitus in a colonial workplace. *Organization Studies, 34*(11), 1655–1674.

Supreme Court 161205.

Taylor, G. D. (2015). Under (Canadian) cover: Standard Oil (NJ) and the International Petroleum Company in Peru and Colombia, 1914–1948. *Management & Organizational History, 10*(2), 153–169.

The Economist. £90 Million Poser for Burmah. June 29, 1963; pg. 1398; Issue 625.

The Economist. Oil and Mr Malaviya. January 28, 1961; pg. 349; Issue 6127.

The Economist. Reagan versus Gandhi. August 29, 1981; pg. 66; Issue 7200.

The Economist. Now It's India. 5 December 1970.

Talbot, I. (2012). *Pakistan: A modern history.* London: Hurst.

Thornton, S. E. (2015). *The history of oil exploration in the Union of Myanmar.* International Conference and Exhibition, Melbourne, Australia. Abstract. Retrieved from http://library.seg.org/doi/abs/10.1190/ice2015-2210594

Tung, R. (1982). Selection and training procedures of U.S., European, and Japanese Multinationals. *California Management Review, 25*(1), 57–71.

Uche, C. U. (2012). British government, British businesses, and the indigenization exercise in post-independence Nigeria. *Business History Review, 86*(04), 745–771.

Vassiliou, M. S. (2009). *The A to Z of the petroleum industry.* Lanham, Toronto, and Plymouth, UK: Scarecrow Press.

Venn, F. (2016). In pursuit of national security: The Foreign Office and middle eastern oil, 1908–39. In J. Fisher, E.G.H. Peadliu, & R. Smith (Eds.), *The foreign office, commerce and british foreign policy in the twentieth century* (pp. 69–87). Palgrave Macmillan UK.

Verma, S., & Abdelrehim, N. (2016). Oil multinationals and governments in post-colonial transitions: Burmah Shell, the Burmah Oil Company and the Indian state 1947–70. *Business History, 59*(3), 342–361.

Webster, A., Bosma, U., & de Melo, J., eds. (2015). *Commodities, ports and asian maritime trade since 1750.* Springer.

Westwood, R. I., & Jack, G. (2007). Manifesto for a post-colonial international business and management studies: A provocation. *Critical perspectives on international business, 3*(3), 246–265.

White, N. J. (2004). *British business in post-colonial Malaysia, 1957-70: Neo-colonialism Or Disengagement?* Routledge.

Yacob, S., & White, N. J. (2010). The 'unfinished business' of Malaysia's decolonisation: The origins of the Guthrie 'dawn raid'. *Modern Asian Studies, 44*(05), 919–960.

Yergin, D. (2011). *The prize: The epic quest for oil, money & power.* New York, NY: Simon and Schuster.

Getting together, living together, thinking together: Management development at Tata Sons 1940–1960

Swapnesh K. Masrani, Linda Perriton🆔 and Alan McKinlay

ABSTRACT

This contribution analyses internal management development activities at Tata Sons during the 1940s and 1950s in India. The existing literature has concentrated on the establishment of management education programmes at universities, and our understanding of in-company managerial training and development activities remains very limited. The contribution challenges the commonly held assumption that the American influence on Indian higher education in the post-war period was decisive in shaping management education in general. After 1947, Tata Sons continued to look to Great Britain for management development models to build the internal capacities and management culture that would make governing a diversified business group practical.

Introduction

Management education in India is widely considered to have formally commenced in 1953, with the opening of the first Indian Business School – the Indian Institute of Social Welfare and Business Management (Jha & Kumar, 2011). This first university-led initiative was soon followed by other degree programmes offered by the Universities of Delhi, Bombay and Madras in 1955, and Andhra in 1957. These early developments in providing formal degrees in management – and the later establishment of the Indian Institute of Management in Ahmedabad and Kolkata – have dominated the scholarly discussion of the development of Indian managers since independence in 1947 (Bandyopadhyay, 1991; Bhattacharya, 2010; D'mello, 1999; Matthai, 1980; Saha, 2012; Sahu, 1991; Sheth, 1991). The interest in the development of, in particular, the Indian Institutes of Management has been in relation to the involvement of the Ford Foundation and the extent of local decision-making about management education approaches, and the degree to which establishing American educational principles were conditions for financial aid (Cooke, 2004, 2006; Cooke and Alcadipani 2015; Kipping, Engwall, & Üsdiken, 2008; Sancheti, 1986; Srinivas 2008; Srinivas, 2012).

Post-colonial perspectives on management education have added an important element of critique to the story of the transfer of management knowledge from the US to other global

Table 1. Tata Staff College timetable. session one, week two (17-2-56 to 24-2-56).

Time	Friday 17-2-56	Saturday 18-2-56	Sunday 19-2-56	Monday 20-2-56	Tuesday 21-2-56	Wednesday 22-2-56	Thursday 23-2-56	Friday 24-2-56
9.15 am to 10.45 am	History of Industrial Medicine & Policies of Industrial Health Dept Dr H.P. Dastur	Accountancy Mr M.P Mistri	Annual accounts of stock companies Mr H.D Katrak	Effective Public Relations Mr F.S Mulla	Role of the Engineer in the Factory Mr C.R Rao	Cost Accountancy Mr S.N. Mathur	Industrial Relations & Personnel Management Mr M.R Masani	FREE DAY
10.45 am to 11.15 am	BREAK FOR COFFEE							FREE DAY
11.15 am to 12.45 pm	Financing the expansion of limited companies Mr N.B Danver	Medical aid, Environmental Hygeine & Welfare Work Dr H.P. Dastur	Mental Hygiene and research work Dr H.P. Dastur	Annual accounts of joint stock companies Mr H.D Katrak	Cost Accountancy Mr S.N Mathur	Industrial Relations and Personnel Management Mr M.R Masani	Early days of the steel company Miss B.J.M Cursetjee	
1pm to 2.15 pm	LUNCH							
2.30 pm to 4 pm	Group Discussion: 'Case Study of an actual event on the shopfloor' Dr H.P. Dastur	Group Discussion: 'A General Problem' Dr H.P. Dastur	Talk & Discussion 'Importance of responsibilities and attitudes in an industrial organisation' Mr B.J. Stedman	Visit to the National Defence Academy, Khardakvasla	Discussion of draft report: Topic 1	Discussion on collective bargaining, Mr M.R Masani	Finalising the report: Topic 1	
4.00 pm	TEA	Service records and promotion procedures in the Railways Mr K.C. Bakhle	TEA	TEA	TEA	TEA	TEA	
4.00pm-7.00 pm	International Labour Organisation Mr N.H Tata / Religion in Industry Prof. Marcus Bach		Some observations on the Personnel Department of Metal Box Co, England Mr. V.E. Bowyer					

7.00 pm	Study Circle "Technique of Executive Control" Ch. XIII	Some aspects of public administration Mr A.D. Gorwala	Historical glimpses of people and places around Bombay and Poona Dr P.M. Joshii
8.30 pm	DINNER		
9.30 pm		Bombay Management Association Mr R. Pierce	Tata personalities of the past Miss B.J.M Cursetjee

North countries before those of the global South. A key point of debate has been the extent to which American management theorists and practice have been privileged, while the existing management praxis of the 'receiving' cultures has been ignored or denigrated (Joy & Poonamallee, 2013). We note the continued importance of examining issues of hybridity, transfer and facadism in the historical accounts of the development of managers, but observe that the majority of such studies have focused on higher education and degree programmes rather than internal management development programmes operated by specific firms. Even when specific firms are considered, for example in Russell's study of Bell Canada, the frame of reference has been the role of management theory rather than the firm itself (Russell, 2015). Undoubtedly, the history of educational institutes is more accessible to researchers than the decisions made by nascent training functions within organisations. However, it is important to examine the history of in-house management development in addition to a nation's higher education provision of management education. The choices made by organisations about how their internal management development programmes were organised, designed and delivered reveals much about institution-building, as well as the transfer of management knowledge globally. Additionally, in internal management development programmes, we see different local adaptations being made in relation to pedagogy, the idea of the manager and practical content.

We focus on the Indian conglomerate Tata and its approach to management development in the 1940s and 1950s. Tata and educational initiatives were closely linked. Tata's founder, Jamsetji Tata, established an educational endowment in 1892 that helped students of all castes to pursue higher education, and his personal wealth also financed the Indian Institute of Science, established in 1911. This was consistent with Tata's business ethic that combined a Parsee stress on societal improvement with an Indian nationalism that emphasised the country's self-reliance (Worden, 2003, pp. 151–2). Later generations continued the connection to education by founding the Tata Insitute of Social Sciences in 1936, which specialised in research on social sciences, public policy and economics (Jha & Kumar, 2011). Tata Iron and Steel executives were also closely involved in the pre-Independence education commissions charged with investigating the options for the establishment of institutes of technology in India (Ganesh, 1979). But it was in the late 1940s, when the company began to gradually move away from the managing agent system, that the company also considered their *internal* training of managers. And whilst, at a national level, Tata were supportive of US educational partnerships, when looking for models of in-house training they preferred to emulate Britain's Administrative Staff College at Henley.

The spread of the Administrative Staff College model is a lesser-examined route in the global spread of management ideas from the Anglo-American centre to the industrialising periphery. Originating from wartime planning in Britain, the residential cohort model is of interest for its pedagogical approach and its ambiguous relationship to the idea that leadership was a matter of character and experience, rather than theory and task mastery. Here, we argue that this pedagogical model was a way of developing managers who operated with high degrees of operational autonomy within Tata's normative framework. In discussing self-managing managers, we can usefully invoke Michel Foucault's concept of governmentality. Governmentality was an unfinished project introduced by Foucault in a series of lectures that has become a vital resource for the understanding of contemporary neo-liberalism (McKinlay & Pezet, 2010). By governmentality, Foucault was enquiring about the genealogy of modern liberal forms of governance; that is, forms of governance that accept the inevitability – indeed, desirability – of individual freedom. Good governance maximises individual freedom *and* the benefits to the population. The benefits and risks of governance are assessed at the level of the population: maximising the responsible decision-making of autonomous individuals becomes the vehicle for effective, efficient governance.

The phasing out of the managing agent system was crucial in triggering Tata's development of cadres of corporate managers and leaders. Management development was a vehicle for establishing a coherent executive culture within a loosely coupled conglomerate.

We begin with an examination of the history of the Administrative Staff College at Henley, its approach to management development and its adoption by, for the most part, Commonwealth nations. The second section examines Tata in the context of the organisational and national developments of the 1940s. Finally, we look at the use of the Henley model by Tata as an adaptation, rather than an adoption, of the Henley model. Here, we stress that Tata's management development was pragmatic in its acceptance of high degrees of operational autonomy for managers and its efforts to construct, rather than impose, a normative framework to regulate leadership practices.

The Administrative Staff College, Henley

The Administrative Staff College, Henley was created as the result of a series of discussions held by the British Government in the last three years of the Second World War. Over a hundred individuals – representing politics, industry, trade unions, the civil service, banking and academia – were involved in discussions about the readiness of British industry for the return to peacetime production. The concern was that 'heavy burdens' would be placed on those individuals who would be moving from departmental management to senior management in the context of post-war recovery (Cornwall-Jones, 1985, p. ix); the college would provide management development opportunities for those managers. Lyndall Urwick was one of the key figures lobbying for the establishment of a national staff college (Brech, Thomson, & Wilson, 2010, pp. 8, 14, 17–18; Wild, 2002). Unsurprisingly, Henley derived much of its pedagogy from military staff colleges, especially the Imperial Defence College. There was a widespread acceptance that military training methods produced results, and that the role of the senior manager was akin to the art of generalship (Nettle, 2014; Ritson & Parker, 2016). But the defining method borrowed from the military colleges was the idea of the 'syndicate', a group of around eight individuals who learn together as a group, sharing their experiences and interpreting theory and ideas in relation to those experiences (Watson, 1984).

Despite the involvement and tacit support of government, Henley was – from its inception – a private, non-profit company, rather than a public body. Keeping Henley outside of the public sector allowed it to remain closely connected to its business sponsors, whilst at the same time being open to civil service and trade union involvement (Guerriero Wilson, 2011). In positioning itself outside of the higher education sector, Henley represented a continuation of British thinking about the basis of managerial effectiveness as necessarily practical rather than theoretical that would not be challenged until the late 1950s (Larson, 2008; Locke, 1989, pp. 155–6). Henley was, in effect, a superior sort of residential offering in the same practical, experiential format favoured by a number of professional associations that existed in the inter-war period. Professional associations such as the Office Management Association, the Institute of Industrial Administration, the Institute of Labour Management, the Works Management Association ran night-schools and offered diplomas related to distinct areas of business (Guerriero Wilson, 2015). The post-war push would be to amalgamate many of these separate provisions into a single broadly recognised Diploma of Management. However, at this time, management education remained the prerogative of the professional associations, the private sector, and with a strong emphasis on practitioner knowledge (Guerriero Wilson, 2011; Roper, 1999).

Dedicated studies of Henley, whether celebratory or critical, say little about the genesis of the pedagogical design decisions of the early 1950s (Allen, 1979; Cornwall-Jones, 1985; Dimock, 1956; Vernardakis, 1982). However, the basic design of the General Management Course is clear. It was an 11-week course, which comprised 10 or 11 men and women in a syndicate, with each course cohort comprising six syndicates. The cohort was known as a session. The Henley programme was considered very short compared to programmes with similar aims, albeit with different pedagogical models, that lasted up to nine months (Cornwall-Jones, 1985). The preferred mix of participants on each session was outlined by Cornwall-Jones, a facilitator on the programme from 1950 to 1957, as individuals from the civil service (6), nationalised industries (8–9), private industry (42–4), overseas – mostly Commonwealth nations (6), local government (1–2), and armed services (1–2). The College took great care to select the members of each syndicate with the aim that they would be able to share different experiences, and to challenge each other:

> [the differences] … would invite, if not compel, the individual to compare his [sic] knowledge, his experience, his outlook, his style, and his capacity … to find out that many of their problems would not be so different from, and indeed would be similar … to his own … Discoveries like these, as they unfolded in the individual member's mind, would broaden his sympathy and quicken his perception, surely leading to a better understanding of other people's way of life and point of view. (Cornwall-Jones, 1985, p. 4)

Before each session, the subjects were reviewed, tasks revised and guest speakers allocated. Each syndicate operated under the chairmanship of one of its members, and a different chair and secretary was appointed for each separate subject covered by the course (Dimock, 1956). Over the 11-week programme, each member of the syndicate would therefore take the chair; and be responsible for co-ordinating the task allocated to the syndicate, ensuring its completion in a fixed time period. The chair oversaw the discussions that went into each project, and reported back to the rest of the session. Each syndicate was allocated a facilitator. The role of the facilitator was not to teach, but to help the syndicate achieve the learning embedded in the subject tasks. The facilitator briefed the chair, but was forbidden to discuss the substance of the subject. The 'higher responsibility', as Cornwall-Jones explained it, was a commitment to preparing the syndicate members to make use of their own talents and to learn as much as they could from the experience (Cornwall-Jones, 1985). Cornwall-Jones experienced a repeated anxiety about what this meant in practice, and developed a rough code of behaviour to guide him as to when it might be appropriate to intervene in, rather than just observe, the group. He felt that it was wrong to intervene when things were going well; appropriate to offer his view if asked directly, but not if he thought that the individual or group needed to uncover the information for themselves; but that he was free to ignore these rules 'just because [he] was human' and 'had something to say' (ibid. p. 11).

Group work was central to the Henley experience. But there were also lectures provided to the whole session, evening talks by invited guests, as well as syndicate presentations on the biographies of key industry leaders, or more 'off the cuff' presentations (Cornwall-Jones, 1985). Case studies were also a feature of the curriculum in relation to specific topics. For example, when studying technological change, a syndicate may visit a company to study how they adapted to international competition by upgrading machinery. Henley also had a large library, and subscribed to the key economic and industrial journals of the day (Dimock, 1956). But, the focus of the development was the experience of chairing the syndicate, and the experience of each syndicate member of adjusting to the group dynamics.

> I wanted them to be able to disagree without being disagreeable … I hoped I had an ally in the chairman, who might know more than I about handling people. Often he and some members of the group were discovering that the handling of groups or equals had charms of its own which were new to them, and I did not want to disturb the process of discovery in this more than I did in anything else. (Cornwall-Jones, 1985, p. 15)

The course was, therefore, less concerned with instruction and the transfer of generalisable knowledge than with providing spaces for experiential learning. The balance of cases, lectures and projects was carefully designed to set the conditions for – but not the content of – learning. The emphasis was on using the experience of other syndicate members as a resource to understand and apply knowledge. This was the purpose behind non-directive facilitation of syndicates. The aim of the learning design was to help each participant 'learn, develop and mature on an individual basis' (Allen, 1979, p. 68). As the programme became established, and the interest shifted to explaining how to establish similar colleges throughout the Commonwealth, the emphasis on personal development receded. But the underlying rationale for focusing on learning rather than instruction was that senior management roles required emotional development more than task mastery, i.e. sharing responsibility, dealing with different professional attitudes, and evaluating specialist inputs (Vernardakis, 1982, p. 28).

Making Tata corporate

Tata Sons began operations in 1868 as a trading company. The company was established by Jamsetji Nasarwanji Tata and traded in textiles and other commodities. It soon moved into manufacturing with the purchase of an old textile mill in Bombay. After selling the mill for a profit, Tata formed the Central India Spinning and Weaving Company at Nagpur. The company was renamed the Empress Mill in 1877, and quickly became the pre-eminent textile mill in India. In the early twentieth century Tata created several new companies, i.e. the Taj Hotel (1903), Tata Steel (1907), Tata Hydro Electric Power Supply (1910), Andra Valley Power Supply (1916), Tata Power (1919), and Tata Oil Mills (1917). A merger of India Cements which had been created in 1912 led to the formation of the larger Associated Cements in 1926. After the creation of New India Assurance (1921), the pace of new company creation slowed, with the 1930s seeing the launch of Tata Chemicals in 1939 and Tata Engineering and Locomotive Company in 1945, later renamed Tata Motors (Lala, 1991, pp. 70–74). Structurally, Tata relied on a form of management at a distance that owed much to the managing agent model. In a conglomerate with a strategy of unrelated diversification, after 1947, professional operational managers replaced profit-sharing agents, but continued to exercise high degrees of operational autonomy.

Tata Sons, in common with many Indian business houses, operated as a managing agency. The managing agency system was the most common form of corporate management in India until the 1950s. It was a system that first developed in nineteenth-century India, but was seized upon in London as a way to manage joint stock companies operating in the subcontinent, and whose shareholders had no first-hand knowledge of the business (Kapila & Kapila, 1995; Kling, 1966). Within India, the managing agency system offered families and partnerships, a way to attract capital investment from local banks into basic joint stock companies (Lokanathan, 1935). Often much bigger than the companies they managed, the managing agent's main responsibilities were to guarantee sound management that allowed foreign capital to be raised to finance the company start up, and then manage its day-to-day operations (Kapila & Kapila, 1995). In return, the managing agents were paid a commission, normally a percentage of revenues, sales or profits. Managing agents were accountable to the board of directors of the company that appointed them, and in most cases the agents formed part of the board of the companies they were paid to manage (Rungta, 1970). Tata Sons were instrumental, therefore, in the formation, financing and management of their portfolio of companies by holding the Chairmanship of the board and by appointing a director-in-charge who oversaw operations by working closely with the management. The managing agency model was popular because it was a way of earning income from a company unrelated to investment or profitability, a feature that eventually led to limits being placed on the number of companies that could be controlled by a managing agent in the Companies Act of 1956, and the complete abolition of this model by 1968 (Kapila & Kapila, 1995). The three major Indian managing companies, of which Tata was the largest, adapted to the change in legislation by the purchase of strategic shareholdings, financed by state-owned banks that also held substantial stakes in the same companies (*ibid.*).

The challenges of running organisations that spanned several different industries – from textiles, to hotels, to steel, and motor manufacturing – had become clear to Tata by the mid-1940s. People management problems prompted Jehangir Ratanji Dadabhoy Tata (JRD), who had become Chairman in 1938, to examine a number of personnel management solutions and introduce greater 'professionalism' in a 'co-ordinated' way (Sabavala & Lala, 1986, p. 117; Lala, 1991, p. 196). JRD created Tata Industries in 1945 in anticipation of post-war expansion. All agency contracts from Tata Sons were transferred to this new company. New board members were appointed based on their professional expertise. Tata Industries became the managing agents for all Tata companies: the directors of all Tata companies sat on the Board of Tata Industries (Lala, 1993, p. 292). However, JRD remained concerned about the lack of attention given to the development of individuals who were current, or future, heads of departments, as well as the supply of future managers into the different companies.

> If our operation required the employment of, say, 30,000 machine tools, we would undoubtedly have a special staff or department to look after them, to keep them in repair, replace them when necessary, maintain their efficiency, protect them from damage etc. But when employing 30,000 human beings each with a mind and soul of his own, we seem to have assumed that they would look after themselves and that there was no need for a separate organisation to deal with the human problem involved. (Sabavala & Lala, 1986, p. 117)

Between 1940 and 1960 Tata adopted a centralised and increasingly strategic approach to management development. The prelude was Tata's involvement in national debates about managerial and technical education. From 1954 Tata deployed internal management development programmes (Lala, 1993, p. 292). Tata's experience is unique in the Indian context because it was deeply involved in national policy-making and was one of the handful of firms to initiate and implement systematic internal management developments in the two decades after Independence (Myers, 1958, p. 112).

Management development

The Indian government turned to its major industrial companies when, in the 1940s, it created a range of advisory committees responsible for planning India's new institutions of state and economic development. Tata was deeply embedded in this process. For example, the National Council for Technical Education was established in 1946 under the chairmanship of T.T. Krishnamachari, a newly elected senator, to explore more 'modern' approaches to management education. In turn, in 1948–49, this committee created the Industrial Administration Business and Management (IABM) Committee, chaired by Sir Jehangir Ghandy, general manager of TISCO and a director of Tata Sons. Ghandy's committee reported to the government in 1953, with three main recommendations. First, it suggested the formation of an Administrative Staff College modelled on Henley's Staff College. Second, to establish a Board of Management Studies to consider partnerships and models for university level management education. Third, it recommended the establishment of a National Institute of Management as a standing committee to coordinate all future management education initiatives (Hill, Haynes, & Baumgartel, 1973, pp. 11–13; Myers, 1958, p. 11).

Between the late 1940s and the early 1950s, several Tata executives travelled internationally, examining a range of options for the development of India's managers, and brought that knowledge back into Tata at the time it was considering its own approach to management development. As part of the continuing research into the applicability of the Staff College model to India, the general secretaries of the IABM committee, a civil servant and a Tata employee – Krishna Khosla, Deputy Agent – spent three months at Henley in 1954 studying its methods (TISCO News, 1954). There were further visits to Henley by Tata staff in 1956 and 1957 by the registrar of the Tata Institute of Social Sciences, and also Sir Jehangir Ghandy.

At the same time as Tata executives were involved in advising the Indian government on how to develop a new type of industrial manager for India as a whole, Tata was concerned about the same issue in their own companies. JRD Tata wanted to create the mechanisms for a common and distinctive Tata management culture based on a sense of consensus and authority based on technical knowledge combined with individual leadership (Lala, 1993, p. 292; Lala, 1995, pp. 72–73). Early experiments focused on personnel management rather than management development, notably the efforts to create 'formal and systematic' approaches to recruiting staff into various Tata firms (Bhabha, n/d). Not all those early experiments were successful. The 1948 'Superior Staff Recruitment Committee' initiative, comprised senior executives such as Homi Modi, Ardershir Dalaal, John Matthai and JRD. Little thought was given into how new recruits would be integrated into the organisation and the three people recruited through the initial scheme all left quickly. Undeterred, JRD relaunched the idea in 1954 as the 'Tata Cadre'. Cadre members were encouraged, upon recruitment, to move between different companies and functional areas, before settling down in one of the companies. Since there was no management college that could produce the sort of junior manager that JRD envisaged, he concluded that Tata needed its own management college that promising recruits could join. This became the Tata Administrative Service (TAS), and recruited direct from university graduates.

Tata held its first 'managers' conference and seminar' in 1955. This 'conference' was both a forerunner of more systematic management development projects and continued as a stand-alone event, provided an opportunity for the 'top echelons' of Tata management to 'exchange notes on subjects of mutual interest, pool their wisdom and draw upon others' experiences' (TISCO News, 1962). The conference was designed to include inputs from senior Tata executives, such as JRD, Jehangir Ghandy, H.P. Dastur and Ardeshir Shroff, as well as visiting academics such as Charles A. Myers, from MIT.[1] The initial idea was for the conference to run for up to three days, and each conference addressed a particular company concern and worked towards a set of recommendations that could be actioned. Whilst the directors were brought together by the Management Conference, and the new recruits were inducted via the TAS, there was still an identified gap regarding the development of middle managers. John Matthai and Rustum Choksi pitched the staff college idea to JRD as a place where existing Tata managers would focus on the 'organisation's own character and spirit, its problems and needs', modelled on – but not reproducing – the Henley experience.[2]

The adaptations made to the Henley model by Tata were consistent with the wider managerial views of JRD and his senior management team. JRD was a student of the Human Relations approach, and delivered an address on the subject in Oxford in 1956 (TISCO News, 1956). He referred to social surveys on internal migration patterns, and urban development around large industrial plants such as those of Tata Steel in Jamshedpur. Industrial and urban development were driving social change such as the loosening of the caste system and improving the status of women. Urban development around large plants drove the creation of markets for outlying villages, increased demand for medical treatment, and offered the possibility of fuller social and cultural lives. JRD saw the human relations 'problem' in developing countries like India as being addressed by providing for the basic material needs of workers, providing inside and outside of the factory the means for self-expression and fulfilment; together with the means for personal recognition through advancement and promotion. JRD considered it possible for industry in general, and Tata in particular, to be much more than a source of employment, but also a community, and a way of life (*ibid.*).

Tata managers were integral to JRD's humanist developmental vision. Training within a community of managers combined self-development with a shared experience, and offered the prospect of the career as an economic and moral project. From the late 1940s onwards, the thinking, and experimentation, of Tata's management development programme reflected these principles. For example, the performance rating form that was used to assess managers who entered via the Tata Cadre scheme listed 20 qualities a Tata manager needed to possess, develop and demonstrate. Of the 20 qualities, only two were task related. The rest were concerned with the individual's attitude and demeanour, e.g. 'What degree of intelligence, speed, accuracy, resourcefulness etc. does he show in performing task entrusted to him? How is he on executive skill, viz, given the opportunity can he plan effectively, arrive at workable solutions and put them into practice? (Anonymous, n/d). In terms of 'character', future Tata managers were rated against ideals of 'favourable general impression[s]', and whether they possessed good carriage, manners, poise, courtesy. Stability of emotions was prized and was best demonstrated by the individual's ability to receive criticism and endure set-backs with equanimity. Managers were expected to be respected *and* liked, sympathetic and understanding to others, and able to listen 'without bias'. A manager of the right character would be the sort of person others would naturally accept as a leader. These judgements were to be reached through inspection and were reported narratively. Judgements were searching about the individual's leadership, despite the absence of numerical coding and statistical comparability.

In summary, the Henley model was adopted and then adapted, for three main reasons. First, key decision-makers in Tata were familiar with the Henley approach through their involvement on the working party that was charged with considering how to develop a national administrative staff college. Second, the Henley model offered flexibility through its emphasis on personal development, as opposed to task or specific forms of knowledge. The third, more nuanced, explanation is that the management ideas of JRD Tata led them towards management development that stressed a collective culture, and an emphasis on individual character, self-awareness and personal development.

Tata Staff College

In many ways, the Tata Staff College was a refinement of the Management Conference approach rather than a variant of the TAS. The Tata Staff College was formed in order – in keeping with the Henley approach and JRD's inclinations – to 'cultivate awareness' rather than to 'supply knowledge and information'. It was not 'subjects but people who matter' (Tata Staff College, 1956a). The college would give opportunity for staff of various Tata companies working in different industries and different parts of country for 'getting together, living together, thinking together, and develop a corporate sense' (Matthai, 1956a). It was thought that the 'staff college' would have achieved its aim if it was able to 'send members back to their work' with 'increased awareness of their responsibilities, a greater flexibility of mind, a more informed understanding of public affairs and with readiness and enthusiasm to meet the needs of a changing situation' (Matthai, 1956b).

The Tata Staff College's objectives were to:

(1) Cultivate an awareness of what Tata stands for;
(2) Realise where [Tata] stand in the changed conditions of modern India;
(3) Provide some opportunity for the study of management and business problems at various levels and in relation to the different companies;
(4) Have a forum for discussion and exchange of information and ideas on 'Tata' problems and projects; and thereby
(5) Create a fellowship amongst ourselves. (Choksi, n/d; Tata Staff College, 1957)

The College, formed in 1956, eventually found a permanent home in Pune in 1966, after a somewhat peripatetic existence. Adopting the residential model from Henley, the property in Pune was an impressive, and extensive, country home built for a wealthy family, set amongst 15 acres of landscaped grounds and capable of housing up to 60 students and staff. The college was expected to function in the cooler season, i.e. the period between December and February, when Pune experienced milder weather conditions thought most conducive to education.

The core educational staff at the college was envisaged to be small, just three full-time facilitators. The main input was to be provided by senior officers from Tata who were identified as having the specialised knowledge to deliver lectures, while always returning to general questions of leadership. As with the Tata 'management conferences', Tata directors and guest speakers would also be invited to address the course attendees. There would be two course 'sessions' of four to five weeks duration in each season, with approximately 12 participants attending each session. A session was limited to 12 participants as this permitted 'close touch' among them and with College staff and Tata's senior officers. Participants would usually be between 30 and 40 years of age, with reasonable levels of managerial experience, and drawn from across various Tata companies. It was the responsibility of individual companies to nominate staff identified as on the cusp of promotion to senior operational roles.

The primary method of training was Henley's 'syndicate method', but in a 'simplified form' (Tata Staff College, 1956a). The training combined lectures and discussion. A wide range of subjects were to be studied, not all of them related to the commercial interests of the Tata Group. Participants on the early sessions had access to books from Tata's Economics and Statistics Department, as well as the Tata Institute of Social Sciences. Programme administrators ensured that books on history, politics and literature were stocked 'since the purpose of the training [was] for more effective service in Tata' (Choksi, n/d). This signalled that management development was something other than technical training. The resources for aspiring leaders were not restricted to training manuals or their practical experience. The schedule for each day of the session comprised three time blocks. Mornings were focused on 'instructional' and commercial topics given by senior Tata executives, with time afterwards for discussion. These were led by senior Tata executives. The block after lunch was dedicated to 'study circles, group discussions ... and even more light hearted extempore speaking'. The evening session, which included dinner, was given over to guest speakers to 'stimulating and enlightening' talk by visiting experts such as Lyndall Urwick, government ministers, and Tata directors, including JRD (Tata Staff College, 1956a). As at Henley, there was a strong emphasis on group assignments. It was expected that this would provide each participant an opportunity of 'initiating and leading discussion or preparing a report'. The underlying belief was that best training is provided by 'contact with one another'. As the session was residential, there was also time provided for activities that would promote the 'art of living together' (Matthai, 1956a; Tata Staff College, 1956c). The temporary community of the Pune college was a metaphor for the permanent community of Tata management.

Sessions one to six: 1956–1960

The first session of the General Management Course was held at the Turf Club, Pune, with 18 participants drawn from eight separate Tata companies. Participants were aged between 32 and 48 years of age, and all were male (Tata Staff College, 1956b). The timetable of the first session (see Figure 1) suggests Tata made only minor changes to the Henley syndicate model. The adoption of the Henley model as a direct result of Khosla's attendance at Henley was acknowledged in the public report of the first session, as was Khosla's role as one of the programme's facilitators. The comments taken from the participants' evaluation forms noted that:

> Mr Khosla (of TISCO) saw the syndicate system in operation at Henley and adapted it to our needs ...

> At Henley, Mr.=Khosla told us, there were often sharp differences of opinion in a syndicate but these were usually ironed out around the College bar – a facility that could not be made available to us at Poona. (Tata Staff College, 1956b, pp. 6–7)

In practice, given that each syndicate appeared to work in exactly the same fashion as it did in Henley, although minus the bar, the adaptation that Khosla made in terms of design was in only having two set syndicates in the programme, which meant that there were fewer opportunities for each participant to lead a syndicate through an extended task and/or to act as secretary. The syndicate teaching model gained general approval:

[Syndicate work] is based on the theory that management cannot be taught as a subject. Management could only be learnt by doing management, i.e. by self-instruction. This method gives incentive to and develops administrative skills.

The mental discipline and training that one acquires from working in a syndicate cannot be over-stressed ... [syndicate work] provides training in the art of working with and through people, of conducting business and integrating differences through the conference method. (Tata Staff College, 1956b, p. 7)

The participants' approval was not altogether surprising, since John Matthai's opening remarks to the first session stressed the value of syndicate work, a message reinforced throughout the course. JRD Tata's final evening address also stressed the importance of syndicates to Tata's management development system. Despite the assertions that management could not be taught as a subject, the emphasis in the first session remained somewhat skewed towards instruction rather than self-discovery sessions.

But whilst the syndicate method might have been a pedagogical decision at Henley, it was a relational decision on the part of Tata and of Matthai, Choksi and JRD Tata. Syndicates were used extensively across the range of middle- and senior-management conferences, training courses and events (Tata Staff College, 1953, 1962, 1964) And all were deployed with the intention that the syndicate method would foster closer relationships, and eventually a common management culture, across all the Tata companies. That the individual *was* and would remain a leader within Tata was signified by their participation in the development programme. Equally, being defined as a leader signified their autonomy, agency and responsibility for modernising the organisation (Jacques, 1996, pp. 114–115). In his address to the first session, JRD Tata insisited that:

he recognised the difficulties faced the organisers in an experiment of this kind ... but the need to establish closer relationships in such an organisation was all the greater. The conference method, which had been adopted in recent years, and the college plan were means to that end. He asked members to carry back to their own places of work the message of fellowship and the gospel of good human relations ... It should be the constant endeavour of sound management to make men at all levels feel that they 'belonged'. (Tata Staff College, 1956b, p. 9)

One other element of the Henley model that Tata adapted was the programme's emphasis on the discussion and study of liberal arts subjects. Session one had invited Marcus Bach, professor of religion and philosophy at Iowa State University, to talk to participants about the role of religion in industry. But subsequent sessions expanded on this element of topics of general interest, science and the arts and humanities. Session six, for example, included discussions on 'Life in central India ca. BC 1000', 'Indian Paintings' and 'International Locust Control'. Suggestions for topics to be covered in subsequent sessions included space conquest, Everest expeditions, and 'women's problems' (Anonymous, 1962). Again, it was an element of the pedagogical design that was explained at the start of the sessions, most notably by John Matthai at the start of session two:

You cannot isolate business from the rest of a community's life ... I am one of those who believe that unless a certain measure of general education is combined with scientific and technical education, you are not fitting yourself properly ... I was very much interested to know that in a place like MIT today, some time is allocated in their syllabus for subjects of a purely cultural character...It seems to me that American educationalists and business men have discovered almost instinctively the needs for integrating the various activities of a community together. (Matthai n/d)

And again at the start of session three:

You may question why such subjects as economic planning … important landmarks in philo-sophical and political thought, and anthropology, which have little bearing on your day-to-day work, should be included on this course… we should endeavour to combine science and culture, and broaden our mind and vision, and seek fullness of life, which alone can lead to wisdom and happiness … I might add that it is for the same reason that the study of humanities receives spe-cial emphasis in engineering courses in the USA. At the Massachusetts Institute of Technology, for example. (Tata Staff College, 1957, p. 9)

The greater part of the papers held by the Tata Central Archive on the Staff College in this period relate to reports of, and reports on, the first session. The 18 participants were inter-viewed at the start of the session, at the mid-way point, and two 90-minute 'looking ahead' sessions were included in the last week of the session designed to provide feedback to the college and executives. Overall, the course was judged to have been a success – although three participants had withdrawn shortly before the start of the course and the resulting loss of fee income meant that the course incurred a loss. Thirty senior officers had attended the session, 11 directors, and 20 external guest speakers. 'Not much importance' was attached to the somewhat uneven distribution of individuals who attended the first session in terms of their age and positions. The report stated that because of the varied companies within the group, varying salaries, and the difficulties of releasing some staff, it was likely that there would always be some clustering of age and companies. Both the participants and the staff reported that the intensive first week of the course and then a gradual tapering off of the workload was important, although the absence of recreation or physical activity was con-sidered mistaken.

The subsequent sessions had a greater emphasis on shared recreation. Session six included time for a participants' cricket match. Increasing the time for cultural discussions, and preparation time for syndicate work were matters of degree, not principle. Participants reported that they felt involved in decision-making about the programme, although the published timetable renders this claim suspect. Perhaps the participants' perception of their involvement came from their sense that they were encouraged to criticise and grumble at design decisions. However, the general view of the participants was that the basic design of the course was sound and it was largely matters of internal planning and financing that required discussion: how best to expand the programme and to maximise the involvement of Tata directors. The overall model for the General Management Course remained stable throughout the 1950s and well into the 1960s. When the college had a permanent home, Tata could look to providing specialist training, but this was to complement the cultural thrust of the inaugural management development programmes (Tata Staff College, 1956c).

The Tata programme deliberately chose not to offer specialised functional training. For Tata and the programme's participants, the course was valuable, but that value was intan-gible. In this sense, Tata's management development was geared towards developing the norms that would guide the actions of senior operational managers beyond the direct control of Tata's corporate centre. Developing a normative framework for Tata was both a recognition of the practical limits of central control and a practical response to the inherent difficulties of managing at a distance in a sprawling conglomerate.

Conclusion

Organisational histories that focus on the development of their management population, and the ideas and pedagogy that support them, are largely missing from the academic field of business history. This absence is regrettable, both for the loss of insight such firm-level studies would provide for the field of human resource development, and also for the complementary information they could provide in mapping the global spread of management ideas and practices in the twentieth century. Without fine-grained studies of management development, we are left with only histories of institutional management education as a proxy for an understanding of how industry was developing its managers in-house.

We stress this element of the Tata approach in order to put both the adoption *and* adaptation of the Henley model in context. The Administrative Staff College at Henley was a much-imitated model. From the first, Henley welcomed participants from international companies, and received a steady stream of interested visitors with whom it was happy to discuss its experience of running and positioning the programme. Requests to release staff to help establish similar institutions in – predominantly – Commonwealth countries were refused on workload grounds until 1953, when staff were occasionally released for extended periods to help at national level (Cornwall-Jones, 1985). There was no policy that supported the release of staff to help individual companies set up internal management training centres. Tata benefitted from their involvement with several Indian government study trips, committees and planning bodies on the subject of national management development and education after 1947. They were able to study models of management development around the world, and to send representatives on courses such as those run by Henley.

But Tata were selective in their use of models that they saw in operation in Britain and the US. Adopting educational models for use in your own organisation is not the same process as negotiating partnerships at national level, or subject to the same dynamics in terms of funding and dealing with organisations such as the Ford Foundation. There was, in the early 1950s, a period of experimentation and ad hoc arrangements in human resource development within Tata, as with the short-lived 'Superior Staff Recruitment Committee' and early management conferences. The exposure to Henley, and its syndicate idea, was useful because it matched the existing management philosophy of JRD Tata rather than influencing it. The syndicate style allowed for the inclusion of local technical concerns and pre-occupations whilst reinforcing JRD Tata's own views on the primacy of character, belonging and self-development within a specific cultural context. Tata's management development programme was based on adaptation, not adoption.

In Foucault, liberalism encounters the intractable problem of how to avoid governing 'too much' (Foucault, 2007, p. 319). In Tata, by contrast, to govern was to accept the practical limits of centralisation in a conglomerate built on the extreme decentralisation of the managing agency system. Equally, accepting organisational decentralisation was consistent with the Tata's fusion of religious and nationalist ideology and its emphasis on self-reliance. For the individual participant, Tata's management development had a dual purpose. First, the recognition and articulation of one's personal experience of leadership. Second, exposure to the emerging norms of Tata as a modernising organisation and how these norms were assessed. Through management development, the manager had to develop new 'arts of self-government' and understand that these were the ways that defined his relations to others and to the organisation (Foucault, 1997, p. 88; Foucault, 2005, p. 252). Tata's management development was consistent with human relations; that is, to consider leadership as a set of individual qualities whose effectiveness are maximised if these were deployed consistently and in a contextually sensitive manner (Miller & Rose, 1990, p. 26). Leadership was, then, no longer to be thought of solely as an individual asset, but also as a collective and organisational resource. Tata's formal system of accountability was incapable of overcoming functional and spatial distance. Tata's management development programme was predicated upon a recognition that spatial and organisational distances could not be collapsed through administrative control from the centre. Developing managers to operate within normative parameters was also the pursuit of a more efficient form of managing Tata as a whole. Tata's management development programme was a way of understanding the diverse vocabularies of managing operationally while developing a shared ontology of management in Tata. The making of 'Tata cadres' was the construction of reliable, responsible proxies for direct personal control from headquarters. Creating 'Tata cadres' was a necessary precondition to developing and centralising knowledge of managers and management practices at the organisation's operational peripheries (Scott, 1998).

Tata's management development stressed the need for the individual to improve their self-awareness as necessary if they were to improve his/her effectiveness as a leader. Syndicate conversations around participants' experience of leading were inherently performative. Debates about common experiences of leadership inevitably carried practical imperatives about *how* the everyday behaviours of leadership. The management cadre became the target of government, simultaneously an object of knowledge *and* a means of government. Participation in conversations about leadership served to enlist the individual in the making of a new language of governing the self, others and Tata as an organisation.

Notes

1. Charles Myers visited India between 1954 and 1955 to study problems facing labour, management and government in the industrial development of the Indian economy. The project was part of a Ford Foundation funded project on Inter-University study of labour problems in economic development.
2. While other Tata executives had visited Henley in early 1950s, John Matthai and Rustom Choksi were responsible for organising the Tata Staff College. Dr .John Matthai received education in law and economics. He joined Tata Sons in 1940 and assumed directorship in 1944. He was on the board of several companies managed by Tata Sons. In addition, he held various government posts including finance member of the Viceroy's executive council in 1946 and India's finance minister from 1949 to 1950. In 1950s he held brief stints as Vice Chancellor of University of Bombay and a member of the first governing board of Administrative Staff College of India. Professor Rustom Choksi was a director of Tata Sons and Tata Industries. Between 1950s and 1980s he was a key decision-maker at the Sir Dhorabji Tata Trust.

Acknowledgements

We would like to thank the two archivists at Tata, Swarup Sengupta and Rajendraprasad Narla, for their guidance, encouragement and patience while conducting this research.

Disclosure statement

No potential conflict of interest was reported by the authors.

Funding

This work was supported by the University of Stirling Seed Funding.

ORCID

Linda Perriton ⓘ http://orcid.org/0000-0002-9109-5767

References

Aldcroft, D. (1992). *Education, training and economic performance*. Manchester, NH: Manchester University Press.
Allen, B. (1979). The administrative staff college, Henley. *Education + Training, 21*(3), 68–69.
Anonymous. (1962). Memo to D Malegamwala, July 26, Box 998, Tata Staff College, Tata Central Archives.
Anonymous. (n/d). Merit Rating Form, Box 998, Tata Central Archives.
Bandyopadhyay, R. (1991). Indian management education: Need for a constructive debate. *Economic and Political Weekly,* 118–M122.
Bhabha, J. J. (n/d). TAS Facilitation Function, Speech by J J Bhabha, Box 998, Tata Central Archives.
Bhattacharya, A. (2010). Mismanagement of Indian management education. *Economic and Political Weekly,* 14–17.
Brech, E., Thomson, A., & Wilson, J. (2010). *Lyndall Urwick, Management Pioneer*. Oxford: Oxford University Press.
Choksi, R. (n/d). Staff College: A Preliminary Note, from Rustom Choksi to John Matthai, Box 998, Tata Central Archives.
Cooke, B. (2004). The managing of the (third) world. *Organization, 11,* 603–629.

Cooke, B. (2006). The Cold War origin of action research as managerialist co-optation. *Human Relations.,* *59*(5), 665–693.

Cooke, B., & Alcadipani, R. (2015). Toward a global history of management education: The case of the Ford Foundation and the São Paulo School of Business Administration, Brazil. *Academy of Management Learning & Education, 14*(4), 482–499.

Cornwall-Jones, A. T. (1985). *Education for leadership: The international administrative staff colleges 1948–1984*. London: Routledge and Kegan Paul.

D'mello, B. (1999). Management education: A critical appraisal. *Economic and Political Weekly,* 169–176.

Dimock, M. E. (1956). The administrative staff college: Executive development in government and industry. *American Political Science Review, 50*(1), 166–176.

Foucault, M. (1997). On genealogy and ethics: An overview of a work in progress, in Foucault, M. and Rabinow, PD (Ed) Essential works of Foucault 1954–1984, vol. 1; Ethics: Subjectivity and truth, pp. 253–280, New York: Penguin Books.

Foucault, M. (2005). *The hermeneutics of the subject*. New York NY: Picador.

Foucault, M. (2007). *Security, territory, population*. Basingstoke: Palgrave.

Ganesh, S. R. (1979). Collaborative institution building: A critique of three experiences in higher education. *Vikalpa, 4*(2), 161–176.

Guerriero Wilson, R. (2015). The loss of balance between the art and science of management: Observations on the British experience of education for management in the 20th century. *Journal of Management Education, 39*(1), 16–35.

Hill, T., Haynes, W., & Baumgartel, H. (1973). *Instituion building in India: A study of international collaboration in management education*. Cambridge, Mass: Harvard University Press.

Jacques, R. (1996). *Manufacturing the employee: Management knowledge from the 19th to the 21st Centuries*. London: Sage.

Jha, S., & Kumar, M. (2011). Management education in India: Issues & challenges. *Journal of Management & Public Policy, 3*(1), 5–14.

Joy, S., & Poonamallee, L. (2013). Cross-cultural teaching in globalized management classrooms: Time to move from functionalist to postcolonial approaches? *Academy of Management Learning & Education, 12*(3), 396–413.

Kapila, R., & Kapila, U. (1995). *Understanding India's economic reforms* (Vol. 3). New Delhi: Acdemic Foundation.

Kipping, M., Engwall, L., & Üsdiken, B. (2008). Preface: The transfer of management knowledge to peripheral countries. *International Studies of Management & Organization, 38*(4), 3–16.

Kling, B. B. (1966). The origin of the managing agency system in India. *The Journal of Asian Studies, 26*(1), 37–47.

Lala, R. M. (1991). *The creation of wealth: The Tatas from the 19th to the 21st century*. Penguin Group.

Lala, R. M. (1993). *Beyond the last blue mountain: A life of JRD Tata*. Penguin Books India.

Lala, R. M. (1995). *The joy of achievement: Conversations with JRD Tata*. Penguin Books.

Larson, M. J. (2008). *The Federation of British Industry and management education in post-war Britain*. Cardiff Historical papers, Published by the Cardiff School of History and Archaeology, Cardiff University.

Locke, R. (1989). *Management and Higher Education since 1940: The influence of America and Japan on West Germany, Great Britain and France*. Cambridge: Cambridge University Press.

Lokanathan, P. S. (1935). *Industrial organisation in India*. London: George Allen & Unwin.

Matthai, J. (1956a). A talk by Dr John Matthai on the opening day of the second session of the Tata Staff College. Box 998, Tata Staff College, Tata Central Archives.

Matthai, J. (1956b). Foreword by John Matthai to the Report on first session of the Staff College, 1956, p 2-3, Box 998, Tata Central Archives.

Matthai, R. J. (1980). The organisation and the institution: Management education in India. *Economic and Political Weekly,* 69–72.

McKinlay, A., & Pezet, E. (2010). Accounting for Foucault. *Critical Perspectives on Accounting, 21*, 486–495.

Miller, P., & Rose, N. (1990). Governing economic life. *Economy and Society, 19*(1), 1–31.

Myers, C. A. (1958). *Labor problems in the industrialization of india*. Harvard University Press.

Nettle, D. J. (2014). Issues of management identity: Attitudes to management within the Australian Institute of Management, 1940–73. *Business History, 56*(2), 287–313.

Ritson, P., & Parker, L. (2016). You're in the Army now! Historical lessons for contemporary management theorists. *Journal of Management History, 22*(3), 320–340.

Roper, M. (1999). Killing off the father: Social science and the memory of Frederick Taylor in management studies, 1950–75. *Contemporary British History, 13*(3), 39–58.

Rungta, R. S. (1970). *The rise of business corporations in India, 1851–1900.* Cambridge University Press.

Russell, J. (2015). Organization men and women: Making managers at Bell Canada from the 1940s to the 1960s. *Management & Organizational History, 10*(3-4), 213–229.

Sabavala, S. A., & Lala, R. M. (1986). *Keynote: JRD Tata. Excerpts from his speeches and Chairman's statements to shareholders.* Rupa Publications.

Saha, G. G. (2012). Management education in India: Issues & concerns. *Journal of Information, knowledge and research in business management and administration, 2*(1), 35–40.

Sahu, K. C. (1991). Reorienting management education. *Economic and Political Weekly,* 133–136.

Sancheti, N. (1986). *Educational dependency: An Indian case-study in comparative perspective* (unpublished PhD thesis, Institute of Education, University of London).

Scott, J. (1998). *Seeing like a state: How certain schemes to improve the human condition have failed.* New Haven CT: Yale University Press.

Sheth, N. R. (1991). What is wrong with management education. *Economic and Political Weekly,* 123–128.

Srinivas, N. (2008). Mimicry and revival: The transfer and transformation of management knowledge to India, 1959-1990. *International Studies of Management & Organization, 38*(4), 38–57.

Srinivas, N. (2012). Epistemic and performative quests for authentic management in India. *Organization, 19*(2), 145–158.

Tata Staff College. (1953). Report on the first session, Box 998, Tata Central Archives.

Tata Staff College. (1956a). Report on first session of the Staff College, p 2-3, Box 998, Tata Central Archives.

Tata Staff College. (1956b). Brochure, Box 998, Tata Central Archives.

Tata Staff College. (1956c). Report to the Chairman and Directors of Tata Industries, Tata Staff College (for session 9th February to 9th March 1956). Unauthored. Box 129, Tata Central Archives.

Tata Staff College. (1957). This is probably Jehangir Ghandy, but the author is not specified. Training for Management, Box 998, Tata Central Archives.

Tata Staff College. (1962). Report on Second Tata Accountants Conference, Box 874, Tata Central Archives.

Tata Staff College. (1964). Report on the first Tata Secretaries Conference, Box 874, Tata Central Archives.

TISCO News. (1954). April 30, Volume 1 (7), p.2, Tata Steel Archives.

TISCO News. (1956). August 17, Volume 3 (15), p. 1-2, Tata Steel Archives.

TISCO News. (1962). March 26, Volume 9 (6), p 2-3, Tata Steel Archives.

Vernardakis, G. (1982). The administrative staff college at henley-on-thames. *International Journal of Public Administration, 4*(1), 23–37.

Watson, K. (1984). *Dependence and interdependence in education. International perspectives.* London: Croom Helm.

Wild, A. (2002). The management college that never was. In Proceedings of the Eighteenth Annual Conference of the Association of Researchers in Construction Management, September.

Guerriero Wilson, R. (2011). The struggle for management education in Britain: The Urwick committee and the office management association. *Management & Organizational History, 6*(4), 367–389.

Worden, S. (2003). The role of religious and nationalist ethics in strategic leadership: The case of J.N. Tata. *Journal of Business Ethics, 47,* 147–164.

Index